WHEN A BABY DIES

WHEN A BABY DIES

Psychotherapy for Pregnancy and Newborn Loss

IRVING G. LEON

Foreword by Erna Furman

Yale University Press   New Haven and London

Designed by Mary Mendell
Set in Palatino type by Brevis Press.
Printed in the United States of America by Vail-
Ballou Press, Binghamton, New York.

Library of Congress Cataloging-in-
Publication Data
    Leon, Irving G.
    When a baby dies : psychotherapy for
pregnancy and newborn loss / Irving G.
Leon ; foreword by Erna Furman.
        p.   cm.
    Includes bibliographical references.
    ISBN 0–300–04575–1 (cloth)
        0–300–05230–8 (pbk.)
    1. Perinatal death—Psychological
aspects.   2. Bereavement—Psychological
aspects.   3. Parent and child.   4. Brothers
and sisters.   5. Psychotherapy.   I. Title.
    [DNLM: 1. Bereavement.   2. Death—in
infancy & childhood.   3. Fetal Death.
4. Pregnancy—psychology.
5. Psychotherapy.   6. Sibling Relations.
BF 575.G7 L579w]
RG631.L47   1990
155.9'37—dc20
DNLM/DLC
for Library of Congress   89–22706
                                        CIP

The paper in this book meets the guidelines of
permanence and durability of the Committee on
Production Guidelines for Book Longevity of the
Council on Library Resources.

10 9 8 7 6 5 4 3 2

TO NANCY

FIRST

You were my first,
a July baby
to be born
in the hot sun,
when the river glistens
and trees are full,
fruit ripe,
ready to drop.

But I lost you
in cold December
under operating lights,
in a river of blood.

I lost you
when you'd just begun,
before the July river,
before first light of day.

And with you
I took
one step closer
to death.

Nancy Grossman Leon

CONTENTS

FOREWORD

Erna Furman

This is indeed a most welcome book. It is welcome above all to the enormous number of mothers who have suffered perinatal loss and to the fathers and siblings who are deeply and inevitably affected by such a death. It is welcome to all of us who have worked with these parents and their surviving children professionally, aware of their unique predicament, assisting them in mastering its hardship, while also trying to alert others to its crucial importance. And it is welcome to all those who as sufferers or as potential helpers find it difficult to acknowledge that this, in Leon's term, "invisible" loss tends to leave shockingly visible and lifelong marks on the personalities of all family members when its significance goes unrecognized and the mental task of coping with it is shelved.

Fortunately, during the past ten years, the concerted efforts of a few have paid off in bringing about a considerable change in general awareness of the impact of perinatal loss and in the approaches to assisting families with it. Recognition, however, is not yet paralleled by understanding, and measures for helping therefore tend to be formally categorized rather than individually attuned to the needs of the particular family. For example, the newly introduced policy of showing the dead baby to the parents and involving them in the funeral arrangements is often pursued as an end in itself rather than as a part of an empathic professional relationship; similarly, definite protocols in predetermined numbers of interviews are used to assist the bereaved parents, without sufficient consideration of the many ways in which the parents deal with their stress or even of just how they use these professional contacts. When the wish to help our patients and ourselves is ahead of our understanding, our means of being really helpful are limited. Here again, this book is most timely. Leon introduces the reader to pregnancy as a developmental step that, like other developmental steps, brings about an upheaval within the personality, with the goal of a new integration and preparation for parenting. The unique tragedy of perinatal loss not only frustrates the outcome of this step but leaves the parents, the mother especially, in a state of mental turmoil. The difference between this loss, so much of it a loss to the self, and other losses through death that mark the end of a mutual relationship is rightly emphasized, as is the effect on the afflicted parents' ability to feel with and parent their other children, those already living at the time of the perinatal loss and those yet to be born.

As for how to help the bereaved parents, Leon is unequivocal in insisting that an empathic relationship is the most crucial prerequisite: "The engine of healing in the psychological treatment of perinatal death is the therapist's empathy with and interpretation of the multifaceted aspects of the bereaved mother's loss," but "a therapist's humanity, rather than his or her erudition, will probably be the best guide in responding to a patient's grief." Leon does not know and does not claim to know everything about perinatal loss. He makes a strong plea for more research, more meaningfully structured and more carefully executed. Judging by my own experience, I believe that increased knowledge will best be gained from empathic work with individuals because this gives us the opportunity to listen and to hear instead of asking questions that are of interest only to us, or telling patients what is good for them.

PREFACE

Perinatal loss has been the grief that knows no words.* Only recently has our society begun to learn what mourning parents and siblings have discovered by experience: in our culture perinatal loss can be a family trauma with potentially serious consequences if unattended. Many handbooks have been written lately (Berezin 1982; Borg & Lasker 1981; Ewy & Ewy 1984; Friedman & Gladstein 1982; Panuthos & Romeo 1984; Peppers & Knapp 1980a) to inform grief-stricken parents and help guide them toward recovery. Dozens of papers in nursing, pediatric, and obstetric journals have traced the course of this special bereavement and begun to outline potentially beneficial, usually crisis-oriented interventions. Major newspapers and magazines have discussed the nature of the loss, providing caregiving advice to the general public. The absence of *any* books in the mental health field oriented toward psychotherapy for perinatal loss has become an increasingly glaring professional blind spot.

This book is intended to be a first step in the psychotherapeutic understanding and treatment of perinatal loss. Chapter 1 reviews the theories of pregnancy in order to highlight

*Although perinatal death, as generally defined in the United States, includes all losses occurring between the twentieth week of gestation and the twenty-seventh day of life (Taylor and Pernoll 1987), I will also view earlier miscarriages as perinatal losses.

the unique context in which the loss occurs. The next chapter explores intrapsychic and interpersonal responses to peri-natal loss, contrasting the death to other reproductive casu-alties and losses. Psychotherapy with the bereaved parent (chapter 3) and with surviving and subsequent siblings (chap-ter 4) is described in detail. Discussions of clinical case ma-terial focus on maladaptive responses to perinatal loss, a variety of interventions, obstacles in dealing with this ther-apeutic population, and the range of outcomes. The final chapter reviews research methodology and considers possi-ble questions for future investigation.

The data source is a clinical sample of forty cases in which perinatal loss appeared to be a significant factor in ensuing emotional disturbance. The clinical sample should not be viewed as representing typical outcomes of perinatal bereave-ment. Because the purpose of the book is to describe dis-turbed reactions to perinatal loss and their treatment, mala-daptive response was a crucial criterion in choosing cases for my sample. Individual therapies were conducted with twenty bereaved mothers, child treatments with nine bereaved sib-lings, and individual therapies with eleven adult siblings of earlier perinatal losses. Although most cases were once-a-week therapies of short to intermediate duration (from a few months to a year), several more infrequently meeting sup-portive cases are included, as are a number of intensive ther-apies that met several times a week over a period of years. The intensity and length of treatment most frequently pre-sented in the sample are those most commonly used by out-patient therapists.

The book explores how perinatal loss can become inter-twined with latent conflicts and how psychotherapy can fa-cilitate both mourning and a greater resolution of those difficulties now associated with the loss. The reverberation of perinatal loss within the family is examined by clinical case illustrations of children struggling to understand the usually hidden facts about these family bereavements. By tracing how adults in treatment are still haunted by privately en-dowed meanings and parentally reinforced attributions surrounding perinatal loss of siblings in childhood, the lasting heritage of perinatal loss across generations can be documented.

My theoretical orientation and wish to provide a wide range of cases, some in considerable detail, will probably make this book most relevant to the psychodynamically oriented clinician. The many traditions of psychodynamic theory and technique represented here, including developmental stage, instinctual (that is, drive), object relations, and Kohut's (1971) self paradigms, as well as elements of a family approach applied in treating siblings of perinatal loss, may broaden its appeal to clinicians of other persuasions. Although this book is geared primarily toward the practicing clinician, it was written with other potential audiences in mind. I especially hope that medical practitioners—obstetricians, pediatricians, nurses, and neonatologists—who are on the "front lines" in facing the tragedy with the bereaved family as it occurs will find the conceptualization of the impact of perinatal loss (chapter 2) useful in understanding their patients and guiding them toward psychotherapy when appropriate. Teachers and ministers whose contact with victims of perinatal loss may be less frequent and immediate may likewise find this chapter beneficial in appreciating why the effects of this loss can be so enduring and its manifestations so disguised. Although the intent of this book is primarily to advance clinical theory and technique, researchers engaged in investigating perinatal loss should be able to pose many unanswered questions provoked by this work. In addition to the chapter discussing the psychology of perinatal loss, the protocols used in organizing data for the clinical sample (see the Appendix) and the final chapter will probably be of greatest interest to these researchers. Empirical research is sorely needed in order to assess not only the long-range impact of perinatal loss but the soundness and efficacy of therapeutic interventions. Finally, the book may offer some helpful insights to those whose lives have been affected by perinatal loss.

I greatly appreciate the contributions of the many people who enriched and supported my writing this book. Many colleagues generously shared their case materials and insights, patiently allowing me to test hypotheses against their own clinical experiences. For this help, I thank Judith Adler, Carol Barbour, Martha Diamond, Mary Gass, Prakash Kamalnath, Fred Kellerman, Carolyn Krone, Jeffrey Last, Susan Miller, Eleanor Rosenberg, William Schafer, and Jean Twomy. Several colleagues provided wise comments and recommendations in reacting to an earlier version of the book. For this help, I thank Judith Ballou, Albert Cain, Cecily Legg, and William Schafer. Gladys Topkis, my editor, and Karen Gangel, my manuscript editor, at Yale University Press, made many useful suggestions that clarified my writing. All of these people improved my book, although I assume full responsibility for its contents.

Several people offered valuable support for my ongoing work in the area of perinatal loss. I am especially grateful to John LaFerla. His immediate (and gently persistent) encouragement to begin reporting my findings on sibling perinatal loss after hearing an early presentation of mine helped motivate my deepening involvement in this area. Mary Schuman provided a forum for me to present my developing ideas.

I owe a special debt to my patients and patients of my colleagues whose stories *are* this book. Although their individual identities have been disguised to preserve confidentiality, their devotion to their children, alive and dead, testifies to the enduring reality and magnitude of their losses. I hope I have understood and communicated their struggles in such a way as to improve clinical work with those who suffer a perinatal bereavement.

I owe the greatest gratitude to my wife, Nancy, who has patiently listened to my thoughts, offered her own keen observations, and, as with all my published work, provided able editing. She has sensitively supported my work while helping me to keep perspective on what is important in life. Her brave struggles with our own pregnancy losses have inspired me, demonstrating how a spirit can be bowed without being broken.

I gratefully acknowledge permission to reprint sections of my previously published papers that have been incorporated in this book: "The invisible loss: The impact of perinatal death on siblings," in *Journal of Psychosomatic Obstetrics and Gynecology*, 1986, 5, 1–14; "Intrapsychic and family dynamics in perinatal sibling loss," in *Infant Mental Health Journal*, 1986, 7, 200–213; "Psychodynamics of perinatal loss," in *Psychiatry*, © 1986 Washington School of Psychiatry, 49, 312–324; and "Short-term psychotherapy for perinatal loss," in *Psychotherapy*, 1987, 24, 186–195.

CHAPTER 1
THE PSYCHOLOGY
OF PREGNANCY

The impact of perinatal loss can best be understood by examining the psychological milieu in which it occurs—that of pregnancy. I shall apply four psychodynamic models in conceptualizing pregnancy: developmental stage, drive,* object relations, and self theories. These models are presented separately to highlight the particular level of analysis and conceptual terminology, but they are not mutually exclusive or necessarily contradictory. Adherents of these schools emphasize important differences among them in understanding personality development and therapeutic process, leading to an often bitter rivalry for the singular "truth." I do not wish to dismiss these differences as insignificant, but I believe the most comprehensive and accurate view of pregnancy is afforded by using all four models. In discussing individual cases, I shall emphasize those orientations offering the most explanatory power.

Pregnancy as a New Developmental Stage

"Pregnancy, particularly the first pregnancy, is a crisis point in the search for a female identity, for it is a point of no

*This approach is currently represented by ego psychology, although the earlier term is used here to emphasize instinctual expression.

return, whether a baby is born at the end of term or whether the pregnancy ends in abortion or miscarriage. . . . It implies the end of the woman as an independent single unit and the beginning of the unalterable and irrevocable mother-child relationship" (Pines 1972, 333).

Grete Bibring was the first theorist to delineate extensively pregnancy as a distinct developmental stage in becoming a parent. In a series of papers, she and her associates (Bibring 1959; Bibring et al. 1961a; Bibring & Valenstein 1976) described pregnancy as a crisis that, while reviving earlier wishes, identifications, and unresolved conflicts, offers the potential for new, more or less adaptive solutions. The specific constellation of conscious and unconscious fantasies, issues, and modes of adaptation activated in pregnancy is unique to each woman and depends upon both her psychic history and her current personal relationships. However, profound psychological and physiological disequilibrium is common to all pregnant women (Leifer 1977). As in adolescence (Blos 1962), the presence of psychological upheaval, distress, and regression may be less an indicator of pathology than an attempt at constructive resolution. Likewise, the absence of turmoil may be grounds for greater concern owing to the individual's refusal or inability to make the necessary internal changes in preparation for the new challenges and demands in her life—separation and independence for the adolescent, mothering for the pregnant woman. Increased symptom formation, including much greater anxiety (Bibring et al. 1961b; Leifer 1977) and obsessional, compulsive, and phobic preoccupations (Colman 1969), is typically reported by pregnant women and is indicative of their state of crisis rather than of psychopathology. In addition to signifying a new developmental stage in preparation for mothering a child (Shectman 1980), pregnancy can represent the attainment of adult status and authority (Ballou 1978), with a greater separation from mother (Pines 1982).

Pregnancy provides the crucible in which both the baby and the woman's motherliness can grow; as such, it is a natural prelude to parenthood. However, pregnancy and parenting need to be distinguished. Motherliness does not depend upon fertility (Deutsch 1945), just as delivering a child is no guarantee of nurturant parenting. And although the father-to-be is unable to experience pregnancy biologically, his psychological journey strikingly parallels that of his wife, with a resurgence of earlier conflicts, potential improvement or worsening of adaptations, and intensification of psychological turmoil and symptoms, again indicative of crisis rather than of emotional disturbance (Osofsky 1982). Men and women can realize similar maturational goals in becoming parents (Deutsch 1945; Jessner et al. 1970).

Parenthood may be understood as a crucial developmental phase of adulthood offering the opportunity to change oneself via the evolving relationship with and development of one's children (Benedek 1959). Parenthood usually provides the vehicle for expressing generativity (Erikson 1963), that is, the basic adult developmental task of guiding the next generation. In addition to the psychosocial tasks involved, Veevers (1973) describes multiple societal meanings to becoming a parent, including fulfilling one's moral, civic, and marital obligations and demonstrating sexual competence. Pregnancy is a vital prelude to parenthood, which, though not indispensable, helps prepare the prospective mother for her future role.

The model of pregnancy as a new developmental stage highlights both repetition and revision. The past is reorganized, and, for better or worse, one is changed in entering a new life phase. Optimally, the individual may find a new sense of purpose and a greater degree of maturity and psychic independence, along with enriched ties with family, within and across generations. Obstacles to entering that stage can result in psychological stagnation and arrested development. Impediments to its successful navigation can have far-reaching effects in reinforcing past hurts and solidifying earlier self-defeating patterns of intrapsychic and interpersonal functioning.

Pregnancy as Instinctual Process

Biology is central in understanding this perspective on pregnancy, although it does not deny the importance of psychological experience. Two complementary paths of this approach may be distinguished—pregnancy experiences determined by hormonal sequences and pregnancy as instinctual regression.

Therese Benedek (Benedek & Rubenstein 1942; Benedek 1949) was the first to contend that a woman's immediate psychosexual orientation varies directly with her hormonal production. Thus, during the estrous phase of her menstrual cycle, prior to ovulation, her heterosexual drives are heightened; during the postovulatory progesterone phase of her menstrual cycle and the whole of pregnancy, she is narcissistically oriented, tending to be self-preoccupied and subject to mild depressive moods in an oral mode of functioning. Benedek and Rubenstein (1942) were able to predict a woman's position in her menstrual cycle accurately on the basis of the heterosexual or narcissistic orientation of her corresponding psychoanalytic material, such as dreams. Women with conflicts over heterosexuality demonstrated considerably more anxiety in the estrous phase, and women troubled by aggression, especially directed at mother, frequently experienced severe depression during the normally tranquil postovulatory phase. Benedek (1960) later modified her view of the centrality of hormonal production in evoking psychological experience, considering hormones as facilitating but not ultimately determining agents in feminine and maternal expression.

As an instinctual process, pregnancy also recapitulates infantile sexuality (Bibring et al. 1961a; Deutsch 1945; Pines 1982). In the first trimester, with the initial attachment of the fetus inside the uterus, oral trends predominate in the woman, who assumes a passive-receptive libidinal position (Benedek 1955, 1956, 1959). The reciprocal interplay of physiological and psychological forces may result in nausea, vomiting, and food cravings (Deutsch 1945; Kestenberg 1976) and activation of unconscious fears and wishes of devouring and being swallowed by one's mother (Lester & Notman 1986). In the second trimester, when the fetus is accorded greater separateness during quickening, anal-retentive trends become prominent (Kestenberg 1956). The pregnant woman may struggle with sadistic wishes to destroy her "fecal" baby, who is unconsciously associated with dirtiness—worms, disgusting animals, and so on (Deutsch 1945). A vital task of this phase is the differentiation of the baby from both the mother and her own "dirty," anal contents (Kestenberg 1976), thereby facilitating a nurturant response (Lester & Notman 1986). Finally, during the third trimester, as the mother prepares for delivery, phallic-aggressive wishes, associated with urethral drives, predominate as her heightened fears that she or the baby may die resonate with her bodily fears of losing control—that is, of urination (Kestenberg 1976). While latent oedipal conflicts are not linked to a particular stage in pregnancy, they may be activated if the pregnancy is experienced as a victory over mother in the competition for father (Ballou 1978; Deutsch 1945). This patterning of instinctual regression is typical; each woman's unique constellation of intrapsychic conflicts, defenses, and fixations will determine the nature and intensity of her fantasies, difficulties, and pleasures during pregnancy (Bibring 1959; Bibring et al. 1961a; Deutsch 1945).

In addition to drive regression, earlier modes of cognition and adaptation are more evident during pregnancy. Ego regression occurs, with impaired reality-testing and freer exercise of magical thinking (Pines 1972; Raphael-Leff 1986). Much like the infant whose psyche and body are not yet differentiated (Spitz 1965), leading to somatic expression of emotions, the pregnant woman is more likely to express her conflicts, wishes, and feelings somatically (Pines 1982), as "psychic contents can utilize the language of the organs" (Deutsch 1945, 135).

Although Kestenberg (1956, 1976) described this sequence of instinctual regression during pregnancy, she emphasized that these modes are not passive recapitulations of the mother's infantile sexuality. Rather, they are new renditions subsumed under a distinctly female stage of "inner genitality." This is the basis of maternal feelings, as distinct from the phallic-oedipal phase, which is viewed as the foundation of female heterosexuality. Instinctual regression therefore provides a reintegration during pregnancy of the mother's maternal aspirations. Although those ambitions could not be realized during their first appearance—in the pre-oedipal phase at three or four years of age—they can now be fulfilled by bearing a child. This instinctual regression may be in the service of a progressive integration of the personality in preparation for motherhood (Benedek 1949; Kestenberg 1976), or it may be a regressive attempt to gratify infantile yearnings (Pines 1972, 1982). Pines has illustrated clinically that the unconscious motivation for becoming pregnant may be to satisfy unresolved dependency and sadistic wishes rather than to create and mother a child.

The instinctual model provides an explanation of both psychological functioning and motive during pregnancy. In early psychoanalytic formulations, Freud (1917a) traced the woman's wish for a baby from an anal association with feces to the long-awaited substitute for a penis as compensation for a fantasized castration. As reviewed by Blitzer and Murray (1964), this narcissistic basis of maternity (that is, to repair body damage by replacing the missing penis) needed to be transformed into an object wish for a child. On a positive oedipal level, maternal wishes are based on the desire to be impregnated by and give a baby to father.

Freud's interpretation of maternity rested principally on the restitution of phallic frustrations and oedipal wishes. Later studies emphasized the crucial role of the little girl's earliest wishes to fuse with her mother (Chasseguet-Smirgel 1984) and the primacy of her receptive genitalia (Kestenberg 1976; Lester & Notman 1986) in organizing maternal activity. Some of these views may amplify and elaborate, rather than contradict, Freud's formulations: "It seems to me . . . that her *capacity for motherhood* enables the woman to realize in fantasy her dual incestuous wish: to recover the state of primary fusion with the mother by means of the union established with the foetus during pregnancy and to keep the love object, the father or his penis, inside herself" (Chasseguet-Smirgel 1984, 170). However, recognizing the importance of early feminine development for maternity can lead to important modifications of Freud's theory. Kestenberg (1976) convincingly argued that a little girl's powerful disappointment in being unable to fulfill her maternal aspirations during the initial inner-genital phase may intensify her desire for a penis as substitute gratification for the child she cannot have and mourns. From this perspective, penis envy is not a basic motive behind maternal wishes but may become, at least in part, a defensive refuge for frustrated maternal strivings. Ultimately, Freud's definition of maternal wishes as secondary reactions to narcissistic injury and heterosexual drives robbed maternity of its primary, life-giving, nurturing focus. A theory of maternity that denies a primary role to the mother-child relationship seems incomplete.

Pregnancy as Object-Seeking

"And yet a special relationship will be established to this child—different from any other earlier or later. It will persist in the form of a synthesis of her relationship to the child, representing a person in his own right, of her relationship to the child, representing her husband, and not least, of her relationship to the child, representing herself" (Bibring et al. 1961a, 17). Pregnancy is the process of making a person. An object-relations perspective highlights internalized patterns of interaction, involving representations of both the self and connected others. It may clarify the exposition to discuss first the pregnant woman's constituent representations of herself as mother-to-be, followed by those representations she has of her child, before attempting to integrate the two.

THE ROLE OF MATERNAL REPRESENTATIONS

"The fate of the identification with the mother is another factor that determines the course of pregnancy. In every instance, the capacity for motherhood is related to this identification" (Deutsch 1945, 145). Many psychoanalytic theorists have highlighted the crucial role of the mother's identifications with her own mother in influencing the psychological course and outcome of pregnancy (Ballou 1978; Benedek 1955, 1956, 1959; Coleman et al. 1953; Deutsch 1945; Kestenberg 1956, 1976; Lester & Notman 1986; Pines 1972, 1982; Raphael-Leff 1986). In the process of becoming a mother herself, the pregnant woman identifies, much more powerfully than before, with the mothering images and experiences of her infancy and childhood. Although identifications with her mother naturally informed her identity throughout her development, an important transformation occurs during pregnancy: former object-representations of her mother (as mother) may now become a part of self-representations (as a mother). She is now able to become a mother, whereas before she could only be a daughter; thus she can fulfill lifelong maternal ambitions (Kestenberg 1956, 1976). These maternal representations range from the earliest identifications with the omnipotence of one's mother (Brunswick 1940) and her active caretaking (Benedek 1955, 1959; Kestenberg 1956, 1976) to possessing mother's prerogatives in her conjugal relationship with father during the oedipal period (Deutsch 1945). Pregnancy wishes may be rooted in the seeking of maternal power, status, and authority through the revival and transformation of maternal identifications, all of which are potentially independent of maternal wishes to nurture a child. Conversely, maternal strivings to care for a baby may be complicated and foiled by conflicts over becoming a mother. Pregnancy makes not only a baby but a mother as well.

In addition to heightened maternal identifications, the mother-to-be experiences the "revival in pregnancy of infantile fantasies about herself as the intra-uterine foetus in her mother's body which are activated by her narcissistic identification with the foetus now concretely inside her own body" (Pines 1982, 311). Benedek showed how pregnancy and early motherhood were oral and alimentary relationships for both mother and child (Benedek 1949, 1955, 1956, 1959); many psychoanalytic theorists who have studied pregnancy have emphasized the importance of the mother's needy, dependent feelings embodied in her sense of herself as a hungry infant (Ballou 1978; Deutsch 1945; Pines 1982). In the process of physiologically making a baby out of a mother, pregnancy intrapsychically makes a mother into a baby.

Perhaps the foremost psychological challenge over the course of pregnancy is to reconcile the mother and the infant within the psyche of the pregnant woman. Although her maternal identifications may fuel her nurturant capabilities, infantile identifications threaten her with profound neediness and dependent yearnings. Before describing how these conflicting identifications may be resolved, we must first consider the elements of the mother's representations of her child-to-be.

THE ROLE OF REPRESENTATIONS OF THE CHILD-TO-BE

Most mothers clearly conceive of their children as "real people" before they are born. By the second trimester almost two-thirds of mothers in one study viewed the fetus as a distinct person (Lumley 1982). Even more striking is the considerable precision and conviction with which mothers imagine attributes of their prospective children by the final trimester. Zeanah and his associates (1985, 1986a) discovered a statistically significant* degree of stability between the way pregnant women imagined their near-term babies along personality dimensions of temperament (that is, activity, mood, intensity, rhythmicity, and adaptability) and the way they viewed the babies postpartum. Another study (Zeanah et al. 1986b) revealed that a mother's postpartum views of her child's personality were more powerfully associated with her prenatal images of the child than with samples of actually observed interactions. Even by six months postpartum, the mother's conception of her infant's personality appeared to

---

*Levels of significance will not be reported for individual empirical findings reviewed because of the variety of statistical tests used in the different studies, making comparisons misleading. Only those results of studies that are likely to occur by chance no more than 5 percent of the time ($p < .05$) will be considered statistically significant and noted as such here.

be more strongly influenced by her prenatal experiences and fantasies about the child-to-be than by actual interactions with her child! Anecdotal descriptions vividly amplify how potently maternal prenatal images can organize her view of her child:

> Mother A—prenatal: I feel this is a very, very emotional and intense child—very active. Very verbal and very intense. I'll know when it's upset and when it's happy. I cried when something beautiful happened at work. I was sure the baby cried, too. The baby kicked and kicked. It felt what I was feeling.

> Mother A—postnatal: Definitely not quiet. He's got a mind of his own. He's very alert. If he had his way, he wouldn't sleep all day. He likes to stay up and observe things. Likes human contact, likes a lot of love. (Zeanah et al. 1985, 208)

These empirical studies are valuable in highlighting the importance of the pregnant mother's image of her child-to-be in her conscious experience. The psychoanalytic perspective can delineate the more unconscious aspects of herself and others that are integrated into her conception of her unborn child. Several theorists have noted how the mother fuses the image of her child-to-be with that of the father, a natural result of the role of sexual intercourse and shared genetic heritage in creating a new being (Bibring et al. 1961a; Deutsch 1945; Pines 1972). The all-too-common occurrence after divorce of a mother's wrath directed at her child may be based less on the current displacement of hostility from the now-absent father than on her earliest representations of her unborn child, which include images of the father.

Clinical studies of unresolved grief and separation difficulties indicate that actual pregnancies (Blumenfield 1978; Gedo 1965), pregnancy wishes (Jackel 1966), and psychosomatic pregnancy symptoms such as lactation (Aruffo 1971) may be attempts to undo earlier losses and deny current separations. The identity of the child-to-be may be linked unconsciously with the memory of a beloved deceased figure. It is the custom in some religions, such as Judaism, that the newborn be named after a deceased relative. In instances where the traumatizing impact of the death is still felt, such as the recent loss of another child, a pregnancy may be unconsciously designed to produce a "replacement child" as an effort to recover the lost child (Cain & Cain 1964; Legg & Sherick 1976; Poznanski 1972).

The woman's images of her child-to-be are based on the vicissitudes of her history of identifications and conflicted object ties. The unborn child commonly becomes a projective screen for the mother's hopes, fears, hates, and loves. Clinical material from psychoanalysis (A. M. Sandler 1988) and psychotherapy (Stack 1987) illustrates the way in which the pregnant woman may experience her child-to-be as representing herself, mother, or sibling. Pines (1972) provides several clinical anecdotes in which the images of unborn children were dramatically influenced by mothers' object and self representations (for example, a mother relinquishes her child in adoption as an unconscious repetition of her own feelings of abandonment as an adopted child; another mother despises her infant son as the embodiment of her "dirty," sexual self, of which she was ashamed; a third mother anticipates rejecting her third child, who personifies her much-envied younger brother).

THE MOTHER'S RELATIONSHIP WITH HER UNBORN CHILD

"In the term 'emotional symbiosis' are conceptualized the ongoing processes of the hungry infant being fed, the feeding mother's need to care for the child, and the intrapsychic precipitates of these processes in the child and in the mother. . . . Each higher integration in the growing individual as well as in the parent occurs through the reactivation and the overcoming of the ambivalent core" (Benedek 1956, 375–376). One of the many paradoxes of pregnancy is that though it is a biological process of differentiation—the creation of a distinct human being—it depends upon psychological processes of integration, that is, the unification of disparate representations. Within the mother's representational system of herself is the opportunity for better integration of her conflicting identifications—that of a nurturing mother and a helpless infant. This integration is realized in the mother's object relationship with her unborn child. Just as a thriving interaction between mother and child simultaneously reinforces the baby's sense of basic trust and the mother's basic confidence in her maternity (Benedek 1956, 1959), so an uncomplicated pregnancy may confirm a woman's earliest faith in herself as a mother. And just as a mother's earliest dependency needs may be gratified or frustrated vicariously in her relationship with her child, so a woman's intense conflicts over wishing to merge with or separate from mother, her fears of destroying or being destroyed by mother, can be activated in her pregnancy, during which time she can alternately identify with her mother or with her unborn infant, as the fetus within her mother (Lester & Notman 1986; Pines 1982; Wyatt 1975). The woman's potential resolution of her early ambivalence is negotiated in her relationship with her young infant (that is, will her maternity be sufficient to satisfy her own dependency, now experienced in identifying with her needy child?), just after it was revived in pregnancy (that is, will her positive maternal identifications based on having been nurtured herself be bountiful enough to gratify her hungry infantile identifications?).

In focusing on the importance of reconciling ambivalence toward one's own mother for the successful outcome of pregnancy, Ballou (1978) provided case illustrations of pregnant women who, unable to tolerate their own neediness, maintained either an intensely ambivalent tie to a mother experienced as dangerous and intrusive or later could not respond empathically to her helpless infant. In the first instance, rage over frustrated dependency was projected onto the mother; in the second, the neediness had to be denied in one's own child.

The pregnant woman's early experiences of having been mothered help to determine her maternity through the revival of maternal identifications, but she may also tap other potential sources of nurturance. In noting the vulnerability of pregnant women to their intensified dependency needs, several theorists have described or provided case illustrations of how a supportive, usually maternal, relationship during pregnancy, whether with a therapist (Bibring et al. 1961b), maternal figure (Deutsch 1945), or husband capable of responding in a care-giving fashion (Ballou 1978), may help alleviate the damaging impact of negative maternal identifications rooted in early experiences of deprivation and frustration. One empirical study reported statistically significant results indicating that maternal attachment during pregnancy was directly correlated with availability of social support and inversely associated with experienced stress (Cranley 1981). Pregnancy is not a closed system, the outcome of which is predetermined by one's past. Rather, it is a new arena in which the course of the drama may be changed by a new cast of characters.

The intrapsychic processes of integration and differentiation complement each other in pregnancy. The integration of competing demands to give as a mother and to receive as an infant facilitates an additional step of maturation and differentiation (Benedek 1959). In uniting her sense of herself with her sense of both her mother and her unborn child, the pregnant woman can more fully differentiate herself from the mother of her childhood during the process of becoming a mother herself (Lester & Notman 1986; Pines 1982). The pregnant woman thus embodies three generations (Benedek 1970). The mother-to-be recapitulates her earlier stages of separation-individuation from her own mother (Raphael-Leff 1983) in the growth and impending delivery of her child.

Pregnancy as Self-Enhancement

Pregnancy may be viewed as the height of both selflessness and self-involvement. While devoting herself to the care of her needy infant, the mother may realize the fulfillment of her most grandiose narcissistic wishes.

PREGNANCY AS OMNIPOTENCE

"So God created man in his own image . . . male and female he created them. God blessed them and said to them, 'Be fruitful and increase, fill the earth and subdue it, rule over the fish in the sea, the birds of heaven, and every living thing that moves upon the earth'" (Genesis 1:27–29). From the biblical account of Creation one may infer that a person's divine aspirations may be most nearly realized through the human act of creation, giving birth to a child. One early empirical study of a child's conscious awareness of the origins of babies reported that preschoolers cited God more frequently than mother as the source of babies (Conn 1947). These literal findings may be outdated by the tendency of today's parents to provide more factual information to their young children. Adult myths about the divine origin of conception, however, may ultimately be based on unconscious infantile fantasies.

Perhaps the earliest roots of the pregnancy wish can be found in the young child's profound yearnings to become the all-powerful mother (Brunswick 1940). The child's inability to realize this ambition later fuels intense envy of mother during the anal and oedipal periods (Jacobson 1968). Maternal omnipotence, for the young child, may be represented concretely by mother's procreative capabilities, as well as by her fertility, symbolizing her power over her young child's dependent existence. Nor is this quest for maternal omnipotence via pregnancy limited to females. Many theorists (Brunswick 1940; Fast 1984; Jacobson 1968; Ross 1975) have noted that a boy's wishes to be pregnant, to give birth, and to develop breasts are initially rooted in early identifications with the omnipotent mother and not with the later feminine identifications in relationship to the phallic father in the negative oedipal constellation. Becoming pregnant may fulfill lifelong wishes of personal power and creativity totally independent of the nurturant aims of motherhood. This sense of omnipotence, which may be achieved in pregnancy, must be tempered after birth, when, no longer completely responsible (biologically) for her child's survival, the mother must cede some of her power and control to her infant's separate fate (Shectman 1980).

PREGNANCY AS DENIAL OF DEATH

"To have an heir to one's own ego, a carrier of one's own blood, a creature who springs from *me*, as fruit from a tree, and secures continuity, immortality, for *my* own transient existence—all these are psychologic motives in the desire for a child" (Deutsch 1945, 167). The literature documenting humanity's everlasting attempts to master the inevitability of death is as voluminous as civilization itself. Manifesting itself as the source of most religious beliefs, with some form of immortality as the goal, and as an important root in familial, cultural, and national identifications, the struggle to find life and continuity beyond one's biological existence is a basic human motivation. Both the creation of another human being and the continuation of one's genetic heritage via pregnancy and birth may somewhat alleviate the finality of death. If facing one's inevitable end is the ultimate narcissistic blow (for what could be more humbling to a sense of personal power and efficacy?), pregnancy may normally serve as a vital narcissistic defense, preserving a sense of self-worth and permanence.

PREGNANCY AS SELF-EXTENSION

"By tender identification, by perceiving the fruit of her body as part of herself, the pregnant woman is able to transform the 'parasite' into a beloved being" (Deutsch 1945, 139). Just as the fetus is physiologically part of the mother's body, so too is the unborn child psychologically part of her. Kohut (1971) has described how an individual may experience other people narcissistically as "self-objects" (p. 26), as if they were an extension of oneself, expected to be under one's control as much as one's own body or thoughts. This view of others explains the demanding and intolerant behavior of narcissistic individuals and young children, who inevitably become enraged when self-objects refuse to comply (Kohut 1971). The unborn child, more than any other human, becomes a self-object for the mother, with her self-experience expanding to include her child-to-be just as surely as her body swells to accommodate the new life within. Other theorists have recognized the mother's narcissistic identification with her fetus (Benedek & Rubenstein 1942; Deutsch 1945; Kestenberg 1976; Pines 1972; Rubin 1975), often noting that her initial acceptance or rejection of the fetus may depend on her level of self-esteem, whether she is capable of feeling that something good and worthwhile can come from and be a part of her.

As Loewald (1982) has described, the mother's narcissistic bond to her unborn child may be compared to the young child's need for the transitional object (Winnicott 1953)—the first external object that is both self and not-self simultaneously, and an important milestone in the child's increasing separation from mother. Benson and Pryor (1973) have described how the transitional object can be conceptualized as a self-object, through which self-worth may be protected by exercising total control over the (narcissistic) object. In fact, the example they provide of a later transitional object, the imaginary companion, seems to correspond closely to the common experience of the pregnant woman communicating, often in open dialogue, with her unborn child. She is entitled to unrestrained fantasies about her child-to-be, while her body in fact enacts dominion over the child's existence. Through her imaginings about her child-to-be, which may assume the voice of maternal conviction, the mother seeks to achieve in fantasy what she has already accomplished physiologically—control of her unborn child. This intense immersion in conscious and unconscious fantasy (Deutsch 1945; Raphael-Leff 1983, 1986), as an example of transitional phenomena such as play (Winnicott 1971), may be a potentially enriching refuge from the ever-present demands of reality-testing.

Rather than being idle self-indulgence, this regressive retreat may serve as a preparation for ministering to her cognitively symbiotic infant, who is unable to distinguish self from other. Thus, the mother's transitional thought processes, which during pregnancy blur the distinction between self and other, anticipate her empathic relationship with her like-thinking baby. The mother's narcissistic bond to her baby as part of herself during pregnancy corresponds to the baby's symbiotic experience of the mother as part of himself.* The experience of maternal omnipotence during pregnancy res- onates with early infantile omnipotence in which the infant experiences reality narcissistically as a product of his own fantasies (Benedek 1937; Winnicott 1945, 1953) and actions (Fast 1985). The blurring of physical boundaries between the pregnant mother and her fetus is the crucible for the blurring of psychic boundaries for the mother—between self and other, inside and out, mother and baby. By experiencing her unborn child as part of herself, the mother makes the baby's needs part of her needs. Her "primary maternal preoccupa- tion" (Winnicott 1956), a highly intensified devotion to her baby beginning near-term, prepares her for the consuming physical caretaking of a needy, helpless infant. The *physio- logical* symbiosis between mother and child during pregnancy facilitates the *cognitive* symbiosis for the mother experiencing her unborn child as a part of herself. This is eventually ac- tualized in the *affective-interactive* symbiosis of mother-infant synchronous play (Brazelton et al. 1974) in early childhood, when each participant reciprocally influences and mirrors the other.

PREGNANCY AS SELF-AGGRANDIZEMENT

"Many an introspective woman admits that the amount of happiness she experienced during her first wished-for preg- nancy (unless it was overshadowed by negative counter- ideas) far exceeded the joys of real motherhood. . . . She had the feeling that *her* pregnancy was something extraordinary, that the child she expected would give her unprecedented bliss" (Deutsch 1945, 155). Kohut (1971) distinguished vari- ations of the narcissistic transferences, with each designed to protect and regulate self-esteem for individuals susceptible

*To avoid both confusion over whether feminine pronouns refer to mother or daughter and inelegant repetition of "him" and "her," the baby will be referred to in the masculine in all instances.

to intense, devastating experiences of worthlessness. In each instance, he traced the emerging transference in treatment to its earlier genesis in the young child's unsuccessful attempts to establish an internalized reservoir of positive self-esteem necessary for a continuous sense of well-being and positive self-worth. With the activation of the "mirror transference" (28), the patient assumes the stance of the "grandiose self" (that is, "I am perfect" [26–27]), in which the analyst is obliged to echo and confirm the patient's glorified self-image. In its counterpart, the "idealizing transference" (28), the patient seeks to bolster self-worth by personal contact with the exalted analyst, who is identified with the early images of parental omnipotence, the "idealized parent imago" (that is, "You are perfect, but I am part of you" [26–27]). These paradigms may be applied as nonpathological, typical versions of how the unborn child participates in the pregnant woman's maintenance of a cohesive sense of self and positive self-esteem.

"To all those who suffer from awareness of their own ego weakness, pregnancy is a welcome opportunity to enhance their own importance" (Deutsch 1945, 156). The pregnant woman's exhibitionistic pleasure in displaying her fullness (if not inhibited by her modesty) partakes of this narcissistic gratification. Her "grandiose self" is confirmed by her unborn child's obvious presence. Fantasies of perfection in a brilliant, extraordinary pregnancy (Deutsch 1945; Raphael-Leff 1986) exemplify the mother-to-be's basking in the fulfillment of lifelong maternal wishes.

"Often it appears as an ideal child, usually representing the dreamer herself endowed with her own best qualities and all those she would like to have" (Deutsch 1945, 162). Although the mother-to-be may be embarrassed to display publicly or even to enjoy privately her "grandiose self," she usually experiences less conflict in savoring narcissistic splendor through the idealized images of her unborn child. Through transmuting internalizations, what formerly had been accomplished in a relationship via the idealizing transference can now be achieved through the formation of an internal, psychic structure, the ego ideal, in which goals and standards may serve to both guide the individual in pursuits and provide narcissistic gratification when fulfilled (Kohut 1971; Tolpin 1971). As an idealized self-object, the unborn child may be viewed as an expression and extension of her ego ideal, around which a large share of her self-esteem becomes organized. Images of her unborn child's perfection therefore become a crucial source of and validation for her sense of well-being and self-worth. The flawless aspects of oneself are personified in the unborn child (Deutsch 1945; Raphael-Leff 1986). To avoid the narcissistic mortification of seeing her real, less than ideal child at birth, the pregnant woman must temper her idealized images of her child as delivery approaches and in the early postpartum period (Solnit & Stark 1961). The inevitable narcissistic disappointment resulting from the discrepancy between the idealized and actual child is typically reduced by now having the compensation of a live, separate child whom one can love, caress, and nurture. However, even a tempered idealization of the fantasized, unborn child cannot accommodate the birth of a handicapped infant, the reality of which engenders an intolerable narcissistic blow.

The woman with sufficient psychological resources for maintaining self-esteem is able to endure the narcissistic vulnerability of investing her unborn child with her own self-worth and to love the child despite actual deficiencies. A narcissistically damaged mother, however, may encounter severe obstacles in loving her child. Depleted of any self-worth, such a woman is unable to feel anything positive can come from herself, often experiencing her child as a reflection of the degraded aspects of herself (Raphael-Leff 1986), whom she must reject. In an attempt to compensate for a profound sense of worthlessness, such a woman may erect desperately and rigidly held idealizations of her unborn child that are shattered by her inevitable disappointment with the actual baby.

An Integrative Summary

The richly woven tapestry of meanings that pregnancy fulfills is applicable to the father as well as to the mother.

> Fatherhood gives him a feeling of triumph: now he can transform the old unconscious identification of the little boy with his father into a real and permanent one. The conflict between the hostile and tender impulses can now be decided in favor of tenderness. Loving care for the new generation helps the mature man to free himself from his own childhood, and the urge to this liberation is one of the motives in desiring a child. The physical proof of his masculine potency strengthens his faith in himself as a man. His unfulfilled aspirations and expectations, now charged with new hopes, can be shifted to the child's future. (Deutsch 1945, 175)

In this passage, Deutsch refers, respectively, to the intrapsychic achievements pregnancy may facilitate—solidifying of gender identification, resolution of oedipal conflicts, reconciliation of ambivalence, further attainment of separation-individuation, narcissistic gratification of omnipotence, and expansion of ego ideal. Although I have presented these and other motives as elements of distinct models, these perspectives are often mutually reinforcing rather than contradictory. A simultaneous examination of these different models may in fact provide a richer texture to understanding pregnancy. As a summary, I shall link these views in a theoretical synthesis.

In order to progress through a new developmental stage, pregnancy fosters a regression in virtually all areas of functioning, including drives (recapitulation of psychosexual stages), object (revival of early representations of mother and self), cognition (immersion in transitional phenomena blurring the boundary between self and other), separation-individuation (repeating earlier stages of establishing psychic independence from mother), and self (reactivating earlier narcissistic modes of experiencing others as self-objects in regulating self-esteem). These processes complement one another. Through the interplay of her maternal and infantile identifications, mediated by her relationship with her unborn child, the woman may further resolve her intrapsychic conflicts (especially dependency) revived in her pregnancy. In seeking merger with her mother, the most primitive object relationship, the pregnant woman satisfies her earliest instinctual (that is, oral) yearnings and realizes her narcissistic ambitions of maternal omnipotence and grandiosity. At the same time, this intensified maternal identification will enable a more complete differentiation from mother and achievement of maturity in motherhood, providing nurturance to her needy infant. Maternal identifications can simultaneously index the sought-object tie with her own mother and the narcissistic aims of fulfilling motherhood. The physiological symbiosis of mother and fetus provides the biophysical foundation for the following interrelated processes: the activation of antithetical maternal and infantile identifications, the psychic blurring of boundaries between the mother and her unborn child, and the inclusion of her child as a narcissistic extension of herself in both forming a cohesive sense of self and regulating self-esteem.

The course of pregnancy traces the transformation of a narcissistic bond into an object relationship. In the first trimester the mother perceives the unborn child as a physical and psychological expansion of herself, in the form of a narcissistic self-object; during the second trimester she increasingly experiences the fetus as a distinct object, especially when it begins to move. This interaction culminates in an object relationship by birth, so that the mother is able to relate to her child as a separate person. Because of the freshness and intensity of the earlier mode of experiencing her unborn child as part of herself, her object relationship to her baby is heavily narcissistic, thus serving as a vital preparation and support for her maternity. The new mother's continued experience of her child as a part of herself both facilitates her empathy with her baby's lack of differentiation between self and other and ensures her devotion to her child as a fulfillment of her own needs. Vestiges of this early narcissistic tie to her child always remain. They are evident in the common, though often unconscious, parental experience of repeating and revising one's own history in the unfolding of one's children's lives.

CHAPTER 2
THE PSYCHOLOGY OF PERINATAL LOSS

Understanding the range of typical responses to perinatal loss is necessary to appreciate the maladaptive responses illustrated in treatment cases in the following chapter. Here I will review the available research and clinical literature as well as present my own formulations on the impact of perinatal loss. In chapter 5 I examine methodological problems that could limit the validity and reliability of research findings and then consider possible areas for future investigation.

A Mother's Need for Her Baby

An infant's need for his mother is both obvious and overwhelming. Not only does the baby's physical dependency require considerable parental caretaking to ensure the child's survival, but his immature cognitive apparatus and the expectations for increasing participation in a complex social network demand long-term, intense relationships between parents and child. Some of the most important developmental contributions of the past thirty years have elaborated aspects of the baby's need for the mother as reflected in innate patterns of attachment behavior to promote close contact (Ainsworth 1973; Bowlby 1969), in the dangers of early separation and loss for later competent functioning (Bowlby 1973, 1980), and in the importance of reciprocal mother-infant interaction for optimal emotional development (Brazelton et al. 1974).

Much less obvious, but perhaps not much less crucial, is the mother's need for her baby. In addition to whatever current and long-standing motives may have impelled a woman to become pregnant, once pregnancy is established, a combination of developmental, instinctual, and psychological processes is initiated. As discussed in the prior chapter, bearing and mothering a child may (1) satisfy progressive developmental forces directed, socially, toward fulfilling a vital function in rearing the next generation and, personally, toward one's further maturation as an adult; (2) provide instinctual gratification of infantile sexual pleasures (including oral, anal, phallic, and oedipal drives) and of one's femaleness through reproduction; (3) offer an opportunity to further resolve latent intrapsychic conflicts and fixations intensified during pregnancy; (4) satisfy a wished-for reunion with mother; (5) effect a greater degree of separateness and individuation from mother; (6) inspire a sense of omnipotence in the act of creation; (7) defy the dreaded inevitability of death through one's participation in the continuity of generations; (8) expand one's boundaries through the experience of merging with another; (9) realize exhibitionistic, grandiose wishes in maternity; and (10) enrich self-esteem through identifying with the accomplishments of one's child. While some of these gratifications may be felt most acutely during pregnancy (for example, the sense of omnipotence in the act of creation), most continue into the mothering relationship, during which a powerful identification with one's child as a part of oneself endures. Perinatal loss not only frustrates all of these potential satisfactions but, because of the regressed state of heightened arousal, conflict, and narcissistic vulnerability during pregnancy, may result in overwhelming and debilitating psychic injury.

In order to appreciate the mother's need for her baby, it is vital to understand that her attachment to her child does not begin at birth. As we have seen, by the third trimester the mother has a well-defined image of her child-to-be's personality, has powerfully identified that child with herself in her mother's body, and has included that child within her narcissistic orbit as a crucial extension that preserves and replenishes her self-esteem. Birth is simultaneously a beginning, a continuation, and an end. It marks the beginning of a person separate in body. As such, it ends the fetus's total physiological dependence on and physical inseparableness from mother. Less obviously, birth is a continuation, or, more precisely, a transformation of the mother's bond with her "inside" child to one with her "outside" child (Lewis 1976). As many theorists have noted, the mother's initial attachment to and relationship with the newborn is predicated on her prenatal fantasies and her bond with the unborn child (Ballou 1978; Benedek 1949; Deutsch 1945; Leifer 1977; Pines 1972; Raphael-Leff 1983).

Klaus and Kennell (1982) have provided fascinating empirical evidence of the potential importance of the first hours after birth. Events during this particularly sensitive period may facilitate the mother's bonding with her newborn. They offer, as one possible explanation, the ethological model of instincts, in which maternal behavior in many animals must be activated by contact with the newborn within a critical period following birth, after which the offspring will be rejected if introduced. Another, more psychological explanation they suggest is the importance of reconciling the image of the fantasized baby during pregnancy with that of the real infant via bonding.

Early contact with the neonate aids in transforming the prenatal bond into a postnatal bond. Both prenatal and postnatal bonds involve elements of a narcissistic tie (as part of oneself) and an object relationship (to a separate person). However, the experience of birth and of viewing one's separate child increases the object (and reduces the narcissistic) nature of the tie. Bonding also transforms a physiological symbiosis into an interactional one; after birth mother and neonate are bound together in a complex web of reciprocal behaviors including touch, eye-to-eye contact, and nursing. "These behaviors seem to be specific and innately programmed to start the process of locking mother and infant together in a sustained reciprocal rhythm" (Klaus & Kennell

1982, 82). The psychological symbiosis with the unborn child also continues postpartum. Although the object status of the infant is promoted by his separate body and unique qualities, the narcissistic nature of the bond (that is, her psychological symbiosis) is reinforced through these interlocking behavioral sequences, her persisting tendency to identify her child as a part of herself, familial resemblance, and, of course, the enduring memories of pregnancy.

The drive, object relations, and narcissistic models may be integrated in portraying the mother's need for her child. Her infantile identification enables an empathic awareness of her baby's needs. In the mother's caring for her child as an extension of herself, her early infantile cravings are satisfied by her maternal need to nurture. Thus, her infantile and maternal identifications are actively enlisted in the process of mothering. The psychosexual basis of this oral bond is expressed in the mother's physical capacity to nurse her infant as well as to soothe him by holding and molding the baby to her own body. The regressive maternal and infantile identifications intensified over the course of pregnancy not only prepare the mother to care for her child but *require* that nurturing bond in order for her maternal and infantile needs to be fulfilled. In a mutually satisfying postpartum symbiosis, the mother fulfills her child's needs and in so doing has her maternal and infantile needs gratified. The smooth operation of maternal and infantile identifications, postpartum, demands the continuity of the mother's relationship with her child.

Intrapsychic Meanings of Perinatal Loss

When perinatal loss occurs, there are multiple frustrations, many disappointments, and much deprivation. The course of the parent's development is derailed, usually abruptly, without warning, sometimes permanently. There is profound deprivation of one's instinctual urges to both give and receive, to nurture and grow, to feed and be fed. A specific person who can never be replaced has died. A part of oneself, an embodiment of the future, and the best one has to offer has died as well. A sense of power, of having defeated death, is extinguished by the occurrence of death when it is least expected.

DEVELOPMENTAL INTERFERENCE

Nagera (1970) has described how a parent's death may distort a child's development by removing an important figure who is needed both to experience and optimally to resolve normal developmental conflicts (for example, the father's involvement as a competitor and object for identification during the oedipal period). Other circumstances such as physical handicaps and injuries may interfere by impairing or preventing developmental achievements in a more or less typical manner.

The crisis of pregnancy is normally resolved, for better or worse, in the birth of a child. By disturbing this natural resolution, perinatal loss may act as a developmental interference. Without a child, the adult is unable to negotiate entrance into parenthood, a process that has already been set into motion in pregnancy. This interference may be partial or temporary as prior or subsequent successful pregnancies may permit establishment of a beachhead in parenthood. Perinatal loss, however, may sorely test the security and vulnerability of that parental identity, potentially impairing one's interactions with children, which further compromises parental identification.

Developmental interference in the successful resolution of adult stages may have less dramatic results than childhood developmental interference owing to the critical importance for the growing child of mastering developmental tasks and the greater availability of sublimatory channels for an adult in achieving developmental goals. A boy deprived of paternal contact during the oedipal period, for example, may face massive obstacles to the normal establishment of a secure masculine identity, a solidifying of conscience, and later a consolidation of heterosexuality. A man or woman deprived of biological parenthood may find substitute expression through adoption or alternative forms of nurturance and through creativity in a career. Nonetheless, the developmental interference caused by perinatal loss may reverberate throughout one's life. Being deprived of the ability or seriously hampered in the attempt to parent may significantly compromise the possibility of adapting effectively to earlier neurotic conflicts (Benedek 1959) by assisting and identifying with a child's navigation through developmental conflicts. Both pregnancy and subsequent parenting provide these "second chances" at more productive solutions, giving truth to the maxim that "the child raises the parent." Cummings (1976) describes how, conversely, fathers who experienced failure in their parenting of handicapped children often displayed a pattern of neurotic constriction, low self-esteem, depression, and intensified compulsive tendencies, suggesting a solidifying of preexisting neurotic traits.

Little has been written about perinatal loss as a developmental interference (Kowalski 1980). Perhaps the more striking and immediate dynamics of loss (both object and narcissistic) obscure this effect. The extent to which perinatal loss acts as a developmental interference may not become evident until years after the event, when parenting has become compromised. Even then, the impact of an earlier perinatal loss on parenting may not be obvious unless illuminated by a parent or child in psychotherapy.

Many usual responses to perinatal loss, such as visualizing or hearing a baby, the intense wish to have another baby as soon as possible, and the feeling of great pain on being exposed to any and all reminders of babies, are often attributed to mourning a specific object loss. These reactions, especially to pregnancy loss in the first trimester, may be due less to loss of a particular object than to the major disruption in developmental progress caused by this loss and the desire to get back on track developmentally by having a baby to secure one's parenthood. This seemingly impersonal wish for a baby is not inherently disturbed, although for some pregnant women, especially adolescents, it may be based on a defensive maneuver to bypass the tortuous straits of separation-individuation by "achieving" adult status via motherhood and not on a genuine wish to mother (Fisher & Scharf 1980). In fact, the urge to mother may indicate a readiness, after much preparation, to assume maternal responsibilities.

The woman whose mothering aims have been frustrated often experiences a terrible sense of exclusion and being different in the company of other mothers, especially if she has no other children. Being with other mothers and babies is often intolerable. The loneliness and perhaps shame of being in this isolated position may, again, be based less on mourning than on the failure to reach this developmental milestone, which is further exacerbated by the success of other mothers. This experience may be akin to that felt by the isolated, physically handicapped child, whose impairment prevents mastery of certain motoric skills, the resulting confidence in his body, and the shared sense of developmental progress with peers exercising that skill together. The bereaved mother is excluded from mothers' groups, which consolidate a sense of identity in entering the new developmental phase of motherhood—much as team sports may offer latency-age children a context in which to master participation in social groups, and as adolescent subculture may offer teenagers a sense of belonging during the separation-individuation process.

INSTINCTUAL FRUSTRATION

Perinatal loss may inspire instinctual frustration both by depriving the person of the satisfaction of powerful oral drives and by reviving earlier internalized conflicts. Although this state is common for all bereaved mothers, the degree of frustration, as well as the variety of conflicts activated, is highly individualized.

Many researchers on perinatal loss have poignantly described the intense, quite visceral yearning of the bereaved mother for physical contact with her dead child (Davidson 1977; Kirkley-Best & Kellner 1982; Lewis 1976). Peppers and Knapp (1980a) noted that "mothers say they yearn to embrace their baby; their arms ache to hold the baby; their breasts ache to nurse the baby" (p. 42). There is a profound and quite literal hunger for the baby—a hunger to give and nurture, which can vicariously satisfy the mother's revived oral needs. The sense of deprivation, neediness, and orality may be understood as a fact of mourning, which has long been known to activate a regression to oral drives and fixations (Abraham 1924; Freud 1917b). It should be recalled, however, that prior to the perinatal loss, the pregnant woman displays an intensely oral mode of functioning in symbiotic attachment to her fetus (Benedek 1949, 1955, 1956). The pregnant woman is deprived of her child, whose nurturance is the sole means of satisfying her intense maternal strivings and infantile needs, in an already heightened state of oral arousal. Not surprisingly, this can provoke additional feelings of deprivation, leading to profound depression. Most researchers have attributed this depression to a specific object loss, overlooking the independent contribution of the orally regressed state of pregnancy in which the loss occurs. The mother's intense need to hold, feed, and care for her child cannot be based on prior memories of those actual interactions but draws on powerful maternal and infantile wishes fueled by both the oral regression within pregnancy and the deprivation caused by the baby's death.

In addition to the regression to orality during pregnancy, earlier intrapsychic conflicts are activated with potentially new resolutions (Bibring 1959), especially regarding unresolved ambivalence toward mother (Ballou 1978; Benedek 1956; Deutsch 1945; Uddenberg 1974). Perinatal loss occurs in the midst of these intensified conflicts, and inevitably the baby's death becomes endowed with personalized meanings. The revival of oedipal conflicts in pregnancy may fuel competition with one's own mother (Ballou 1978; Deutsch 1945). If oedipal conflicts in pregnancy have led to the woman's fear that she or her baby will die (Deutsch 1945), she may interpret a subsequent loss as punishment for her prohibited oedipal strivings. The pregnant woman who struggles with sadistic impulses is likely to experience a subsequent perinatal loss as punishment for her aggressive wishes. Multiple instinctual drives may operate together; the bereaved mother's intense envy of other mothers may represent the exacerbation of her newly disappointed oedipal wishes as well as her profound hunger for a baby, the only person who can satisfy her maternal longings. The nature and degree of earlier intrapsychic conflicts will be a crucial determinant of the individual meanings and outcome of the loss.

OBJECT LOSS

The unique relationship of the mother to her child-to-be makes the loss of an unborn or recently born child different from any other. The object, as opposed to narcissistic, experience of the fetus is increasingly established during the second half of the pregnancy, particularly owing to the baby's movements in the womb. This object relationship is quite special in that it coexists with an intense narcissistic attachment to the child and is much more heavily laden with projective contents than are other object relationships because of the relative lack of concrete stimuli (that is, interaction with an "outside" baby) and the activation of maternal and infantile identifications. The object loss is thus colored by the loss of the fantasized child-to-be and needs to be further distinguished from the narcissistic loss. The extensive literature on bereavement is a useful guide to understanding perinatal loss, but it is also important to appreciate the special aspects of this unique object loss.

The essence of mourning a loved person—that is, of painfully recalling memories of the deceased in detaching oneself from that relationship and of identifying, finally, with certain features of the deceased—was described by Freud (1917b). Later investigators described a sequence of three stages of mourning (Engel 1964; Lindemann 1944). Upon learning of the death, the bereaved is quite shocked or numb, especially if the death was unexpected. An initial lack of reaction usually signifies denial, a disbelief of and refusal to accept the fact of the beloved's death. After a period of internal disorganization and chaos, frequently with lapses in memory, anxiety, restlessness, irritability, and somatic distress, which may persist for several weeks, the bereaved actively grieves for his loss. During this second phase, the mourner yearns for the return of the deceased, is inconsolably saddened by that person's absence, and is preoccupied with memories of the beloved. The bereaved usually feels lonely, empty, and hopeless at this time, and possibly guilty, as a result of anger toward the deceased. Recovery is gradual over the next year(s), signaled by a resumption of everyday activities, a renewed interest in other relationships and the world in general, and a restored capacity to experience pleasure.

While this pattern is typical among the bereaved, more recent investigators have emphasized how unique and individualized mourning is: "Because each relationship is different, each grief is different and it is not possible to adopt a rigid time frame for bereavement. Also there is no clear end to grief" (Parkes 1985, 12). Zisook and DeVaul (1985) similarly noted that the recovery process often requires years, as opposed to the few months outlined in Lindemann's (1944) classic study, and is sometimes never completed. A recent empirical study demonstrated statistically significant impairment in many areas of functioning from four to seven years after the accidental death of a spouse or child (Lehman et al. 1987). Many researchers, having become cognizant of the intense, seemingly disturbed reactions during both the initial shock/denial phase and subsequent active grieving, believe it may not be possible at first to discern whether such responses indicate adaptive grieving or a pathological process (Engel 1964; Zisook & DeVaul 1985). Virtually all investigators maintain, however, that a broad distinction can and should be drawn between mourning as a self-limited, healing process in which a resumption of prior functioning is achieved and the multiple forms of unresolved grief, either as an arrest at one of the phases of bereavement (for example, inhibited grief or chronic mourning) or as a pathological variant (for example, hypochondriasis), in which serious impairment in functioning persists (Bowlby 1980; Engel 1964; Freud 1917b; Knapp 1986; Lindemann 1944; Parkes 1985; Raphael 1975, 1983; Rubin 1984; Volkan 1970; Zisook & DeVaul 1985).

Most studies view perinatal death in terms of the bereavement reaction outlined above. The bereaved parent, especially the mother, is shocked to learn of the child's death and may be in a state of disbelief for a number of weeks, at times hallucinating the baby's cries. Intense grieving for the lost child usually follows, often with an overwhelming sense of responsibility and guilt for the death. Even in sleep, dreams of the child haunt the parent. After about six months and usually within a year, hopelessness begins to abate and a more positive outlook toward the future emerges (Dunlop 1979; Elliott & Hein 1978; Ewy & Ewy 1984; Forrest et al. 1982; Giles 1970; Kennell et al. 1970; Kirkley-Best & Kellner 1982; LaFerla & Good 1985; Outerbridge et al. 1983; Panuthos & Romeo 1984; Peppers & Knapp 1980a; Phipps 1981; Saylor 1977; Scupholme 1978; Seitz & Warrick 1974; Standish 1982; Wilson & Soule 1981; Zahourek & Jensen 1973). Although this pattern is typical of perinatal loss, investigators have recognized considerable variation in individual responses (Clyman et al. 1980; Ewy & Ewy 1984; Outerbridge et al. 1983), much like that reported for bereavement in general.

Some investigators, noting the intensity of grief, have emphasized the similarity between mourning perinatal death (especially a stillborn or neonatal death) and any other family bereavement (LaFerla & Good 1985; Morris 1976; Outerbridge et al. 1983). Other researchers have focused on the uniqueness of this death, the loss of a fantasized person who was to be rather than of a consciously known individual (Davidson 1977; Lewis 1976; Wilson & Soule 1981). Some of the major difficulties in resolving perinatal loss may be directly due to the differences between this death and other losses.

Mourning the death of a person who has lived for some time requires the painful recollection of past interactions with that individual, heightened by intolerable yearning for his or her presence—the image, voice, odors, and touch of the deceased. The most agonizing feature of this process—that is, evoking visceral memories of the deceased—is a key element in resolving grief. Mourning a perinatal death, however, requires the painful recall of *fantasies* about (versus interactions with) one's child-to-be in the *absence* (versus excruciating presence) of visceral memories. Mourning a perinatal loss is exceedingly difficult because there is little or no tangible evidence of the child's existence. The grieving process can be facilitated if those fantasies and actual experiences of the baby's movements become concretized in the form of the dead baby's body. Interacting with the dead baby—seeing, touching, holding, and kissing him—may facilitate mourning in several important ways. The separate, object (versus narcissistic) status of the child is heightened by seeing his distinct body and features. Just as in the usual bonding process, there is a transformation from one's attachment to an unseen, "inside" baby to a visible, touchable, "outside" child. In fact, Kowalski (1980) noted that bereaved mothers interacted with their dead babies in ways quite similar to bonding with their live babies, first touching fingertips before moving to full-hand contact with the head and trunk. Parents are better able to accept the reality of their child's death if they view the baby's body. The mother's heightened attachment to her unborn child as he begins to move within her body may make the touching and holding of his lifeless body especially important in facilitating mourning; grieving through touching may be most effective when bonding has occurred in a similar kinesthetic mode. Finally, loving interaction with one's dead child creates unforgettable memories for later recall, thereby allowing the mourning of a perinatal death to approach the more usual bereavement process. By linking her feelings and wishes about her fantasized child-to-be with her actual, dead baby, the mother may be better able to grieve. Viewing the dead baby provides a tangible form through which her love for her unborn child can be expressed and mourned.

It is not surprising, therefore, that virtually every researcher or clinician who has worked with victims of perinatal loss has recommended that the parents be given an opportunity for contact with the dead baby in order to facilitate the grieving process (Adolf & Patt 1980; Beard et al. 1978; Cohen et al. 1978; Davidson 1977; Dunlop 1979; Elliott & Hein 1978; Ewy & Ewy 1984; Furlong & Hobbins 1983; Furman 1978; Hallet 1974; Helmrath & Steinitz 1978; Jolly 1976, 1978;

Kellner et al. 1981; Kirkley-Best & Kellner 1982; Klaus & Kennell 1982; Kowalski 1980; Kowalski & Osborn 1977; Krone & Harris 1988; LaFerla & Good 1985; Lewis 1976, 1979a; Lovell 1983; Mahan & Schreiner 1981; Osterweis et al. 1984; Outerbridge et al. 1983; Panuthos & Romeo 1984; Parrish 1980; Peppers & Knapp 1980a; Phipps 1981; Raphael 1983; Rappaport 1981; Russell 1975; Seitz & Warrick 1974; Speck 1978; Stierman 1987; Taylor & Gideon 1980; Worlow 1978). Most of these investigators emphasize parental contact with the dead baby as one important way to make both the child's life and his death more real. Providing additional concrete evidence of the child's existence (for example, pictures and footprints) and death (funeral service and burial) may similarly facilitate mourning. Case (1978) eloquently describes how religious ceremonies help parents grieve by fostering a clearer sense of their child's identity (through baptism and naming rituals) and death (through a funeral). Although parental contact with the dead baby may be the most effective means of facilitating mourning, there is no empirical evidence to indicate that it is the only method or even the best one for all parents.

Most mourning is retrospective—a remembrance of a person in one's past. But perinatal bereavement is prospective mourning—relinquishing wishes, hopes, and fantasies about one who could have been but never was. In a very real sense, perinatal death is a loss of the future (Lewis 1976; Wilson & Soule 1981). On the anniversary of the death, parents often recall how old the child would have been (Lockwood & Lewis 1980). Mourning the older fantasized child continues as the years pass and the would-have-been child reaches the age of the child in their earlier fantasies. Perinatal mourning may thus be more prolonged than other object losses, extending throughout the parents' lives until they must finally face the disappointment of those earlier fantasies. A mother who yearned for an adult offspring as a companion in her elderly years may mourn that particular loss dozens of years after the death. Several clinicians have described mothers who never fully recovered from perinatal loss, even when the death had been mourned and their functioning had returned to more or less normal (Furman 1978; Raphael 1983). A "shadow grief" (Peppers & Knapp 1980a, 22) often persists in the form of a lingering and transient sadness years after the loss has occurred. In tracing parents' bereavement after Sudden Infant Death Syndrome (SIDS), Rubin (1981) distinguished the typical reorganization of personality within a year after the death from the persistent, highly charged memories of the dead infant, which diminish much more gradually. Prospective mourning without any clear-cut end is not unique to perinatal death but seems typical of parental loss of any child.

One might argue that perinatal mourning involves no true object loss at all because the prenatal bond is merely a narcissistic tie and an object relationship based on fantasies rather than on actual interactions. This approach, however, overlooks the obvious fact that pregnancy is quite real. From her first awareness of having conceived, the pregnant woman begins an object tie with her future child (overshadowed, at first, by the narcissistic experience of her offspring). A central goal of pregnancy is the mother's intrapsychic preparation to engage in an intense, lifelong object relationship with her child. The vivid fantasizing about her child fosters an object tie when, at birth, the baby becomes totally dependent on parental care for survival. Therefore, to view pregnancy as solely a fantasized relationship ignores both the biological reality of the fetus in the womb and the intrapsychic purpose of the mother's intense prenatal bond—the eventual care for her infant. Fantasies of one's child-to-be during pregnancy are grounded in intrapsychic and physiological realities directed toward a real child.

One of the most serious obstacles to the successful resolution of grief is the suddenness of object loss. Unexpected death is usually much more traumatizing than anticipated bereavement, much more likely to be experienced as overwhelming loss, followed by potentially long-term maladaptive defenses and pathological variants of grief. This finding has been frequently reported by bereavement researchers (Parkes 1985; Volkan 1970) and has been supported by empirical research that reveals a statistically significant increase in psychiatric morbidity among those who were suddenly bereaved compared to those who expected the death (Lundin 1984). The psychological danger of a sudden bereavement is applied in the concept of anticipatory grieving; mourning an expected death often results in less devastating grief and a more benign outcome post-death than does a sudden loss (Bourke 1984; Rando 1986a). Studies examining the impact of an older child's death on the parents and the course of their mourning have convincingly demonstrated less overwhelming grief and a much greater likelihood of eventual recovery if the parents allowed themselves to begin grieving about six to eighteen months (Rando 1983) prior to the child's death (Bergman 1974; Binger et al. 1969; Chodoff et al. 1964; Easson 1972; Friedman 1974; Friedman et al. 1963; Knapp 1986; Lascari & Stebbens 1973; Martin et al. 1968; Solnit & Green 1959).

Anticipatory grieving before perinatal loss is usually not possible because the death is typically quite sudden and unexpected, a factor that has frequently been cited as exacerbating the resolution of grief (Kirkley-Best & Kellner 1982; Peppers & Knapp 1980a; Stack 1984). Although miscarriage in the first trimester is not uncommon—comprising about 20 percent of all pregnancies of which women are aware—the relative infrequency of near-term intrauterine deaths, stillbirths, and neonatal deaths (accounting altogether for only about 2 percent of all pregnancies [Newton & Newton 1988]) usually makes this a totally unexpected, potentially traumatizing event. One possible psychological casualty of the success of modern medicine in dramatically reducing perinatal losses may be a widespread reduction in normal anticipatory grieving. Ours is a death-denying society (Becker 1973; Freud 1915; Fulton 1967; Gorer 1965; Hallet 1974; Kubler-Ross 1969), one that attempts to isolate death in hospitals, away from everyday contact and experience. When perinatal loss was both more common and more accepted as a part of life, such death was perhaps less shocking and could be more readily integrated into one's everyday reality, especially with the emotional support of others who had shared a similar loss.

Anticipatory grieving as a cushion against the traumatizing impact of perinatal death may be less available, therefore, owing to both the reduced incidence of this loss and a societal unwillingness to face and prepare for the inevitability of death.

The common fear that the baby or oneself will die during delivery (Deutsch 1945; Kestenberg 1976) may in part be a usual form of anticipatory grieving as preparation for a dreaded but possible outcome (Hallet 1974). The typical experience of heightened anxiety during a pregnancy following a perinatal loss (Kowalski 1980; Phipps 1985; Seitz & Warrick 1974) may also be viewed as a potentially adaptive form of anticipatory grief, a defense against another traumatizing blow by preparing for the worst. Similarly, a temporary blunting of maternal attachment during pregnancy following infertility (Shapiro 1986) or immediately prior to learning a prenatal diagnosis from amniocentesis or chorionic villus sampling (Siögren & Uddenberg 1988) may be an attempt to soften the anticipatory disappointment of losing the baby when a pregnancy is experienced in jeopardy. Obviously a mother who learns of her child's intrauterine death prior to delivery tends to have a more subdued reaction at delivery than a mother who discovers her loss at birth (Kowalski 1980; Parrish 1980). However, the denial of death is a powerful, persistent defense, often requiring that the mother see her dead child in order to be convinced of this reality—even after being told of the death many times prior to delivery (Grubb 1976a). Clinicians may promote the adaptive use of anticipatory grieving to reduce the trauma of death and thereby facilitate mourning by delaying the onset of delivery, when feasible, in cases of intrauterine death (LaFerla & Good 1985), and providing a supportive hospice program for parents of dying neonates (Harmon et al. 1984; Whitfield et al. 1982).

The difficulty of recognizing a life and mourning a death for which there is no visible body, the nature of prospective grieving for a fantasized child, the suddenness of the death, allowing no opportunity for anticipatory grief—these distinguish perinatal loss from most other kinds of bereavement and help explain why perinatal death may be especially complicated to resolve. In addition to the actual baby, earlier, unresolved losses may become identified with the fantasized, unborn child during pregnancy. When a pregnancy that was unconsciously used as an attempt to undo an earlier death ends in failure, the degree of object loss is compounded. Even if the pregnancy was not designed as a replacement for an earlier object loss, it is not unusual for older griefs to find new expression in the object representation of the mourned unborn child. The common fate of death and the mother's tendency to confer on her child-to-be the heritage of her earlier object ties and losses promote this emotional connection (Orbach 1959). While a living child has an opportunity to establish an identity of his own through development, thereby becoming a more distinct, separate object for mother, a perinatal death "freezes" that process at its inception. At his death, the baby represents for the mother various identities, including her own and the child's father's, her history of object relationships (especially parents), and the child himself.

Not only must the baby be mourned, but the loss or damage to one's sense of maternity and one's infantile identification with that baby must also be brought into the bereavement process.

NARCISSISTIC INJURY

First, and usually foremost, perinatal death is a loss of part of the self. Although several researchers have noted this aspect of perinatal death (Grubb 1976b; Hagan 1974; Klaus & Kennell 1982; Krone & Harris 1988; Palmer & Noble 1986; Stack 1984; Turco 1981), few, I believe, have emphasized its centrality. Erna Furman (1978), more than any other, has eloquently described how such a death is literally like losing a part of one's body, a potentially devastating blow to one's self-esteem; unlike object loss, this death cannot be resolved by an adaptive identification and therefore is more difficult to conclude. Just as pregnancy serves multiple narcissistic purposes, perinatal loss causes multiple narcissistic wounds to a woman's sense of omnipotence, immortality, femininity, selfhood, and self-esteem.

In becoming pregnant, a woman may finally realize a life-long wish for omnipotence via successful identification with the all-powerful, life-giving, pre-oedipal mother. This sense of power is replaced by profound feelings of inadequacy and failure when she loses her baby. The depressive experience of defeated omnipotence during the initial inner-genital phase when the three-year-old girl faced the intense disappointment of being unable to reproduce, in contrast to her mother (Kestenberg 1956, 1976), may be painfully reevoked by perinatal death. Following such a death, the bereaved mother frequently struggles with intense envy of other mothers, wishes to steal their babies, experiences a pervasive sense of inadequacy, and feels hopeless about the prospects of a future successful pregnancy, regardless of the actual medical circumstances. Early childhood wishes to steal a child as a means of securing maternal omnipotence, along with a consuming envy of mother and a sense of one's parental unworthiness (Frankel 1985), may be important dynamic roots for these typical sequelae to perinatal loss.

Virtually all mothers after perinatal loss report some degree of guilt and self-blame, varying in intensity from mild to relentlessly severe (Benfield et al. 1978; Cain, Erickson, et al. 1964; Clyman et al. 1980; Condon 1986; Hagan 1974; Helmrath & Steinitz 1978; Peppers & Knapp 1980a; Seitz & Warrick 1974; Stack 1984; Taylor & Gideon 1980). It is not uncommon for women who are not otherwise psychotic to maintain irrational causal beliefs based on primitive, magical thought processes (for example, a mother's blaming herself for her child's congenital heart defect because she did not adequately protect herself from a solar eclipse during pregnancy) (Clyman et al. 1980). Although unconscious aggressive wishes and ambivalence about becoming pregnant may account in part for this guilt, common reasons for guilt during mourning (Cain, Erickson, et al. 1964), these are generally not the primary causes. Both the mother's narcissistic experience of omnipotence in pregnancy and the deepening maternal identification that prepares her to assume total care for her helpless infant contribute to her enormous sense of responsibility and resulting guilt for her child's death. As the mother of her child, she feels that she is to blame for what has happened. This view may also explain why several empirical studies have found a statistically significant greater degree of guilt in mothers than in fathers after perinatal loss (Benfield et al. 1978; Smith & Borgers 1988; Wilson et al. 1982). Unfortunately, scientific ignorance about what causes most perinatal deaths (Ewy & Ewy 1984; Kirkley-Best & Kellner 1982) limits the adoption of more accurate causal explanations, which might reduce maternal guilt. In fact, parents suffering perinatal loss (Clyman et al. 1980; Schreiner et al. 1979) and parents of a terminally ill child (Bozeman et al. 1955; Chodoff et al. 1964; Friedman 1967; Friedman et al. 1963) often have a great need to learn all they can about their child's illness or death, perhaps in an attempt to mitigate their sense of guilt or helplessness. Gardner (1969) discovered unconscious hostility operating in only 20 percent of those parents experiencing guilt over their seriously ill children and suggested that the parents' wish to master their sense of helplessness may be a more important motive for their self-blame. This view is supported by the defensive-attribution hypothesis in social psychology, which suggests that self-blame may be adaptive if it facilitates perceived control of future events (Janoff-Bulman 1979). One study examining maternal reactions to perinatal complications revealed a statistically significant association between maternal self-blame and positive mood, when mediated by a belief that the problem could be controlled should it recur (Tennen et al. 1986). Affleck and his colleagues (1985) discovered a statistically significant increase in adaptation in improved maternal mood, caretaking, and responsiveness to their developmentally disabled children at nine and eighteen months if there was more behavioral self-blame for the handicap occurring; this implies a heightened experience of control over whether a subsequent handicapped child will be born. Irrational guilt over perinatal

loss may therefore result directly from the powerful revival
of one's experience of omnipotence during pregnancy or indirectly from one's deflation, from a sense of helplessness
motivating a defensive belief in one's responsibility in order
to feel greater control in the situation. The statistically significant increase in well-being reported by parents who participated in the medical decisions (Benfield et al. 1978) or
actual care (Mulhern et al. 1983) of their terminally ill children
versus those parents who did not may be based on a greater
sense of mastery in the situation as opposed to feelings of
debilitating helplessness. Other studies (Dorner & Atwell
1985; Walwork & Ellison 1985) have demonstrated no negative long-term repercussions of parental decisions to withhold medical care from their fatally damaged newborns.

Perinatal loss deals a profound blow to a parent's sense of
omnipotence. It is felt in the loss of one's child, by whom
the parent would have been idealized. Also, because parents
view their child as an expression of unrealized omnipotence
(Cooper & Ekstein 1978), that child's death assaults their
sense of efficacy.

By robbing a woman of motherhood, perinatal loss defies
maternal omnipotence. By destroying the parents' link with
future generations, perinatal loss undoes the denial of death
embodied in giving birth. Facing the reality of death causes
massive narcissistic mortification and acute anxiety over a
basic tenet of existence. Perhaps no other event can evoke
human mortality so brutally as the shocking coincidence of
pregnancy, the process of giving life, with death.

Regarding the mother's revived identifications during pregnancy, perinatal loss is a dual narcissistic injury. Producing
a dead child, particularly if it is her first pregnancy, can be
devastating to a woman's feeling of self-worth. Her positive
maternal identification is challenged by a sense of failure.
Reciprocally, her infantile identification cannot be gratified
by seeing her child develop. Perhaps in an attempt to identify
with her lost child, she feels dead and empty inside.

Perinatal loss usually fills a woman with a terrible sense of
having failed as a mother and as a woman (Cain, Erickson,

et al. 1964; Furman 1978; Peppers & Knapp 1980a; Seitz & Warrick 1974; Stierman 1987). For she has not fulfilled a basic bodily function, reproduction, around which her femininity is organized, and in addition has experienced the intense disappointment of her revived maternal identifications, which seek a child to nurture when there is none. Perinatal loss is often experienced by a mother as punishment for some, usually unconscious, misdeed or guilt (Deutsch 1945; Lockwood & Lewis 1980). For some women this may revive an earlier belief that the lack of a penis is castration, a punishment for prohibited wishes or deeds (Cullberg 1972). The intense envy and hatred toward other mothers frequently described by women after perinatal loss (Hagan 1974; Lockwood & Lewis 1980; Peppers & Knapp 1980a) may, in part, be embedded in feelings of profound inferiority because of the failure to procreate and be inflamed by the presence of other mothers and their babies. The bereaved woman experiences enormous shame and humiliation, as do victims of other narcissistic losses that involve bodily injury. At the same time, the persistence of the bereaved mother's maternity can be quite poignant: she may become distraught on cold, rainy days, feeling that she should be tending to the child's grave.

Perinatal death constitutes a loss of part of the self because literally a part of the mother has died. Furthermore, through her infantile identification she links the image of that child with herself as an unborn child. Grubb (1976b) described a case in which a baby's intrauterine death led to a reversal of the mother's process of separating from her fetus at quickening, leading to fears that she too would die. Indeed, in some cultures this identification is taken quite literally. T. Lewis (1975) described a severely depressed Amerindian woman of Surinam who had no desire to live and anticipated dying after the death of her newborn. She believed that

> an infant who dies goes beyond the trees, to the circling horizon, to the sky where the souls stay. It has an invisible cord attached to the umbilicus and extending to the mother. The cord functions to nurture both until the

child can care for itself, until it can walk and talk and eat by itself. If the child dies before this, it misses its mother and keeps pulling on the cord. She misses the child, and responds by giving up that which keeps her on the earth. (pp. 92–93)

Intended to illustrate how a clinical syndrome may be conditioned by a particular culture, this case history may, ironically, demonstrate the universality of grief over perinatal death, based on the truly symbiotic maternal need to care for her child and, in so doing, satisfy infantile cravings ("The cord functions to nurture both").

Mourning a perinatal loss does not, of course, demand such complete and ultimately fatal identification. Rather, it involves the mother's emotional linking with her offspring as a part of herself rather than as a nameless, anonymous body. Through the process of identifying with her dead child in mourning, the mother gradually relinquishes her symbiotic tie to *this* child and achieves sufficient separation to attempt another pregnancy and to form a psychological symbiosis with *another* child. While her attachment to the unborn child may never fully end, her maternal and infantile identifications may be sufficiently mourned to permit new, different objects of maternal care. Much as the mother's maternal identification during pregnancy eventually permits a further degree of separation-individuation from her own mother, so her identification with her dead child in mourning enables a certain differentiation and resolution of the psychological symbiosis with that child.

Viewing and interacting with one's dead baby not only may facilitate grieving the object loss but may help resolve the narcissistic losses as well. By seeing one's self reflected in one's child, one is more able to mourn the part of oneself that has been lost. Parents typically note family resemblances in their dead baby, much as they do with their live newborn, to reestablish the original narcissistic basis of their bond with their now-visible child (Krone & Harris 1988). Conversely, the mother's maternal identification may find some satisfaction and closure through holding and caressing her child, perhaps providing a special blanket as a token of her enduring wish to comfort and care for her child. As one of the few concrete opportunities to demonstrate her devotion to her child, funeral services may serve as a crucial means of memorializing her maternal actions.

In addition to being experienced as an extension of the mother's self, the unborn child occupies a vital position as an expression of her ego ideal, upon which much of her self-esteem is based. Kohut (1971) has described how a traumatizing disappointment in the idealized self-object may lead to a massive regression in the narcissistic personality manifested by severe bodily worries, extreme shame reactions, and near-delusional fantasies. The hypochondriacal concerns, intense shame, and hallucinations of baby cries often reported by mothers grieving perinatal loss may be understood in part as sequelae to their massive narcissistic injuries and attempts at restitution. As both a reflection of her exhibitionistic pride in her feminine, procreative body during pregnancy (that is, mirror transference) and a source of perfection in compensating for her failings (idealizing transference), the unborn baby may replenish her self-esteem immensely. Producing a dead baby delivers a profound blow to both these sources of narcissistic enrichment just when her narcissistic vulnerability is heightened. Viewing her baby may again offer narcissistic repair. When parents see their dead baby, even if there is some deformity, they usually feel tremendous relief that he is not the monster they may have imagined—a fear only encouraged by the reluctance of medical practitioners to have parents see their dead child (Davidson 1977; Jolly 1978; Lovell 1983). If the mother is able to cherish some aspect of the child she produced, her wounded self-esteem may begin to heal. By viewing her real baby, the dangers of either excessively idealizing the fantasized child (thereby making future children inadequate substitutes) or denigrating him (thereby impairing her self-esteem) may be alleviated.

Maternal rage after perinatal loss is often interpreted as an

externalization toward others of intolerable guilt (Cain, Erickson, et al. 1964; Hagan 1974; Kirkley-Best & Kellner 1982).
Since one important root of this self-blame is the revived
experience of omnipotence during pregnancy, it should not
be surprising that physicians, whom our society endows with
omnipotence, are a common target of this rage. My own clinical experience similarly suggests that rage at others persisting years after the death is most often an expression of
unconscious guilt in unresolved mourning in which the
mother has never allowed herself to feel *any* guilt. Maternal
rage during the active grieving process is not necessarily a
defensive expression of guilt but may be a direct discharge
of the profound and multiple narcissistic hurts the bereaved
mother endures. She is furious over being deprived of the
one being she most desperately needs. Rage is the natural
response to the profound disappointment of her maternal
and infantile longings, to the body blows to her self-esteem,
and to the frustration of her sense of omnipotence and immortality.

Researchers and clinicians in the field of perinatal bereavement tend to view grieving the object loss as the critical psychological task. This obscures, I believe, the often greater
importance of repairing the narcissistic damage resulting
from this death. LaRoche and her colleagues (1984) reported
that although bereaved mothers' test scores on depression
and mourning were statistically significant and positively associated, the degree of mourning for the dead child could
account for only about 20 percent of the extent of depression.
Perhaps the multiple narcissistic assaults on the mother's
self-esteem contribute more powerfully to her depression
than does the loss of a distinct other.

Although most of the research and clinical work on perinatal
death uses the concept of object loss as an organizing theoretical framework, other perspectives can be usefully applied.
Perinatal death not only signifies the loss of another person
but may block adult development, revive earlier, instinctual
conflicts, and impair self-esteem. Reactions to perinatal loss

may be multiply determined. The intense envy a bereaved mother often feels toward other mothers with babies may be based on feeling excluded from this important phase of life (that is, experiencing a developmental interference); feeling jealous of the prerogatives her mother possessed with father (reviving latent oedipal struggles); feeling deprived of her maternal and infantile longings to nurture and be nurtured (deepening maternal and infantile identifications); wishing to recover the sense of maternal power experienced during pregnancy (securing omnipotence); and yearning for that (self-) object who could repair her damaged self-esteem (re-establishing her narcissistic equilibrium through restoration of the ego ideal). Psychoanalytic investigation may determine which combination of dynamics is central in an individual woman.

In light of the multiple ways perinatal loss may inflict psychological harm on bereaved mothers, it becomes more understandable why this loss can be so difficult to resolve. Bereavement researchers have identified three factors often associated with unresolved mourning: ambivalence toward the deceased (Barry 1981; Engel 1964; Freud 1917b; Lindemann 1944; Parkes 1985; Raphael 1975, 1977, 1978; Volkan 1970); extreme dependency on the deceased (Engel 1964; Parkes 1985; Raphael 1975, 1978; Volkan 1970); and the sudden, unexpected nature of the death (Bourke 1984; Lundin 1984; Parkes 1985; Volkan 1970). The revival of intense ambivalence toward mother during pregnancy, the manifold ways in which the pregnant woman needs her baby to fulfill maternal and infantile wishes, and the usually shocking, totally unanticipated occurrence of perinatal death make perinatal death a particularly difficult loss to mourn.

Interpersonal Responses to Perinatal Loss

"Miscarriages do not occur in a uterus, but in a woman; and . . . miscarriages do not occur solely in a woman, but in a family" (Cain, Erickson, et al. 1964, 65). One might add that perinatal loss usually occurs in a hospital and, in the largest sense, within a community. It is not enough to consider only the intrapsychic meanings of perinatal loss. The reactions the bereaved mother receives from medical caretakers, family members, and friends influence her experience of the loss and the eventual psychological outcome.

REACTIONS OF MEDICAL CARETAKERS

Until about ten years ago, the medical profession had demonstrated a startling lack of sensitivity and responsiveness to the often traumatizing impact of perinatal loss. Physicians typically denied or minimized the significance of the loss, avoided discussing the death with parents, prescribed sedatives to reduce expressions of maternal shock and grief, discouraged or prohibited contact with the dead baby, and recommended having another child as soon as possible rather than recognize the necessity of grieving in resolving the death (Cullberg 1972; Giles 1970; Jolly 1978; Klaus & Kennell 1982; Knapp & Peppers 1979; Lewis 1976; Peppers & Knapp 1980a). Bourne (1968) was first to document the fact that physicians repressed stillbirth as a "non-event" and that they were, to a statistically significant degree, less able to recall their stillbirth deliveries than their live ones. He later observed (Bourne 1977) the continued professional blind spot in this area, as evidenced by the lack of research and publications on perinatal loss. Medical personnel help shape the societal definitions of both bereaved mothers and their unborn children by deciding "when the products of conception are deemed to be a baby and a woman deemed to be a mother" (Lovell 1983, 760). Many researchers have noted that unconscious guilt, based on a failure to act omnipotently as expected by patients, society, and themselves, may promote the tendency of physicians and nurses to deny the loss by distancing themselves from parental feelings and questions (Bruce 1962; Klaus & Kennell 1982; Knapp & Peppers 1979; Kowalski 1980; Panuthos & Romeo 1984; Seitz & Warrick 1974; Zahourek & Jensen 1973). The medical caretaker's own sadness over this loss, which may persist for months (Adolf &

Patt 1980), may further motivate a retreat to a coolly detached position. Adopting an unemotional, "professional" attitude, therefore, may serve to defensively block both medical caretakers' grief and their narcissistic hurt in feeling their efficacy challenged by an unexpected death. Unable to mourn their own sense of loss and inadequacy, physicians and nurses have had considerable difficulty displaying empathy with the mother's sorrow and feelings of failure. Professional attitudes, advice, and behavior that actively discourage or prevent bereaved mothers from mourning their children's deaths are clearly not in the mothers' best interests.

Just as unconscious maternal guilt may be externalized when mothers attack medical caretakers, the converse may also occur: as a means of defending against their own unresolved guilt and grief, medical practitioners may subtly or directly blame bereaved mothers for their children's deaths (Cullberg 1972), attributing miscarriages to maternal psychopathology. Simon and his colleagues (1969) suggested that the mothers' unresolved sadomasochistic conflicts may have been acted out in miscarriages, and Kaij and his co-workers (1969) inferred that poor feminine identification led to spontaneous abortions. Although most miscarriages have been found to result from early fetal abnormalities, without any psychological etiology (Schneider 1973), both studies used samples of women who, in the great majority, had had only one miscarriage, which was likely of organic origin. Neither study collected psychological data prior to the loss. Findings interpreted as causal factors were more likely consequences of maternal perinatal bereavement. In light of the narcissistic rage ignited by perinatal loss, it is not surprising to discover sadomasochistic conflicts during the mourning period (Simon et al. 1969). Likewise, the damaged feminine identifications reported by Kaij and his colleagues (1969) may have resulted from the narcissistic injuries these women sustained from their loss, as well as from their inability to resolve earlier conflicts with mother revived during pregnancy, perhaps owing to the devastating impact of these losses.

Dissatisfaction with medical caretakers, who were viewed

as insensitive and aloof (Jolly 1978; Knapp & Peppers 1979), as misunderstanding the intensity of the grief (Estok & Lehman 1983; Smith & Borgers 1988), or as providing inadequate information (Helström & Victor 1987; Rowe et al. 1978), has been commonly reported by parents after perinatal loss. On the basis of what has just been discussed, this perception of medical responses is likely more accurate than distorted. A disruption in the doctor-patient relationship may ensue (Knapp & Peppers 1979); one study (Wolff et al. 1970) found that about half the bereaved mothers in the sample changed their physicians for their next pregnancy. The disappointment and fury of bereaved mothers may target even the most empathic caretakers, who were nonetheless unable to safely deliver their child. The ultimate breach of faith and trust between doctor and patient, however, may be caused by the caretaker's inability to provide a healing, comforting, supportive relationship with the mother who has just lost the most personal and intense bond of her life.

Current medical training and practice are guided by a greater appreciation of parental grief for perinatal loss. More recent pediatric and obstetric textbooks now recognize the importance of assisting parents in perinatal mourning (for example, Behrman & Vaughan 1983; Sciarra 1983). Obstetricians attending a professional conference on an unrelated topic demonstrated widespread awareness of profound grief following stillbirth (Kirkley-Best et al. 1985). Hospital and medical practices now help bereaved parents to accept the reality of their loss and to mourn their child, while discouraging the prescription of sedatives and tranquilizers that may interfere with the grieving process. Within less than twenty years there has been a virtually complete reversal of the prevailing medical wisdom, from denying the loss to facilitating its complete expression and thereby promoting its resolution. Medical practitioners and investigators recommend that concrete reminders of the baby's existence—both birth and death—be rendered for parents by physically viewing and touching the baby, naming the child, participating in a funeral service and burial, and preserving keepsakes from the hospital.

Medical caretakers in hospitals have recently developed extensive protocols in an attempt to implement these practices on a regular basis (for example, Carr & Knupp 1985; Maguire & Skoolicas 1988). While these innovations are a clear improvement over the earlier medical indifference to parental grief, there is a new danger in the institutionalization of bereavement. If a caregiver is preoccupied with a checklist of information given, photograph provided, recording of parental interaction with the dead child, and dozens of other instructions instead of with genuine, emotionally demanding interaction with the bereaved parents, the caretaker will again fail to meet the parents' need for understanding. Although no doubt well meaning, these daunting protocols may homogenize bereavement into a normative syndrome that could seriously interfere with the elaboration of the special meanings of and feelings for that particular loss for these parents and siblings—as a family, couple, and individuals. Interestingly, one study reported that "grief guilt"—a perceived failure to grieve correctly or appropriately—accounted for a large proportion of the guilt by bereaved parents, figuring more importantly than survivor guilt, guilt over recovery, or a moral guilt over the death experienced as punishment for imagined wrongdoings (Miles & Demi 1984). Perhaps parental preoccupation with appropriate grieving is becoming an iatrogenic product of society's regimentation of mourning behavior. Schiff's (1977) wise guidance for bereaved parents emphasizes the importance of doing what is most helpful for oneself in mourning rather than of satisfying others' expectations.

Klaus and Kennell provided the basic model of preventive intervention after perinatal loss in their pioneering study on mourning neonatal death (with Slyter 1970) and work on bonding (1982). They recommended a series of three meetings with the bereaved parents to facilitate mourning. Immediately after the death, the doctor meets with the parents to give the tragic news, offer comfort and support, encourage parental contact with the dead baby, answer whatever questions parents may have, and explain the normalcy of the intense grief that can be anticipated (including rage, irrational guilt, and somatic symptoms). Because the parents are usually in a state of shock at this time, another meeting is scheduled for a few days later to discuss many of these same issues and to continue to provide support and empathy for their feelings and concerns. The importance of sharing their grief and feelings is emphasized, as is the fact that no one is to blame. From three to six months later, a third meeting is scheduled to review the autopsy findings, address any additional concerns, and assess whether or not each parent appears to be recovering—and, if not, to determine whether additional meetings or psychiatric referrals are necessary. Throughout the course of these meetings, the caretakers' concern and availability are crucial in providing a supportive atmosphere in which parents can talk freely about their feelings, with the sense of being understood and accepted. Parents are usually encouraged not to attempt another pregnancy until enough time has elapsed to mourn this loss (usually at least six months). Eventually, parents may need to be gently given permission to relinquish their grief and allow themselves to enjoy their lives again. With some variations, especially scheduling a fourth meeting after one year to assess resolution of grief and discuss anniversary reactions, this approach has been advocated by most clinicians and investigators involved with perinatal loss (Benfield et al. 1978; Clyman et al. 1980; Elliott & Hein 1978; Furlong & Hobbins 1983; Giles 1970; Hagan 1974; Helmrath & Steinitz 1978; Ilse & Furrh 1988; Kellner et al. 1981; Knapp & Peppers 1979; Kowalski 1980; LaFerla & Good 1985; Lake et al. 1983; Lockwood & Lewis 1980; Peppers & Knapp 1980a; Phipps 1981; Schreiner et al. 1979; Stierman 1987; Taylor & Gideon 1980; Zahourek & Jensen 1973). When death can be anticipated, Harmon and his staff (1984) have developed a neonatal hospice program within the hospital to facilitate mourning among both families and caretakers. Woods and Esposito (1987) offer a comprehensive guide to managing perinatal loss in the medical setting, describing the roles of obstetrician (as outpatient counselor), nurse, genetic counselor, peer support group, and others.

This kind of crisis counseling may be accomplished most effectively by the mother's obstetrician, with whom she should have already established a trusting relationship. Leppert and Pahlka (1984) provide a useful model for this form of counseling in a private outpatient obstetric practice. Woods and Klein (1987) formulate a similar approach in a perinatal support service associated with the University of Cincinnati. Continuity of care provides a logical continuation between the formation and mourning of the pregnancy bond, as well as enabling the mutual sharing of grief by medical caretaker and parent, who experienced the pregnancy and its loss together.

There is increasing empirical evidence suggesting the value of this supportive-counseling approach in shortening the duration and softening the intensity of perinatal bereavement. One study reported a statistically significant decrease in psychiatric problems such as anxiety, depression, somatic complaints, and impairments in interpersonal functioning six months after a perinatal loss among bereaved mothers who were randomly offered and accepted supportive counseling compared to those who did not receive such care (Forrest et al. 1982). Reassessment fourteen months after the loss revealed no significant differences between these two groups. Schreiner and his co-workers (1979) compared the emotional reactions of parents contacted in a fifteen- to forty-minute phone call within the first ten days after a neonatal death with those of parents who were not contacted at all. The phone caller reviewed the nature of the grieving process, emphasized the importance of sharing feelings, and answered any questions the parents had concerning the death. By two to six months after perinatal death, the parents who had had the follow-up phone call to review the grieving process demonstrated a statistically significant decrease in loneliness, depression, and guilt, and had fewer questions about the cause of death than the group without benefit of telephone follow-up.

Other investigations have indicated that about 75 percent of parents who suffered a perinatal death wanted to discuss

the details of the death or to come in for a follow-up appointment two to four months after the loss (Clyman et al. 1979,
1980; Kellner et al. 1984). In her literature review, Stierman
(1987) observed that studies using multiple meetings after
perinatal loss tended to report fewer cases of unresolved grief
than studies relying on only a single interview.

Psychotherapy has rarely been considered and discussed
in detail as a worthwhile treatment for perinatal loss. Condon
(1986) recently recommended individual therapy as the optimal treatment for a bereaved mother seeking help one or
more years after her perinatal loss. His bereavement counseling, however, exclusively addresses the current dimensions
of the loss, as has that of other therapists who have worked
with mothers suffering perinatal death (Corney & Horton
1974; Lewis & Page 1978). Only Turco (1981) has emphasized
the importance of a full developmental history to understand
the personalized meanings of this loss. Psychotherapy treating perinatal loss in the intrapsychic context of the bereaved
mother's developmental goals, internalized conflicts, and
narcissistic vulnerabilities has scarcely been explored.

REACTIONS WITHIN THE FAMILY

The father's response to the death of his child is crucial, both
for the effect on his emotional well-being and as an important
influence on his wife's course of bereavement. Unfortunately, my clinical sample of bereaved parents seeking individual therapy for themselves included no fathers. This
discussion will therefore be based primarily on the available
literature and secondarily on reports of paternal reactions by
mothers in my adult sample. The impact of parental interaction on the family following perinatal death will be explored in detail in chapter 4.

Fathers grieve for their unborn, stillborn, and newborn
children who die. Their mourning, however, tends to be less
intense and long-lasting, with generally less guilt and depression, than their wives' (Benfield et al. 1978; Helmrath & Stein-

itz 1978; Saylor 1977; Smith & Borgers 1988; Theut et al. 1989; Wilson et al. 1982). Peppers and Knapp (1980a) have noted that the likelihood of the mother becoming attached to the child-to-be earlier and more powerfully than her husband may cause marital tensions after perinatal loss because of "incongruent grieving" (p. 66): mothers' prolonged and profound grief may inspire anger and hurt over their husbands' seemingly superficial mourning; fathers resent their wives' depression and are ready to resume their prior lives sooner than their wives. Furthermore, fathers may be more inclined to suppress their own grief because of more private emotional expression (Elliott 1978; Ewy & Ewy 1984) as well as their need to assume a protective role in view of their wives' heightened vulnerability (Mandell et al. 1980; Peppers & Knapp 1980a). Sexual relations often suffer because of a fear of or an obsession with becoming pregnant, guilt over pleasure, and denigrating one's attractiveness (Peppers & Knapp 1980a).

Both the physical creation (in conception) and the psychological relinquishing (in mourning) of one's unborn child are naturally expressed in the conjugal relationship. Not only is the sharing of feelings by the couple a vital ingredient in the eventual resolution of grief, but mourning their child's death together often strengthens and deepens their marital bond (Harmon et al. 1984; Helmrath & Steinitz 1978; Peppers & Knapp 1980a; Stringham et al. 1982). Lockwood and Lewis (1980) reported that most women felt their husbands were their greatest source of comfort. More recently, studies reporting statistically significant results (Forrest et al. 1982; LaRoche et al. 1984; Toedter et al. 1988) and impressionistic findings (Conway & Valentine 1987; Dorner & Atwell 1985) have indicated that marital closeness and communication are positively associated with a more benign recovery from perinatal loss.

Most of what has been discussed regarding maternal reactions to perinatal loss applies, perhaps to a lesser degree, to paternal responses as well. In fact, recent empirical studies demonstrate much more similarity than difference in the manner in which expectant fathers and pregnant women bond to their unborn children (Condon 1985; Weaver & Cranley 1983) and grieve for their dead infants (Feeley & Gottlieb 1988). The father's vicariously grieving through his wife's mourning (Panuthos & Romeo 1984) may not only reflect cultural differences in emotional expressiveness between men and women; rather, it may also indicate the continuation of the father's vicarious experience of pregnancy through his wife. For the father, both the formation and the loosening of the prenatal bond may be mediated via the pregnant mother; this perhaps explains why he may find her prolonged mourning emotionally taxing and even experience it as an imposition of grief on him. The bereaved mother's fury at her seemingly unempathic husband's eagerness to resume their prior life before she is ready to end her mourning may be based largely on the narcissistic experience of her loss. *She* feels personally rejected and abandoned when her husband finishes mourning her child. Although Klaus and Kennell (1982) described how some husbands resorted to overactivity to defend against their grief, this style may be an adaptation to their own sense of narcissistic injury in perinatal loss. A father may unconsciously intensify the importance of his career to obtain narcissistic gratification and restitution after experiencing phallic damage through the death of his child-to-be.

The participation of bereaved siblings in the outcome of parental bereavement as well as the impact this event can have on these children's development will be discussed in chapter 4. I know of no empirical studies that have focused on the reactions and influences of parents and siblings of the bereaved parents in perinatal bereavement. The available material suggests that extended family were usually unable to provide much support or empathy for the bereaved parents. They tend to discourage intense grieving and in some instances to deny the reality of the loss (Grubb 1976a). Much of the discussion regarding reactions of friends applies to extended-family attitudes as well.

RESPONSES BY THE COMMUNITY

The support, sympathy, and understanding of friends and neighbors, traditionally available to other mourners, are usually absent for parents suffering perinatal loss. Discussion about the baby is usually replaced with a deafening silence that seems to say, contrary to the mother's grief and turmoil, that nothing has happened and no one has been lost (Berezin 1982; Borg & Lasker 1981; Davidson 1977; Ewy & Ewy 1984; Friedman & Gladstein 1982; Hagan 1974; Helmrath & Steinitz 1978; Peppers & Knapp 1980a). Cohen and his co-workers (1978) argued that the mother's recurrent dreams and images of the child and the hospital experience may be an attempt to affirm the reality of the pregnancy and the baby's existence in the face of societal pressure to deny the loss. Grief may be prolonged or unresolvable because of the maternal fear that her child would be denied reality were her mourning to end, given societal unwillingness to recognize the actuality of her loss (Peppers & Knapp 1980a). Well-meaning advice intended to comfort and distract the bereaved is more likely to impede mourning by encouraging suppression ("Don't think about it and you'll feel better"), reinforcing maternal guilt ("It was meant to be"), and denying the loss ("Try to have another child soon"). Peppers and Knapp (1980a) suggested that societal support for perinatal bereavement is unavailable because the unborn child has not yet acquired an identity or reality in the community, but Furman (1978) believed the lack of recognition is based on an unconscious understanding of the narcissistic nature of the loss and on a tendency to recoil in anxiety, in much the way that one ostracizes amputees. Funeral directors, who might be expected to appreciate the elements of grieving, usually hold attitudes likely to impede mourning, such as discouraging close contact with the dead baby and any viewing of a deformed child, limiting maternal options for participation in the funeral, and believing an autopsy is generally unnecessary and unimportant (Benfield & Nichols 1984). An autopsy may serve many useful functions, including confirmation of the reality (and aspects of normalcy) of the dead child, while addressing a mother's erroneous belief that she caused the death and her concerns about the risks of future pregnancy (Kellner et al. 1984; Stierman 1987).

The most helpful source of social support and understanding for perinatal loss has been self-help groups in which bereaved parents reaffirm for one another the normalcy of grieving and provide a place where those feelings may be freely expressed (Ewy & Ewy 1984; Klaus & Kennell 1982; Lamb 1986; Parkes 1988; Peppers & Knapp 1980a; Wilson & Soule 1981). Self-help groups for perinatal loss (for example, AMEND, PEND, and SHARE) may fulfill functions similar to those of groups designed to support parental mourning for older children (such as Compassionate Friends): isolation is relieved by sharing one's grief with others who are willing to listen and able to understand, thereby helping to establish a sense of community; grieving openly facilitates mourning; learning that others have similarly intense and disorganizing reactions may reduce the common fear that one is "going crazy"; and concrete approaches to solving problems common to bereaved parents may be gained in group discussion (Fischhoff & O'Brien 1976; Klass 1985; Knapp 1986). Self-help groups for parents experiencing perinatal loss may be particularly important because of the lack of social support available elsewhere in the community* (Herz 1984) and the greater difficulty of sustaining the memory of a child who never lived, unlike that of an older child with a recognized identity. Such groups may offer benefits at different points in the grieving process just as it is possible to trace the stages of group membership from affiliation to helping others (Klass 1985). For the recently bereaved, a self-help group may be the only place where their grief may be openly expressed and tolerated without discouragement and criticism. For those whose grief has abated as mourning proceeds, these groups may provide a valid channel for expressing maternal nurtur-

---

*Crawford and Schuman (1988) have prepared a very useful logistical guide for parents seeking to form their own support group.

ance by caring for others. Videka-Sherman (1982) similarly concluded that participation in a self-help group for older-child loss frequently results in transforming self-preoccupation into altruism as a coping mechanism. Professionally facilitated support groups for bereaved parents may provide many of these same functions found in the nonprofessionally led self-help groups (Cordell & Apolito 1981; Soricelli & Utech 1985). Klass and Shinners (1983) advise, however, that in order to preserve the vital self-help efficacy of building a community of responsible people, it is necessary for the professional to abandon his or her natural inclinations to provide abstract understanding, distinguish pathology, and provide referrals.

Self-help groups provide an invaluable function in facilitating the expression and resolution of grief. However, the revival of individual conflicts during pregnancy and its loss can limit the utility of a group approach for many women. In this area, the mental health field continues to lag behind medical caretakers in providing psychotherapy for mothers who could benefit at this vulnerable time. This void is particularly striking considering the widespread recognition of the value of psychotherapy and counseling in assisting the recovery of other victims of bereavement (Horowitz et al. 1984; Parkes 1980; Raphael 1977, 1978), especially those suffering the death of a child, independent of perinatal fatality (Pine & Brauer 1986; Schiff 1977; Williams 1981; Woodward et al. 1985).

Intrapsychic, circumstantial, and interpersonal forces may unite to make perinatal loss especially difficult to mourn and ultimately resolve. The tendency to fantasize the image of the child, the absence of evidence that the baby once existed, the totally unexpected occurrence of the event, and the encouragement by family, friends, and sometimes medical caretakers to deny the loss may all combine to make the death seem insignificant or even unreal. Many investigators have described how disoriented and confused parents feel after the loss, doubting not just the death but the reality of the pregnancy (Cohen et al. 1978; Davidson 1977; Kellner et al. 1981). "With no acknowledgment of the infant's existence, keeping the baby real became a major task. Most parents wished they had a picture of their baby to affirm to themselves that the child had existed" (Helmrath & Steinitz 1978, 788).

Contrasting Perinatal Losses

Many circumstances are subsumed under the term *perinatal death*, including miscarriage, ectopic pregnancy, stillbirth, and neonatal death. These various perinatal losses have potentially different meanings and effects.

Most investigations of perinatal loss examine responses to stillbirth and neonatal death. Studies of miscarriage describe a similar bereavement reaction, characterized by guilt, a sense of failure as a woman, anger, and helplessness (Herz 1984; Leppert & Pahlka 1984; Panuthos & Romeo 1984; Pizer & Palinski 1980; Seibel & Graves 1980). Stack (1984) argued that a miscarriage may be *more* difficult to mourn than a later perinatal loss because of the lack of a visible body and a funeral, which could have facilitated grieving. Peppers and Knapp (1980b) were unable to find significant differences in the duration and intensity of maternal grieving based on the duration of the pregnancy, whether it was an early miscarriage or a neonatal death. However, Kirkley-Best and Kellner (1982), in their literature review on the psychology of stillbirth, persuasively argued that methodological problems with Peppers and Knapp's study may invalidate this finding. (That is, a self-selected sample that used retrospective analysis of losses suffered up to thirty years earlier may not have distinguished reliably between different kinds of losses owing to the distortion of memory over time and the possibility that more "severe" miscarriage sufferers were motivated to participate in their study.)* Kirkley-Best and Kellner (1982)

---

*In fact, in another work Peppers and Knapp (1980a) suggested that grieving for a miscarriage may be as intense as for a later pregnancy loss but is usually of shorter duration.

indicated that more intense grief usually followed a later versus an earlier pregnancy loss, a hypothesis that has been confirmed by statistically significant results in two recent empirical studies (Theut et al. 1989; Toedter et al. 1988). The statistically significant, positive correlation between gestational age and the decision to seek counseling after perinatal death (Woods 1987) similarly suggests a more intense grief reaction following a late-term loss.

A crucial determinant of the extent of object loss experienced is the degree to which mother has become attached to her child-to-be. Although Lumley (1980, 1982) discovered that most women did not experience their first-trimester fetus as a "real person," as usually occurred during the second trimester after quickening, the few women who reported an attachment to their unborn child in the first months and described no ambivalence about the pregnancy showed a statistically significant increase in their likelihood to fear and to anticipate mourning a miscarriage. The great variability of reactions to early miscarriage, ranging from apparent unconcern to profound grief, may be based on the differences in mothers' attachments to their unborn children at this early stage (Outerbridge et al. 1983). Similarly, neither differences in the amount of mother-infant interaction nor the lifespan of terminally impaired infants influenced the degree of maternal grief in two empirical studies of neonatal death (Benfield et al. 1978; Kennell et al. 1970). In both the early and the final setting of perinatal loss (that is, miscarriage and neonatal death, respectively), the mother's prenatal attachment to her unborn child appears to be a crucial determinant of maternal grief.

My clinical experience similarly suggests that a miscarriage is likely to be felt as a major loss in the context of infertility due to chronic inability to conceive or prior miscarriages. When a desperately wanted and expected baby dies, he is powerfully missed, no matter how early the loss. Thus, it is not surprising that women confident of a successful pregnancy through in-vitro fertilization often have an intense grief reaction should implantation fail (Greenfeld et al. 1988).

The greater guilt and sense of failure as a woman reported after miscarriage versus later losses (Ewy & Ewy 1984; Peppers & Knapp 1980a) may be directly based on the perception of the loss as a narcissistic injury, a blow to the female's sense of power and self-esteem. The nonviable fetus is experienced as part of her now-damaged self-representation (Grubb 1976b). Later perinatal losses such as stillbirths and neonatal deaths are recognized as significant bereavements, but miscarriages may still be overlooked as potentially traumatic events with important psychological consequences (Seibel & Graves 1980). Elements of object loss are more likely to influence bereavement the later intrauterine death occurs during the pregnancy, corresponding to the greater degree to which the fetus is usually experienced as a separate person to whom mother becomes increasingly attached.

There have been no studies that I know of on the psychological sequelae of ectopic pregnancy, although the incidence of this hazard has increased by more than 50 percent over the past five years because of the increase in pelvic inflammatory disease (Durfee 1987). In addition to the usual unexpectedness of ectopic pregnancy, its traumatizing potential is considerably heightened by the need for emergency surgery and the threat to the mother's life from internal bleeding if the pregnancy is not removed. Although there may be some experience of object loss—especially if the baby was much wanted and the mother believed all was normal before learning of the ectopic pregnancy—the primary impact is likely to be profound narcissistic injury. The intrapsychic wounds to her self-image as a woman because her reproductive organs did not perform satisfactorily—wounds that are likely to revive any earlier feelings of gender inadequacy and body damage—are compounded by the external scars she has suffered from surgery. The rupture and surgical removal of a fallopian tube, a common outcome of ectopic pregnancy, may be experienced as a castration. The early loss, usually by the twelfth week of pregnancy (Durfee 1987), typically does not allow object representations of the unborn child to be more fully elaborated; the mother's, as well as the father's, immediate concerns about her physical well-being and recovery usually take precedence over the loss they have endured. The much higher incidence of infertility resulting from ectopic pregnancy (about 50 percent [Durfee 1987]) is likely to make this event a more serious developmental interference with attaining parenthood than other perinatal losses.

Perhaps more than any other perinatal loss, mourning a stillborn requires the transformation of a narcissistic tie (with the "inside" child) to an object relationship (with the "outside" child), facilitated by viewing the dead baby. The narcissistic blow to one's sense of immortality and vanquishing death may also be particularly acute with a stillbirth, when one gives birth to death rather than to the anticipated life. The stage during pregnancy when the loss occurs may influence not only the degree of maternal attachment but the kinds of instinctual issues and conflicts that are revived. The degree of maternal attachment and the resulting experience of object loss is usually greater in a later perinatal loss such as stillbirth or neonatal death, causing longer, more intense grief. The difficulty resolving early pregnancy loss such as miscarriage and ectopic pregnancy may be compounded when there is no body to identify, no child to name, nothing concrete to mourn.

Perinatal Death Compared to Other Reproductive Casualties and Losses

ABORTION

Although abortion is a pregnancy loss, its circumstances, meaning, and outcomes are quite different from those of unwanted perinatal loss. Virtually all of the empirical research (and there is much by now) indicates that in almost all cases voluntarily chosen abortion is a relatively benign solution to the crisis of unwanted pregnancy. Guilt and depression in the short-term response were usually transient and outweighed by relief; there have been few lasting, damaging consequences reported from elective abortion (Barnes et al.

1971; Ekblad 1955; Ford et al. 1971; Greer et al. 1976; Harris 1986; Kummer 1963; Lask 1975; Niswander & Patterson 1967; Olson 1980; Osofsky & Osofsky 1972; Pare & Raven 1970; Patt et al. 1969; Peck & Marcus 1966; Perez-Reyes & Falk 1973; Senay 1970; Simon et al. 1967; Smith 1973). Those women who suffered long-term negative reactions to elective abortion, generally some form of unresolved guilt, were likely to have had a prior, ongoing psychiatric disturbance (Ekblad 1955; Ford et al. 1971; Lask 1975; Peck & Marcus 1966; Simon et al. 1967) or to have been pressured to abort the child against their will (Ekblad 1955; Patt et al. 1969; Perez-Reyes & Falk 1973; Senay 1970; Wallerstein et al. 1972). The only subgroup of aborters who experienced intense, persistent grief comparable to that of victims of unwanted perinatal loss did not, in fact, voluntarily choose to abort but were compelled to do so for medical reasons (for example, the pregnancy would have jeopardized the woman's health or, more commonly, it was learned that the baby would have serious birth defects) (Blumberg et al. 1975; Donnai et al. 1981; Freitag-Koontz 1988; Jörgensen et al. 1985; Lloyd & Laurence 1985; Niswander & Patterson 1967; Pare & Raven 1970; Peck & Marcus 1966; Simon et al. 1967; Van Putte 1988).

Research on elective abortion confirms and complements our understanding of unwanted perinatal loss. A woman who chose to abort her pregnancy generally did not fantasize about and become attached to her unborn child (Senay 1970; Wallerstein et al. 1972). When the woman did not want a child and made the decision to abort freely, she felt little loss and achieved a sense of mastery in the situation; when a very much wished-for child died against a woman's will, she experienced tremendous loss and multiple sources of narcissistic injury in her body's failing her. Elective abortion is likely to have more deleterious consequences for the woman when it is an ambivalent choice, approximating the circumstances of unwanted perinatal loss (that is, abortions for medical reasons or pressure from others); there is a greater attachment to and wish for the unborn child, with more regret and guilt over his death.

Clinically oriented research and case studies often empha-size that unconscious ambivalence and maladaptive solutions underlie unwanted pregnancies and the destructive conse-quences of subsequent abortions (Blumenfield 1978; Calef 1972; Cavenar et al. 1978; Pines 1982; Simon et al. 1967). These cases appear to correspond mostly to the subgroup of emotionally disturbed individuals for whom abortions could be problematic. However, the assumption that unconscious ambivalence will always result in long-term negative conse-quences for all freely elective abortions is contradicted by much research on the benign outcome of abortions and by other studies (Baetson et al 1985; Olson 1980) indicating that those seeking abortion were not more emotionally disturbed than their peers.

INFERTILITY

When a couple wishes to have children, infertility is usually a major, lifelong disappointment. Like perinatal loss, infer-tility is a bereavement of one's wished-for child, leading to profound grief, depression, anger, guilt, despair, and yearn-ing (Bresnick & Taymor 1979; Falik 1984; Frias & Wilson 1985; Kraft et al. 1980; Lalos et al. 1985; Menning 1980). Narcissistic denigration of one's masculinity or femininity may be partic-ularly great, with an acute sense of worthlessness, shame, inadequacy, and failure to live up to one's expectations (Hochstaedt & Langer 1959; Kraft et al. 1980; Platt et al. 1973). Resulting sexual dysfunction is common (Bell 1981; Elstein 1975), tending to confirm behaviorally a self-image of impo-tence. When women freely choose sterilization as a means of birth control after child-bearing, these negative repercussions are not reported—rather like the benign outcome of a truly elective abortion. In fact, empirical studies typically report a statistically significant increase in well-being, with less anx-iety over sexual relations after elective sterilization (J. Cooper et al. 1985; P. Cooper et al. 1982; A. Smith 1979).

The assumption commonly held thirty years ago that in-fertility was often psychodynamically rooted in emotional conflicts (especially unconscious guilt, anger, and fears associated with motherhood) that prevented conception (Benedek 1952; Deutsch 1945; Ford et al. 1953; Kroger 1952) is now widely regarded as erroneous (Shapiro 1988). As medical knowledge has advanced, the incidence of psychogenic infertility (that is, infertility attributed to emotional factors) has declined over tenfold, from about 50 percent of cases of infertility to less than 5 percent (Mozley 1976; Seibel & Taymor 1982). What formerly had been viewed as a cause of infertility may now be better understood as the psychological effects of being deprived of one's reproductive capacity (Mai et al. 1972; McGuire 1975; Rosenfeld & Mitchell 1979; Seibel & Taymor 1982). In light of the massive narcissistic injury to one's gender identity and the serious developmental interference from being unable to bear children, it is not surprising that infertile women have been found to have more serious conflicts in feminine identifications and attaining a sense of adult status than their fertile peers. Yet there are no significant differences in chronic psychiatric disturbance that distinguish fertile from infertile women (Mai et al. 1972; Seward et al. 1965). At the same time, it is clear that stress may affect fertility via both the endocrine and autonomic nervous systems (Bos & Cleghorn 1958; Karahasanaglu et al. 1972; Mozley 1976; Seibel & Taymor 1982). It is possible to accept the contributing role of psychological factors such as the psychosomatic expression of stress in the maintenance of infertility (Morse & Van Hall 1987) without resorting to the older psychoanalytic position—still espoused by some (Bydlowski & Dayan-Lintzer 1988)—which teleologically assumes unconscious conflicts associated with infertility are necessarily causal.

The course and outcome of infertility differ in some important ways from those of perinatal loss. The acute and potentially traumatizing occurrence of a perinatal loss may initially intensify the defensive use of denial to cope with this sudden, unexpected death. But the specificity of this event, even in an early miscarriage, usually overrides the tendency to continue denial, as the bereaved mother eventually grieves her loss. This is in sharp contrast to infertility, in which there has been no pregnancy that has been lost and, as is often the case, no clear-cut explanation for the inability to conceive. Under these circumstances, one's infertility may be chronically denied, unless there has been conclusive medical confirmation of this condition. Although increasingly sophisticated reproductive technology (for example, in-vitro fertilization) has enabled some formerly infertile women to bear children, lack of success using such procedures may indefinitely prolong denial of one's infertility as one is continually offered the chance of success (no matter how small). Until the finality of infertility has been accepted—a finality that is becoming less certain through modern medicine— mourning infertility cannot proceed. The infertile couple's decision to stop pursuing additional medical procedures may be, paradoxically, a positive act of mastery and control in the face of the helplessness of being infertile; this is analogous to the greater sense of adequacy reported by parents who decide to withhold or end extraordinary measures for their terminally ill babies (Benfield et al. 1978).

Mourning the particular loss is usually a major feature of grief in perinatal death. In infertility, despite the absence of a unique object loss, the parent feels intense sorrow and yearning for the fantasized child. It is expected that narcissistic damage to competent gender identity and developmental interference with attaining parenthood will be more profound with infertility than with perinatal loss. Narcissistic reparation cannot be accomplished by bearing a child, as after perinatal loss; restitution may be achieved through finding different areas other than reproductive capacity upon which to base one's self-esteem (Menning 1980) or through successful adoption, in which the adoptive child is not denigrated as an expression of the parents' persistent sense of worthlessness and inadequacy (Kraft et al. 1980; Rosenfeld & Mitchell 1979).

For these reasons, grieving infertility may be more chronic and less readily resolved than mourning perinatal loss. The mental health field has responded to these hazards. Although there is widespread recognition of the benefits of counseling and psychotherapy to deal with the repercussions of infertility (Abarbanel & Bach 1959; Berger 1977; Bresnick & Taymor 1979; Klemer et al. 1966; McGuire 1975; Rosenfeld & Mitchell 1979; Seibel & Taymor 1982), the need for and utility of such treatments for perinatal loss are not yet acknowledged.

GIVING BIRTH TO A HANDICAPPED CHILD

Delivering a handicapped baby is a massive narcissistic wound for parents, filling them with shame, guilt, anger, and worthlessness over what they have created; their child's congenital defect is experienced as their own personal failure, an indictment of their inadequacy, profoundly impairing their self-esteem (Lax 1972; Mintzer et al. 1984; Solnit & Stark 1961). As these and other investigators (Bentovim 1972; Drotar et al. 1975; Fost 1981; MacKeith 1973) have noted, mourning ensues as parents grieve for the loss of the normal child they expected and were denied. If mourning the loss of the wished-for, healthy child is inhibited, the parent may be unable to form an attachment to the actual, handicapped child (Fajardo 1987; Lax 1972; Mintzer et al. 1984; Naylor 1982; Solnit & Stark 1961). Anything less than an optimal delivery, even if it is without lasting organic damage, as is the case with many premature births (Klaus & Kennell 1982) and Cesarian sections (Panuthos & Romeo 1984), constitutes a narcissistic blow to maternal self-worth. Parenting a handicapped child demands the additional burden of reconciling oneself to the ongoing and repeated disappointments and special care required by that child's limitations over the course of development, frequently leading to chronic sorrow and, often, depression (Bentovim 1972; Burden 1980; Byrne & Cunningham 1985; Dorner 1975; Olshansky 1962; Wikler et al. 1981).

Although giving birth to a handicapped child involves object loss of the fantasized, normal child, narcissistic injury is even more profound and enduring because of the permanence of the growing child's impairment, an ever-present reminder of one's defective act of creation. Object loss assumes greater importance in perinatal loss, especially in stillbirth and neonatal death, when the opportunity for continued interaction with one's offspring is denied. As with perinatal loss, the regressive revival of earlier conflicts in pregnancy may result in the reinforcement of earlier maladaptive solutions and understandings when a handicapped child is born (for example, neurotic guilt and depression over experienced punishment for imagined misdeeds). The bereaved mother may obtain narcissistic reparation by treasuring those normal aspects of her dead baby with which she can identify positively; similarly, the mother of a handicapped child may replenish her maternal self-esteem by appreciating the ways in which her child is normal and like herself, as well as by taking pride in her mothering and by participating in her child's accomplishments (Drotar et al. 1975; Fajardo 1987; Mintzer et al. 1984; Solnit & Stark 1961). Perinatal loss can cause an immediate, albeit temporary, developmental interference with the achievement of parenthood. Although producing a handicapped child does not prevent one from attaining parental status, the greater vulnerability of these mothers and fathers to failure in parenting (Bentovim 1972; Drotar et al. 1975; Lax 1972; Mintzer et al. 1984; Solnit & Stark 1961) may ultimately preclude the successful negotiation of this developmental phase. Residues of grieving for perinatal loss may linger indefinitely, but a more or less complete resolution is typically achieved within about a year. The disappointment and grief over creating a handicapped child generally persist much longer than the response to perinatal loss (D'Arcy 1968; Solnit & Stark 1961), becoming, it appears, a crucial ingredient in the lifelong task of parenting.

RELINQUISHING A CHILD FOR ADOPTION

Over the past ten years researchers have increasingly examined a case of perinatal loss that does not involve death—giving a baby up for adoption. Several studies have indicated that this loss often results in intermittent but persistent un-resolved mourning; mothers struggle with depression, guilt, and low self-esteem while dreaming (both literally and fig-uratively) of reuniting with their birthchildren (Deykin et al. 1984; Millen & Roll 1985; Rynearson 1982). Most of these trou-bled mothers recalled being pressured by others to relinquish their children (Deykin et al. 1984; Rynearson 1982), as in the cases of mothers whose abortions led to an intense grief re-action. Despite the uniformity of their findings, these three samples may not be representative of the entire population of relinquishing mothers and may exaggerate the negative impact of placing a child for adoption: two of the studies (Millen & Roll 1985; Rynearson 1982) used psychiatric out-patients exclusively; Deykin and her colleagues (1984) col-lected their sample primarily from a support organization for relinquishing mothers.

As in perinatal death, the frequent unavailability of mem-ories of one's baby, the absence of mourning rituals (Millen & Roll 1985), the uncertainty of exactly what and who has been lost (Millen & Roll 1985), and the prospective nature of the loss may all prevent the completion of mourning a relin-quished child. Several studies have emphasized that releas-ing a child for adoption is a narcissistic loss in which part of the self is sacrificed. Although a living child has been relin-quished, the loss may be experienced primarily narcissisti-cally (rather than as an object loss) because of the lack of visible contact with the child after birth; mother-infant inter-action would have facilitated the transformation of a basically narcissistic bond into more of an object relationship. Unlike perinatal death and other forms of loss, the narcissistic blow is not experienced in terms of body damage, assuming that a healthy child has been born. Instead, the woman's image of herself as a mother is compromised by the feeling that she has abandoned her child. As already discussed with regard to infertility, denying the finality of loss is more available as an obstacle to mourning the relinquished child than is the case with perinatal death. The continued existence of the adopted child prevents reunion fantasies from being completely relinquished because of the realistic possibility of meeting one's birthchild.

THE DEATH OF A CHILD

Probably the most painful and overwhelming grief—usually more debilitating than even the death of a spouse—is the death of one's child (Edelstein 1984; Knapp 1986; Rando 1986b; Raphael 1983; Sanders 1980; Schiff 1977). The intensity of the parent-child relationship, from the infant's complete dependency on his parents through the passage of successive developmental stages, generates cherished memories, regrets, and pleasures for each participant. The depth and complexity of the relationship makes this object loss intolerable. In fact, the guilt, depression, and rage are usually so crushing, unbearable, and ultimately traumatizing that long-term coping with this loss appears to depend more on the opportunity to gradually accept this brutal reality through anticipatory grieving before the actual death than on any other factor. Parents typically denied an initial diagnosis of terminal illness in their child (Bozeman et al. 1955; Chodoff et al. 1964; Easson 1972; Friedman 1967; Friedman et al. 1963), suggesting the trauma of learning this news. Studies reporting an ultimately benign outcome described parents who were eventually able to grieve, realistically accept, and plan for this inevitability before the child died (Lascari & Stebbens 1973; Rando 1983; Spinetta et al. 1981). Conversely, investigations revealing a much bleaker outcome—one in which there was no recovery—have focused on sudden deaths from accident, acute illness, suicide, or homicide for which anticipatory grieving was not possible (Friedman 1974; Knapp 1986; Martin et al. 1968; Videka-Sherman & Lieberman 1985). Mourning the sudden death of one's child is never fully concluded in terms of returning to prebereavement functioning but involves major transformations in self-definition, values, and priorities (Edelstein 1984; Schiff 1977), as well as an ongoing relationship with the memories of the dead child (Rubin 1985). The overwhelming parental shock, guilt, and grief following SIDS and resulting difficulties in coping with this loss (Bluglass 1981; Cornwell et al. 1977; Defrain & Ernst 1978; Halpern 1972; Limerick 1976; Rubin 1985) may similarly be traced, at least in part, to the abruptness of the death, which prevents any anticipatory grief.

Usually, the magnitude of grief in perinatal bereavement is not as severe as that of mourning the older child. The existence of an object relationship may intensify the loss of the older child, although memories of interactions, as painful as they are to recall, provide an outlet to complete mourning that is not available with perinatal loss. Death of the older child involves a greater degree of object loss than that of perinatal bereavement. Even if an infant has died of SIDS, for example, I believe the sense of narcissistic damage is generally not as acute as with perinatal loss. Once a healthy child has successfully crossed the birth canal, a mother usually experiences narcissistic pleasure in her maternity that is denied the victim of perinatal loss. Subsequent child losses, at no matter what age, will always involve a measure of narcissistic loss (Edelstein 1984; Klass & Marwit 1988; Knapp 1986; Raphael 1983). This loss, though, will emanate from her child's having originally come from herself as opposed to her additional failure to bring her child safely into the world.

Typical Outcomes

Our understanding of the usual outcome of perinatal loss is deficient. Not only has the empirical research conducted in this area been meager, but of the few studies that exist most have serious methodological flaws, which limit their reliability. Having provided that caveat, I shall review the available data and theories about the resolution of perinatal loss.

Recovery from perinatal death is usually described in terms of having sufficiently grieved one's loss. Most investigators indicate that recovery occurs six to twelve months after the death and that the earlier grief typically revives in intensity as the first anniversary approaches (Behrman & Vaughan 1983; Harmon et al. 1984; Klaus & Kennell 1982; Kowalski 1980; Lockwood & Lewis 1980). Other researchers (Outerbridge et al. 1983; Ewy & Ewy 1984) suggest that it may take a number of years for a resolution of mourning to occur. Recovery does not mean returning to one's earlier mode of functioning, as if the death never happened. Values, friendships, religious beliefs, and self-concepts are often reassessed and sometimes changed (Ewy & Ewy 1984; Panuthos & Romeo 1984). The unique aspects of perinatal loss may prevent a final conclusion to mourning, with a transient "shadow grief" persisting indefinitely. However, recovery is usually signified by a renewed vitality in activities and pleasures without preoccupation with the loss and by the capacity to maintain and develop other significant relationships.

It is not yet clear how often perinatal loss leads to later emotional disturbance. Although several nonstatistical studies report no major psychiatric problems following the resolution of grief (Helmrath & Steinitz 1978; Wolff et al. 1970), other empirical investigations discovered increased depression (Jensen & Zahourek 1972) and such other psychiatric symptoms as anxiety (Cullberg 1972) persisting one year after the death. Empirical research has not yet reliably isolated predictors of negative (or positive) outcomes. However, certain factors that might have been expected to produce or indicate a more pathological solution had no such effect. Several clinical studies demonstrated that bizarre grieving behaviors or seemingly maladaptive defenses against grief did not portend unresolved mourning or later psychiatric disturbance (Barglow et al. 1973; Lewis 1976). Sustained suppression and denial of feelings after the loss, however, were associated with a statistically significant prolonging of disturbance (indicated, for example, by a longer interval before returning to work [Cullberg 1972]). Although one might have expected that parental involvement in the decision to withhold medical care for a terminally ill baby would exacerbate later guilt and complicate grief, no such effect was found. In fact, parents who participated in such decisions appeared to feel more effective (Duff & Campbell 1973) and reported fewer symptoms (Benfield et al. 1978) to a statistically significant degree than those parents who did not participate.

Subsequent children may play a vital inhibitory or facilitative role in the resolution of mourning. Most researchers and clinicians strongly recommended that parents wait at least six months to a year before attempting another pregnancy, concerned that an impulse to become pregnant immediately after the perinatal loss would be intended to replace rather than mourn the dead child. Not only may the motive for a replacement pregnancy be predicated on avoiding grief, but the nature of pregnancy itself may further inhibit mourning because maternal self-absorption during pregnancy interferes with the preoccupation with the deceased, which is necessary for mourning (Lewis 1979b). A loss occurring shortly before or during pregnancy may result in unresolved grief or difficulty attaching to the subsequent child (Geller 1985; Swanson-Kauffman 1988). Lewis and Page (1978) described how the unresolved mourning of a stillborn impeded a mother's attachment to her next child, conceived soon after her first loss. Only after this mother was able to experience the guilt, shame, and rage over her first child's death could she begin to love her new baby. In a study examining maternal resolution of perinatal death, Rowe and her colleagues (1978) reported that five of the six mothers who displayed a morbid grief reaction one to two years after the loss had had either a surviving twin or another pregnancy within five months of the loss; this was the only statistically significant difference between unresolved and completed mourning. Yet other research indicated that neither a pregnancy within six months of a perinatal loss (LaRoche et al. 1984) nor the perinatal death of one twin (Wilson et al. 1982) was associated with unresolved mourning. These studies reinforce the idea that a perinatal loss cannot be replaced by another baby but also suggest that the processes of mourning a loss and bonding to another child may not necessarily be inherently incompatible. Perhaps difficulties are more likely, though not inevitable, for the woman developing another attachment soon after a perinatal loss, thus indicating the greater need for some form of treatment. In fact, one study (Forrest et al. 1982) reported a statistically significant increase in psychiatric disorder among women who became pregnant within six months of earlier perinatal losses *and* did not have benefit of supportive counseling.

Severe depression during the subsequent pregnancy may be viewed as evidence of unresolved grief (Dunlop 1979), although many investigators believe that some sadness at this time is a normal part of the mourning process (Beard et al. 1978; Ewy & Ewy 1984; Kowalski 1980); the mother's growing attachment to her current child-to-be revives thoughts of her prior loss (Bourne & Lewis 1984), not unlike the intensification of grief at anniversaries. Although a pregnancy subsequent to perinatal loss is associated with a statistically significant increase in maternal anxiety compared to a pregnancy without a prior loss, this anxiety is not generalized but is specifically related to concerns about the course of pregnancy (Theut et al. 1988). Phipps (1985) described how a task-oriented, unenthusiastic attitude during a pregnancy following a stillbirth is typical. Mother's heightened anxiety over dreaded negative outcomes and her delay in allowing herself to become attached to her unborn and later newborn child was not associated with later impairment in parental functioning (Phipps 1985). This pattern may be understood as an adaptive readiness to forestall another traumatizing loss through anticipatory grieving (that is, "expecting the worst"). Anticipatory grieving may become maladaptive if, in a more extreme fashion, it prevents attachment to the live child for fear he will die (Naylor 1982). The most complete resolution of perinatal loss may be achieved through the birth of a subsequent child designed not to replace the earlier loss but as a successful reaffirmation of maternal strivings despite the previous death (Kirkley-Best & Kellner 1982; Peppers & Knapp 1980a; Stringham et al. 1982; Theut et al. 1989). Similarly, a mother who helps her surviving children understand and cope with their feelings regarding the death of their sibling may heal her own wounded self-esteem by effective mothering (Furman 1978).

Chronic depression is the most likely outcome of unresolved perinatal loss. Depression can be distinguished from mourning: grieving does not demand the harsh self-criticism and loss of self-esteem so characteristic of depression (Freud 1917b), although the two conditions share the sad, pleasure-less experience of the present and hopeless attitude toward the future. Coping with perinatal loss, however, appears to *require* grappling with self-blame, as is not necessarily the case with mourning other losses. The universal experience of guilt; multiple blows to one's self-esteem in terms of omnip-otence, immortality, and femininity; deprivation of lifelong developmental aspirations; and the instinctual, regressive pull of pregnancy toward orality—all unite in the aftermath of perinatal loss, constituting a potentially massive assault on one's self-worth and sense of adequacy. If reparation in some form cannot be accomplished, depression, founded on earlier depressive issues, may linger indefinitely.

The resolution of perinatal death is interwoven with the fate of the maternal and infantile identifications intensified over the course of pregnancy. The mother is reconciled with her infantile identification by mourning the loss of her child. Her maternal identification endures narcissistic injury in her sense of failure in not giving birth to and not being able to nurture her child. This identification with damaged mater-nity, however, can be repaired by caring for existing children and finding alternative expressions of nurturance. The de-gree of strain caused by the perinatal death will depend on the overall psychological health of the mother, especially the nature of her infantile and maternal identifications, as well as on the circumstances of the loss and avenues of narcissistic support and restitution.

Giving birth to a healthy child once her earlier loss has been sufficiently mourned may be a crucial ingredient in the mother's adaptive recovery from perinatal loss. Especially when her sense of maternity has not been securely estab-lished (for example, if there are significant problems with existing children, damaged and devalued maternal identifi-cations, or no prior healthy births), successfully mothering a subsequent child may help repair the enduring narcissistic wounds of perinatal loss. It must be emphasized that the urge to quickly become pregnant again, especially following an early miscarriage, may be an adaptive wish to repair one's sense of damaged maternity and not a wish to circumvent mourning an object loss by having a replacement child. Although a pregnancy primarily designed to mend narcissistic damage may be disastrous to the subsequent parenting relationship and the development of the child, a successful pregnancy not long after an early miscarriage may provide most women much needed narcissistic healing. When there are no other children, a subsequent pregnancy overcomes the developmental interference of perinatal loss. In the most benign outcome, however, the memory and sadness of the loss of her unborn, or of her child who lived only briefly, survives. To forget her loss would be a form of abandoning her own.

CHAPTER 3
PSYCHOTHERAPY FOR
PERINATAL LOSS

Because of the unique features of perinatal death, certain aspects of the treatment process and the patient-therapist relationship need to be highlighted. I shall introduce this chapter with an overview of psychotherapy for perinatal bereavement. Since clinical practice can best be taught by case illustration, I shall present and discuss six psychotherapy cases drawn from my clinical sample. These patients were selected to represent a range of issues, degrees of disturbance, therapeutic interventions, and potential hazards and outcomes that may be expected. Each case illustrates therapeutic issues for a particular category (for example, psychotherapy for recent loss, treatment for unresolved grief, supportive therapy, and so on). The discussion following each case includes similar patients within that subsample.

Technical Aspects of Treating Perinatal Loss

As has been discussed, perinatal death constitutes a major loss and includes certain features that impede resolution of mourning. Furthermore, the possible exacerbation of lifelong conflicts during pregnancy may result in enduring maladaptive changes independent of and exceeding the effects of the unresolved grief. Psychotherapy in these cases may be conceptualized as not only ameliorative (in facilitating mourning and reducing the dangers of unresolved grief) but also preventive (by addressing revived, latent conflicts that may become chronic if ignored). Owing to an individual's greater potential to change during a crisis, lasting therapeutic benefits may be obtained from brief but timely interventions, much like the considerable gains from short-term therapy during a difficult pregnancy or certain junctures in adolescence.

Seemingly maladaptive reactions to the death should not be the sole criterion for recommending psychotherapy. It can be difficult to know for certain if apparently disturbed bereavement responses indicate adaptation or maladjustment or if an ostensibly benign reaction masks deeper problems. A bereaved mother expressing a need for help is sufficient grounds, I believe, for assuming a potential value of psychotherapy. It is presumptuous and callous to discourage psychotherapy for a grieving mother who is actively seeking help by viewing her mourning solely as a "normal" aspect of bereavement. The view that "these are not people who need the expertise or expense of a psychologist or psychiatrist" (Woods 1987, 184) overlooks the frequency with which reactions to this death become interwoven with revived conflicts and difficulties in a manner suitable for psychotherapeutic intervention. This does not mean that perinatal loss usually leads to a pathological outcome requiring psychotherapy but, instead, proposes that psychotherapy may be useful to the bereaved mother who is motivated for treatment.

Careful evaluation is a necessary part of treatment planning for perinatal loss. This will require several sessions, often more than are necessary with other therapy cases, especially if the loss is fresh and the grief still acute. In these instances, listening to and understanding the patient's immediate feelings are the first priority. Although a patient's great distress may engender helplessness in the therapist, evoking a desire to actively "take control" in crisis intervention, this is rarely helpful to the patient.* Unless the patient

*This refers to evaluation and preparation for expressive psychotherapy. It

is overtly psychotic or clearly threatening suicide*—circumstances I have not encountered—concrete action beyond setting up the next appointment within a week is usually
unnecessary.

A full discussion of the loss and the therapist's empathy
with the intense feelings often expressed are critical in fostering the positive therapeutic alliance that is crucial in cases
of perinatal loss. Although I believe the therapist's self-dis-
closure of his or her personal losses is rarely if ever beneficial
to the patient, the therapist's emotional responsiveness is
vital in communicating awareness of the depth of this loss
for the mother. A therapist's natural tendency to cry quietly
with a grieving parent at particularly poignant moments, as
long as this does not become an additional burden on her,
may support both the bereaved mother's mourning and the
therapeutic alliance. A therapist's humanity, rather than his
or her erudition, will probably be the best guide in responding to a patient's grief. At the same time, providing excessive
support regarding the patient's normality or eventual recovery is usually not useful to the patient and is based on the
therapist's own anxiety over patient distress and need to feel
helpful or powerful. It can be useful to inform the parent that
intense grieving over perinatal loss is not unusual or indicative of serious disturbance, especially if one senses her inhibition to express her grief frankly for fear of being viewed
as very disturbed. However, attributing highly personal feelings and fantasies to a generalized, common mourning reaction denies the patient's individuality and interferes with
understanding the unique meanings of *that* death for *that*

---

is not a critique of a more active form of behavioral-cognitive counseling—
providing direction and concrete advice in order to improve coping and
communication skills in managing this loss (Shapiro 1988)—which I am not
in a position to assess.

*Serious suicide threats need to be distinguished from the commonly ex-
pressed wish to die after these losses. Hopelessness, guilt, and an imagined
reunion with the dead child fuel suicide ideation. Suicidal danger can be
assessed by the usual criteria of conscious intent to harm or kill oneself,
history of suicidal behavior, reality-testing, impulsivity, and existence of an
actual plan.

woman. A practitioner who adopts a crisis-intervention approach may encourage the mother to suppress, and thereby bury, her irrational fantasies of self-blame in an attempt to mitigate the relentless guilt she feels. An ultimately more useful approach in psychotherapeutic intervention, I believe, is to explore the roots of irrational guilt in order to understand their meanings and thereby permit more lasting relief.

Only after the bereaved mother has had the opportunity to tell the story of her child's death and to begin to share her grief is it appropriate to acquire an individual and family history. The history of previous losses and degree of resolution, narcissistic vulnerabilities, earlier instinctual conflicts, childhood and current relationships with parents (especially mother), pregnancy history of the patient and her mother, and marital relationship are some of the key factors that must be considered in assessing the impact of this perinatal loss. The protocol used in organizing case data (see Appendix) may be adopted for clinical purposes to highlight important areas for therapeutic inquiry. As in all clinical investigation, one is as interested in the fantasies as in the facts. Although it is usually best to allow the patient's own associative process free reign in obtaining historical material, active inquiry is necessary if important subjects or details are omitted.

Many women who seek psychotherapy after perinatal loss may appear more acutely and chronically disturbed than they actually are because of the revival and intensification of earlier conflicts and issues in pregnancy. This apparent magnification of pathology has been similarly noted in pregnant women who present themselves for treatment or are in crisis (Bibring 1959). It becomes especially important, then, in assessing the overall degree of maladjustment to consider prior levels of achievement and adaptation in relationships, work, and self-definition, and not only current depression or seeming evidence of major disturbance.

Even when long-term, intensive psychotherapy is clearly indicated by a bereaved mother's history of emotional problems, rarely is the woman able to accept and successfully follow up on that recommendation at the time of bereavement. In my experience, short-term therapies are usually successful in such cases if the therapist is willing to accept the patient's more limited treatment goals. Otherwise, an abortive treatment may follow in which an initially compliant patient soon chooses to stop a long-term therapy, often without overt discussion. There may be many reasons for this difficulty in enlisting recently bereaved mothers in intensive therapy. This should be distinguished from the greater likelihood of success of a patient entering long-term therapy with different presenting problems long after the death and eventually working on unresolved issues from an earlier perinatal loss. The inner turmoil and massive disruption in functioning signalled by any crisis, such as usually occurs with recent perinatal loss, are not an auspicious climate in which to begin an intensive, uncovering psychotherapy. Furthermore, the psychological injuries sustained from perinatal loss may, ironically, militate against an intensive treatment plan. Even if the need for frequent sessions over a long period of time is clearly explained as a measure not of pathology but of chronic disturbance, these patients usually interpret such recommendations as another blow to their self-esteem. In addition to the multiple narcissistic wounds of losing her child, the woman must now endure the sense that not only her body but also her psyche is defective. Once again, she feels she is being singled out for ridicule and punishment; "being in therapy" is often experienced as a mark of shame and inadequacy rather than as a search for understanding and relief. The bereaved mother feels (and is often told by family and friends) that she should be "strong," whereas coming for therapy often means to her that she is "weak." Furthermore, the regressive thrust of intensive therapy may be especially threatening to women who have suffered recent perinatal loss and are still struggling with the unresolved regressive pull of pregnancy, with the revival of infantile identifications, oral issues, and earlier conflicts. The all-consuming preoccupation with her loss limits the degree of libidinal investment in the transference, which is usually a major source of the interpretive work in intensive psychotherapy. As is true of adolescents, the bereaved woman may feel she is already so close to her intensified dependency wishes that it becomes intolerable to have such needy, infantile feelings both heightened and exposed by the experience of intensive treatment. The sense of enforced immaturity resulting from the developmental interference of not being able to attain parenthood may be exacerbated by the regressive process of intensive treatment. Finally, the woman often lacks motivation. Even if significant conflicts and maladaptive patterns are obvious to the therapist (and to the patient), there may be an unwillingness to consider personality change at this time. These patients do not seek treatment to change who they are but to regain some earlier sense of well-being. Instead of feeling taken apart in therapy, they need to feel whole again.

For these reasons, short-term therapy is best suited for women who have recently suffered a perinatal loss. The revival of earlier conflicts and loosening of defenses during pregnancy facilitate a rapid engagement in the uncovering process, with potentially greater acquisition of insight than is usually possible with other short-term adult cases. Perhaps the most important prerequisite for effective short-term psychotherapy is determining the focus of the work (Malan 1976; Mann 1973; Strupp & Binder 1984; Wolberg 1980). The crystallization of often crucial, lifelong issues during the pregnancy and subsequent loss typically provides an ideal focus for the treatment. I believe, however, that claims for pervasive, enduring modification of chronic characterological disturbance through short-term psychotherapy (Davanloo 1980) are wildly exaggerated and need to be tempered. Short-term treatment may facilitate mourning and a significant improvement in functioning, but it is doubtful that the patient will acquire lasting solutions to chronic intrapsychic conflicts and deficits. I believe that the working-through process of applying insight to the multitude of irrational experiences and maladaptive patterns in one's life (and the transference) is crucial to pervasive personality change and cannot be fully achieved under the constraints of short-term or infrequent therapy.

The formal structure of time-limited psychotherapy addresses some of the central features of perinatal loss. Establishing the termination date early in treatment highlights the finality of separation and challenges the tendency to adhere unconsciously to magical, limitless expectations (Mann 1973). Time-limited psychotherapy provides an excellent context for resolving the bereaved mother's denial of the finality of her child's death, symbolized by termination. Moreover, by preparing for the termination date in advance, the bereaved mother is better able to work through the loss. The traumatizing impact of a totally unexpected death, inducing a debilitating sense of helplessness, may be healed by anticipatory grieving in mourning the planned termination of therapy. This affords a paradoxically greater measure of control and mastery over the dreaded inevitability of death.

For patients who from the outset appear to need more time, it is important to keep the termination date open-ended. Otherwise, setting a premature termination may destructively repeat the deprivation experienced in the perinatal loss. As long as the termination date is set sufficiently far in advance (which in these cases means at least a month), I believe many of the benefits of Mann's time-limited approach can be realized. Allowing the patient to decide when she is ready to stop may further promote her sense of mastery over the traumatizing loss.

In treating perinatal loss, the important functions the therapist fulfills vary not only with different patients but with the same patient at different points in the therapy. In facilitating the resolution of grief—both narcissistic and object loss—the therapist encourages mourning, empathizes with the profound loss, and sensitively confronts those defenses used maladaptively to block grieving. To help resolve revived intrapsychic conflicts, the therapist interprets the defended, unconscious wishes, especially as they emerge in relationships, both within the transference and outside the treatment.

If the bereaved woman has been open enough to allow the therapist to respond empathically to her grief, an intensely positive bond will often develop, in which the therapist is warmly regarded as someone upon whom she can depend. This expression of positive transference is an important ingredient in repairing her loss. The mother mourns her object loss not only by recovering memories of her unborn child but also by reliving with the therapist her infantile identification with this child. Through the therapist's serving as the caretaking "mother" of the patient (not through any concrete giving but through empathic understanding), the patient's infantile wishes activated in pregnancy may find some resolution. By then identifying with this caretaking therapist, she may find a restoration of her earlier thwarted maternity, typically by finding others upon whom to invest her care. *The uniquely intimate bond formed in pregnancy and shattered in perinatal loss may be most completely mourned in the revived formation and dissolution of the therapeutic relationship, and not only by the solitary recollection of memories and fantasies.*

Similarly, she is able to mourn her narcissistic loss during therapy by expressing her sense of bodily mortification, damage, and shame. Interacting with the therapist, who serves as the idealized maternal figure (condensing the images of her fantasized perfect child and omnipotent mother), replenishes her depleted self-esteem to a more self-sustaining level. Reestablishing narcissistic equilibrium for the bereaved mother (whose prior narcissism was not seriously damaged) through this relatively brief therapeutic relationship may approximate the process of transmuting internalization in the resolution of the idealizing transference. Again, the value of short-term psychotherapy is highlighted in the dyadic re-creation and ending of a relationship, recapitulating the establishment and disintegration of the pregnancy bond in perinatal loss.

Termination, a crucial part of the psychotherapy, highlights how completely the death has been resolved, while allowing additional opportunity in the transference to directly work on loss issues. Even when significant progress has been accomplished, ending therapy before the planned termination usually indicates the patient's unwillingness to complete mourning. An abrupt decision to terminate psychotherapy repeats the suddenness of the earlier traumatic loss. "Bolting" psychotherapy may be a desperate attempt to undo the helplessness experienced during perinatal loss by "turning passive into active": instead of being left by her dead baby, the bereaved mother is now the one who leaves, with no time to say goodbye. As a defense against remembering and resolving the trauma, the abrupt termination may be an unconscious attempt by the patient to provoke in the therapist the feelings of abandonment, confusion, anger, and guilt associated with her perinatal loss. By not attending the final appointment, the bereaved mother unconsciously denies the finality of her baby's death. Maintaining an unpaid balance long after treatment may signify unresolved anger and dependency, as well as the wish to preserve a connection with the therapist—yet another refusal to acknowledge the finality of loss.

The Clinical Sample

"Each parent reacts to the tragedy in a unique way, consistent with his or her particular personality structure, past experiences, and the individualized meaning associated with the loss. It is important that doctors do not project onto a family what they think the family should be feeling, instead of listening to what they are feeling" (Clyman et al. 1980, 218). Although many researchers (Ewy & Ewy 1984; Outerbridge et al. 1983; Panuthos & Romeo 1984; Phipps 1981) have emphasized this idiopathic approach to understanding perinatal loss, few case histories are available in the literature (for example, Corney & Horton 1974; Lewis & Page 1978; Turco 1981), and generalizations abound.

My research on maternal perinatal bereavement is based on a clinical sample of twenty women, each of whose perinatal deaths was a significant focus in their treatment. This sample is not representative of all women experiencing perinatal loss, because most do not seek professional help. This does not necessarily mean, however, that my clinical sample was significantly more disturbed than a nontreated population. Help-seeking studies have indicated that the degree of psychiatric disturbance was usually less important in the decision to seek mental health care than such other variables as help-seeking attitudes, subgroup membership, access to a referral source, and psychological orientation (Greenley & Mechanic 1976; Kadushin 1969; Leon 1983). However, because disturbed reactions to perinatal loss were crucial in selecting cases, this clinical sample should not be viewed as representing typical responses to perinatal loss.

The sample was largely white (90 percent), middle- to lower-middle-class (95 percent), and married (95 percent). The women were over 21 years of age when seen, and all but one suffered the perinatal loss as an adult. All the women who sought treatment within two years after the loss, comprising 65 percent of the sample, viewed this death as a significant part of their presenting problems. The remaining 35 percent had not initially attributed much importance to the loss occurring several years earlier and not mentioned at the beginning of therapy. The circumstances of their losses varied considerably: nine had at least one first-trimester miscarriage; seven had experienced at least one late-term intrauterine death; four had had stillbirths; two had had neonatal deaths; one had had two ectopic pregnancies; and six had suffered multiple perinatal losses. Of the twenty women, seventeen were seen or evaluated for individual psychotherapy in a private outpatient clinic or in private practice, two were seen intermittently for supportive counseling by an outreach worker affiliated with a hospital, and one was seen in marital therapy in private practice. I treated eleven of the cases; the remaining nine were seen by three psychologists, a social worker, and a nurse.

Although a common clinical protocol was used to gather data on history and treatment as well as to organize clinical conceptualizations on these patients, the unsystematic availability of data across variables prevents meaningful inferential statistical analysis. As with most clinically oriented research based on case reports, generalizations are tentative and subject to further case study and, if possible, to empirical validation.

The Immediate Grief: Psychotherapy for Recent Perinatal Loss

In the midst of the mother's fresh, unrestrained grief—behavior, thoughts, and affects that in another context might be considered disturbed—it may not be possible initially to distinguish adaptive from pathological mourning. Emanuel Lewis (1979a) offered the poignant example of how a newly bereaved mother's seemingly mad behavior of trying to "walk" her dead baby and frantically kissing his navel, mouth, and penis enabled her to mourn her child more effectively by

> attempting to come to terms with the baby's lost future. In her mind she maintained the continuity of the cycle of life. By kissing the umbilicus she was remembering her creative link with the baby *in utero*: kissing the mouth may be linked to the kiss of life, to the resuscitation. The mother longed for her son to grow teeth and learn to walk, and kissing his penis could be considered a wish to restore her dead son's potential capacity to create life. Creating memories about her baby in this way facilitated mourning. (304)

The therapist should encourage the mother's concrete description of the events around the time of loss in order to make both the child's existence and his death as real as possible. Just as *memories* of the beloved must be mourned at the end of a long-standing relationship, so *wishes* and *fantasies* of the child who will never be must be mourned in perinatal loss. Thus, perinatal grieving requires remembering the emotionally laden, fantasized interactions with one's child-to-be in the painful recognition that they will never come to pass.

The therapist needs to be able to accept the often dramatic expression of maternal grief as both normal and necessary. For fear of being viewed as insane, the newly bereaved mother may be reluctant to reveal such reactions as transient hallucinations of a baby crying, wishes to die, and powerful urges to steal another mother's infant. She may consciously suppress her tendency to cry in response to any reminders of babies, fearing that if she is not able to control her grief, it will overwhelm her and never end. The therapist may need to reassure her that such perceptions, wishes, and feelings are a natural expression of grief, mindful of her greater likelihood to pathologize her grieving on the basis of the fact that she is in psychotherapy.

At the same time, the meanings of these wishes, thoughts, and fantasies should be explored and understood in the context of a patient's individual history and psychodynamics and not disregarded as the epiphenomena of grief. The potentially valuable role of the therapist as an interpreter of unconscious conflicts should not be overlooked in facilitating the bereaved mother's mourning. The therapist should help illuminate the unique way in which she grieves for her child, with her particular blend of irrational self-blame, narcissistic mortification, rage, and denial, in order to prevent the beginning or deepening of emotional disturbance. It is particularly important to uncover her often-distorted and potentially pathogenic explanation for the child's death in order to present a more accurate and realistic understanding.

MRS. A

Mrs. A,* a thirty-three-year-old married woman studying to be a medical technician, was seen weekly for twelve sessions in short-term psychotherapy. Born and reared in rural Canada, Mrs. A had two younger brothers. She resented the fact that males seemed to be valued more than females in her family—and chose a male-dominated profession. She reported an unremarkable childhood, with positive feelings about her parents. Her relationship with her mother was warm, although designed, it appeared, to avoid conflict. She left Canada as an adult, without having had any serious romantic involvements there, and eventually married an American.

*The author thanks Carol Barbour, Ph.D., for providing case material on this patient.

She contacted the therapist on what would have been her delivery date had her child not died in utero seven weeks earlier. She appeared demure and somewhat inhibited, more like a shy schoolgirl than a young woman. This was her second pregnancy. She had a healthy four-year-old son who appeared well-adjusted. She was happily married to a successful businessman. This pregnancy had been carefully planned and much wanted.

Following her loss, Mrs. A's immediate response was to defensively immerse herself completely in her studies. She believed at first that she should not be grieving and should be handling things better, especially because she was in the medical field. Though her husband had been supportive, he seemed to be at a loss as to how to help her and how to respond to her grief. Her therapist invited her to share her feelings about her child's death.

Her grieving dominated the first half of treatment. She mourned the loss of the child she had desperately wanted. She felt great bitterness and a terrible sense of injustice that she should lose her baby, yet other women could have children. She felt a failure as a woman, exclaiming that "even cows can have babies." Therapy was the only place she could express these feelings after the "unspeakable" and "unthinkable" had happened. She first noticed that the baby had stopped moving while on vacation and felt guilty over not going to a physician at once instead of waiting until she returned home several days later. She believed she should somehow have known something was wrong and was afraid she might have done something to hurt her baby. She was angry at the doctors, who did not know how the baby had died, a fact that was particularly painful for her. Unfortunately, the baby's remains were mistakenly destroyed, and, not having seen the baby, she did not even know if it was a boy or girl. At first, she felt enormous pressure to become pregnant again quickly but decided to postpone that decision as she began to recognize that she had suffered an irreplaceable loss.

As the therapy progressed, her competition with other

women intensified. She felt she had received a personal blow when she learned that a good friend had just become pregnant. Adding insult to injury, this woman was married to a Canadian. Mrs. A's sexual inhibitions seemed to have prevented her from finding a husband in her home country. It became clear that she was unable to share her grief with close female friends because of her great competition with them. Her transference was marked by both admiration and envy of her female therapist. She had the powerful conviction that everything desirable and valuable was in her therapist's domain.

At this point in the treatment, an important memory emerged. Mrs. A recalled a wonderful night during her summer vacation when she felt that she had everything—the man she loved, the pregnancy she wanted, and, rare for her, an orgasm during sexual intercourse with her husband. When she lost her baby soon after, she felt that she was being punished for having experienced total fulfillment that night. With much feeling, she described how she felt she wanted and had received too much and thus had to lose it. The therapist interpreted how she experienced herself as being punished for pleasures and satisfactions that she felt were forbidden to her. Although Mrs. A could acknowledge long-standing sexual inhibitions in her marriage, describing her marriage as a "brother-sister" relationship at times, she was reluctant to explore this area in greater depth, protesting against having her therapist "in my bedroom."

As the intensity of her sadness and anger subsided by the latter half of her treatment, Mrs. A was motivated to help others cope with death. She attended seminars on grief and organized discussion groups for medical technicians on death and dying. As her own grief lessened, she was able to help another bereaved mother who had suffered perinatal death understand and cope with her loss.

As Mrs. A better understood her conflicts over competition with women and her internal prohibitions against sexual satisfaction, there was some loosening of her inhibitions. She began to feel more attractive, to present herself in a more feminine manner, and to express more self-confidence as a woman. At the same time, she decided not to examine more fully her conflicted sexual wishes. Although emotionally satisfied with her husband, she was seldom orgasmic. She still seemed to believe that it would be asking too much to have everything.

As Mrs. A prepared to terminate therapy, there was a renewed optimism and the sense of a new beginning. She felt better able to cope by herself with her grief, which had diminished considerably. With her therapist on vacation, "getting through" Christmas day—the anniversary of learning she was pregnant—felt like a milestone. Although she still wanted to have another child, the need was not as urgent, and she decided to wait a while longer. She ended her treatment with a warm and appreciative feeling toward her therapist.

This case exemplifies many of the immediate responses to perinatal loss, such as irrational self-blame for the death, anger over the injustice of the loss, tremendous yearning to regain the dead child, the massive blow to the sense of omnipotence in pregnancy, and the woman's devaluation of her feminine and maternal competency. Her child's death represented an object loss and multiple narcissistic injuries, as well as being experienced neurotically as a symbolic castration and punishment for prohibited oedipal wishes.

The resonance of grief with time is particularly noteworthy and common with perinatal death. Mrs. A sought help when her sense of loss was most acute, on the day that she would have been reunited with her baby by the child's birth. This underscores the potency of denial in the mourning process of perinatal death; the full impact of the loss emerged only as the delivery date passed with no baby there. Conversely, the ending of treatment is bracketed by the anniversary of learning of the pregnancy one year before, once again intensifying her sense of loss. An integral part of the mourning process is accepting the demise of the wishes and fantasies of the child-to-be that were powerfully nourished during the pregnancy.

In denying mortality the two vehicles by which the inevitability of death is expressed—bodily deterioration and the ceaseless passage of time—may be transformed into psychosomatic symptomatology and anniversary reactions, respectively. That is, psychosomatic complaints may unconsciously deny the ultimate helplessness of our will over our physical destiny; anniversary reactions may paradoxically challenge the irreversibility of death by unconsciously making one psychically reexperience the loss (although as Pollock [1970] suggested, anniversary reactions may be used in some instances as an adaptive attempt to master an earlier trauma). In another case, a woman who had not overtly grieved over her miscarriage five months earlier sought treatment for psychosomatic symptoms (especially a fear of vomiting and stomach pains) that simulated pregnancy as her delivery date approached. Another woman experienced anxiety attacks around the first anniversary of a very disappointing miscarriage, which was her first conception after attempting pregnancy for more than two years. Her anxiety attacks, which began on Good Friday while meeting with her interior decorator, seemed to express symbolically unconscious wishes for narcissistic restitution by her own bodily repair on a day associated with the vanquishing of death itself.

The case of Mrs. A illustrates that it is possible to mourn a perinatal loss without concrete evidence of the baby. Although the potential benefits of viewing and interacting with the dead baby should not be minimized, this experience is not indispensable for mourning one's loss. I was impressed with the creative abilities of many of these women to memorialize their dead children in unique, personalized ways without having seen them. One woman who steadfastly refused to view her stillborn made an elaborate embroidery on woven fabric of her son's name, proudly displayed on the mantel with those of her surviving children. For a number of these women, viewing the child's remains or establishing a permanent resting place was especially important in order to convince themselves definitively that the child would never return and to repair their sense of damaged maternity. One patient who had viewed her stillborn daughter needed to have the child's ashes to fully accept the finality of her loss. Another woman had viewed her daughter who died in utero in the eighth month but was distraught over not knowing where the hospital had buried the child. Her considerable guilt was markedly relieved when she was able to locate her daughter's grave and fulfill her maternal wishes to care for the site, thus providing assurance that she had not abandoned her child.

Mourning the perinatal death accomplishes the resolution of both the loss of an object tie and the intensified infantile identification with the baby's dependency. The lack of major unresolved dependency issues may explain the relative ease with which Mrs. A was able to mourn her child's death and seems to be confirmed by her comfortable and appropriate expression of dependency on her therapist. More serious conflicts over dependency and separation-individuation would probably have resulted in more withdrawal and counterdependent maneuvers in the treatment as she felt threatened by her neediness. Instead, she allowed herself to feel and to appreciate a sense of being mothered through a relationship with an empathic therapist. Mourning perinatal loss may be accomplished not only in the patient's recollection of wishes and fantasies of her child-to-be but also in a therapeutic process that re-creates the maternal bond through the therapist's empathy; the mother is able to internalize this bond as a reparation for the one that was never realized with her child.

The sense of feeling nurtured by an empathic therapist, who can help the bereaved mother better understand and accept her grief, may also help to repair the damage to her maternal identification. Mrs. A's positive identification with her therapist may have enabled her to help others as she had been helped. Once her grieving had abated, she found alternative avenues of nurturing by helping others with similar losses cope with grief. Her maternal identification revived in pregnancy, which could not be fulfilled in caring for this child, could now find some satisfaction by aiding others facing similar losses. Many of the other women in my sample also repaired their injured sense of maternal nurturance by helping others, often by empathizing with the pain and suffering of similarly bereaved mothers. Self-help groups may also provide a valuable outlet by offering complementary roles for bereaved mothers over the course of mourning: the newly bereaved mother's dependency in grieving her infantile identification may be gratified by the need of other bereaved mothers to satisfy their persisting maternal identification by offering nurturance. And by helping surviving siblings deal with their inevitably confused and ambivalent feelings, the bereaved mother may also find a valid means of fulfilling her maternal strivings.

Psychotherapy with the bereaved mother also provides an opportunity to work on latent, long-standing conflicts that have been refueled during the pregnancy and its tragic conclusion. Her psychological functioning during pregnancy and her distorted understanding of the cause of the intrauterine death demonstrate that Mrs. A was grappling with both phallic and oedipal issues. Although not enough data were available to fully delineate the regressive elements of this pregnancy, the material suggested that during the final trimester she was a more sexually responsive woman. An increasingly positive maternal identification and differentiation from her mother may have enabled her to experience sexual satisfaction at that time, not as an oedipal victory over mother, but as an adaptive attempt to resolve oedipal conflicts and feel proud of her femininity in maternity.

Her perinatal loss, occurring at a time when she was especially vulnerable to those revived phallic-oedipal conflicts, reevoked in full measure those struggles: this child's death was experienced by Mrs. A as a symbolic castration, the punishment for sexual enjoyment, which became forbidden to her once again. Competition with women and her feeling of inferiority compared to both women and men once again intensified as the prohibition against sexual satisfaction increased. In a sense, her distorted interpretation of her perinatal loss undid the adaptation that was being accomplished during her pregnancy. Her increased sense of adequacy as a woman independent of her mother was replaced by prohibitions against her sexual fulfillment as a woman because of her conflicted competition with mother. Her sense of having failed as a woman by losing her unborn child may have reinforced related narcissistic injuries of feeling defective and deficient in lacking a penis. The wish to become pregnant immediately after her loss probably represented the wish to recover her budding mastery of long-standing oedipal and phallic conflicts achieved during this pregnancy more than the need to replace an object loss.

The resolution of Mrs. A's perinatal loss may be considered adaptive insofar as she was able to mourn her child's death and accomplish enough work on revived oedipal and phallic conflicts to allow a more positive and less inhibited feminine identity than existed prior to her pregnancy. The opportunity for an even more complete and adaptive resolution of these conflicts, as was beginning to emerge during this pregnancy, was not attempted because Mrs. A declined further psychotherapy.

Unresolved Grief: The Timeless Aftermath of Perinatal Loss

We have noted many aspects of perinatal loss that may make mourning this death especially difficult to resolve: the suddenness of the death; the mother's intense dependency on caring for her baby to fulfill many object, narcissistic, and developmental needs; the resurgence of oral issues in pregnancy; and the revival of ambivalent feelings toward her own mother. In treating unresolved grief, bereavement experts have advised careful review of the circumstances of the death and relationship with the bereaved in an attempt to understand the issues inhibiting grief as well as to facilitate its full affective expression (Raphael 1975, 1983). Volkan's (1971, 1985) "re-grief" therapy emphasizes distinguishing the mourner from the deceased and uncovering the "linking objects" that tie the mourner to the deceased so that the dead person can be finally relinquished. Major unresolved losses, such as the death of a child, may eventually lead to depressive breakdowns many years later, which can mistakenly be diagnosed as biologically based depression or borderline personality (Geller 1985).

MRS. O

Mrs. O was an attractive, forty-five-year-old, married white woman. The most striking aspect of her self-presentation was her depleted, unemotional voice, pitched at a barely audible volume. In her initial psychiatric evaluation, she presented as moderately depressed. This appeared to be due primarily to the recent upheaval in her life: she had remarried a few months earlier and moved to Michigan from her home state of Montana. She very much missed her adult sons, aged nineteen and twenty-four, who had stayed in Montana. Hyperthyroidism (Grave's disease) had recently been diagnosed and managed by medication. She had been divorced eight years earlier, followed by two years of heavy alcohol use. Upon completing a thirty-day residential treatment program for alcoholism, she became an active participant in Alcoholics Anonymous (AA) and had been abstinent for five years. Just prior to her referral, she had returned to drinking heavily and made a suicide gesture by ingesting several Inderal tablets.

In her initial appointment with the psychotherapist, Mrs. O reviewed what she had discussed in the evaluation and complained about marital difficulties caused by her husband's angry, controlling, demanding behavior. It seemed that whatever she did was met with his criticism. Her current husband was a heavy drinker, as was her first spouse. She was trained as a physical therapist, especially enjoyed working with the elderly, and was in the process of finding a job. She struggled against her depression but frequently succumbed, isolating herself and refusing to leave the house for weeks.

It was not until her second appointment that the history

of her perinatal losses emerged—after direct questioning. She had two surviving children from six pregnancies. Her first pregnancy was uneventful and successful, followed by the stillbirth delivery of a girl two years later. After suffering a miscarriage, she completed a second healthy pregnancy, about two years after her first stillbirth. This was followed by another stillbirth and then a late-term intrauterine death. The final loss had taken place over fifteen years before her present therapy. None of the perinatal losses could be explained medically, and there were no visible defects. All of the pregnancies were planned except the final one, which occurred after her husband's apparently ineffective vasectomy. She was in the process of adopting a child when she learned of this pregnancy. With considerable anxiety she went ahead with the pregnancy, regretting the loss of the adoptive baby she would have received shortly. All three late-term losses had been named and given funeral services and burials.

With considerable emotion, Mrs. O described the horrible pain she felt over her dead children: despite proper precautions during the pregnancies, she blamed herself and felt like a failure. For many years she had tried not to think or talk about her losses, fearful that dwelling on them would make matters worse. In the midst of expressing her profound sense of loss over these deaths, she vented her rage at women who purposely end their pregnancies by abortion. She felt enormous jealousy toward other mothers and strove to be close to relatives who were the age her dead children would have been.

Several days after these powerful revelations and before her next scheduled appointment, she came in asking to be admitted to an alcohol treatment program. She had returned to drinking during the past two weeks but stopped the day after her emotional appointment. She agreed with her therapist's view that she needed to work on her unresolved grief and that seeking residential treatment at this point might be an attempt to avoid her mourning. She was able to follow the recommendation that she actively resume attending AA meetings and was able to remain abstinent for the duration of psychotherapy. She felt that talking about her losses was important, something that had always been in the background but was never discussed. Her first husband had told her to forget about them, and she rarely brought up her losses at AA meetings.

Mrs. O blandly described how there had been "death in the house" throughout her childhood. Her mother had suffered a heart attack when Mrs. O was five, followed by open-heart surgery when she was seven and multiple heart operations afterward. When Mrs. O was twenty-two, her mother died. She remembered her mother as sickly throughout her childhood but felt particularly close to her, especially after her first heart attack. She did not at first believe that her childhood was particularly unhappy. As mother's condition worsened during childhood, her father withdrew into stony silence and heavy alcohol use. A paternal aunt and uncle as well as one sister were reportedly alcoholic in addition to her father. She was never close to her sisters, who were five and seven years her senior.

Time-limited psychotherapy was planned because of financial problems and her uncertainty about how long she would remain in the area, especially if there was a marital separation. She recognized that enduring difficulties related to her alcoholism and deprived childhood would require long-term treatment for more complete resolution. The focus would be on the unresolved grief and terrible sense of failure caused by her perinatal losses; the themes of loss of mother, failure as a wife, and addiction to alcohol were considered lifelong struggles for her to overcome. She was seen for seventeen sessions in weekly psychotherapy with a planned termination date.

She grieved her perinatal losses, particularly the last child, James, throughout the first half of her therapy. Soon after the treatment plan was established, she presented a recurrent dream. There was a dead baby with blood at the back of her head. She recalled a swinging accident when she was a child, resulting in stitches in the back of her head. She was increasingly anxious about her seventeen-month-old granddaughter dying. The dream was initially understood as her wish to sacrifice her life so that her dead child might live in an attempt to preserve some measure of maternal self-worth.

She recalled the last loss as the most difficult. Totally unexpected and seemingly impossible because of her husband's vasectomy, the pregnancy was regarded as a gift from God. When she learned of the baby's intrauterine death in the final trimester, she felt she was being punished and was enraged at God. For her own health, it was recommended that labor not be induced; as a result she carried the dead baby for about five weeks before delivery. Unlike her other dead children, whom she clearly remembered, she could recall nothing of James—neither his face, which she knows she saw, nor the funeral, which she knows she attended. She could not cry for weeks after his death but began to drink heavily. A friend's accusing her of being selfish for abandoning her responsibility toward her two surviving children helped to revive her.

She began to understand more clearly how her ambivalence toward this pregnancy contributed to her difficulty in accepting the death and mourning the loss. The joy of learning of this pregnancy was mixed with the disappointment of losing a soon-to-be-adopted child and the fear of another perinatal loss. She could not help but want and not want this child. She said that carrying the dead baby made her feel like a casket, and that she felt ashamed to be seen in public. At this time a part of her denied the reality of her child's intrauterine death, while another part desperately wanted to be rid of the burden of carrying death. She began to understand how the simultaneous denial of his death and wish to be rid of him compounded the terrible sense of having murdered her son. She did not want to hear the physician's explanation of the death, convinced that she would be blamed. Likewise, her guilt was externalized in anticipating that her husband would accuse her of this death. Her inability to recall James was understood as a need to deny his death in order to alleviate the overwhelming burden of guilt. When death cannot be acknowledged, mourning cannot proceed. To facilitate the completion of grieving for James, she planned to return to the hospital in Montana to clarify several questions about his death.

Mrs. O began to recognize that her anxiety and sadness over leaving her adult children represented, in part, a repetition of her perinatal losses, as well as the dread that she could not protect them from harm. When her younger son was about to leave Montana for an out-of-state college, she fretted over his going to a strange city and having to make decisions on his own. She felt she was abandoning him, as if he were a helpless child. Mrs. O recalled how frightened she was of losing this son to Sudden Infant Death Syndrome when he was an infant, even though he had no health problems. Just having had a stillbirth and a miscarriage, she was terrified that he would die if she left him alone.

In the latter half of her treatment, Mrs. O began to tentatively approach her unresolved childhood issues. Her family had avoided the topic of death at all costs. A family secret that was never openly discussed was the stillbirth of a son one year prior to Mrs. O's birth. This was the much-wanted and unplanned boy in the family. In her youth, Mrs. O became a tomboy who could lick any guy in the neighborhood. She began to recall the constant dread of her mother dying while she was growing up. When Mrs. O was eight, she was afraid that mother might bleed to death should she get a small cut because she was taking a blood thinner. Memories of being lonely and sad as a child returned. She resented how much the household had changed as a result of mother's condition, how quiet and well-behaved she had to be lest she jeopardize mother's precarious health. She began to appreciate her belief that her anger at mother had to be totally buried lest it harm or kill her. When, as a teenager, she had once angrily shouted that she hated her mother as she stormed out of the house, she needed to return quickly to make sure her mother was safe.

Mrs. O was unable to resolve her guilt over rage at mother, especially at the deprivation she had experienced in an emotionally neglectful household. She could report warm memories of mother with ease but carefully censored expressing anger over mother's unavailability. She viewed her sisters as bitter and selfishly demanding, especially the elder one, whose anger at mother, Mrs. O was convinced, worsened mother's condition. She recognized that powerful prohibitions against her anger continued and began to realize that her choosing and provoking angry, critical husbands both vicariously expressed and directly punished her anger. Rather than express her neediness of mother more directly in the transference, she sought and found comfort in dependent attachments to a stepdaughter and a female sponsor at AA, whom she would call if in crisis.

Similarly, as the termination date approached, she could express her gratitude over how therapy had helped her resolve her children's deaths but was unable to explore her rage and hurt about ending. She recognized that the treatment meant a great deal to her and worried about how she would cope without the meetings. She made tentative plans to join a grief group to continue her perinatal mourning, and the therapist suggested that her formulating this idea at this time might be designed to avoid the loss she was experiencing in terminating. Mrs. O realized that she wanted to delay thinking about ending therapy and would discuss the matter only when directly questioned.

During her final session, Mrs. O described how her anxiety about her children had considerably lessened because of a heightened awareness of its association with her perinatal losses. Both she and her therapist began to appreciate that this overprotectiveness represented an attempt not only to undo the tragedy of perinatal loss but also to vicariously satisfy her own unmet dependency needs suffered as a child. She reported that because she was more able to express her anger at her husband and not flee from it, he seemed less angry and the relationship was more stable. She reported a nightmare in which children were being shot and were falling into a river. It reminded her of a movie she had seen the previous day in which Jews were shot; she recalled that she had fallen into a river when she was four. Her continuing need to punish herself over feeling responsible for her children's deaths was reviewed. The association of this issue with her sense of responsibility for mother's death became clear as she concluded the session and therapy by describing her guilt over causing her mother's "heartache," implying that her anger had wrought physical damage.

Many factors contributed to Mrs. O's unresolved grief over perinatal loss. The family's avoidance of the ever-present topic of death complemented her own reluctance to introduce her perinatal losses. She seemed to share her family's fear of the overwhelming affects that would accompany any discussion of death. Her inability to mourn her own perinatal losses mirrored her parents' failure to grieve her older stillborn brother. By identification, her unresolved grief continued the family legacy of unresolved perinatal mourning.

The revival of maternal and infantile identifications in her pregnancies effected a powerful dependency on her children, making them difficult to relinquish in mourning. Identification with a frail, sickly mother, who herself experienced pregnancy failure as well as having had her mothering compromised by a debilitating cardiac condition, could not provide a solid foundation of maternal self-confidence that could withstand multiple perinatal losses. Her infantile identification with her child-to-be reawakened her powerful sense of deprivation as a little girl who could not regularly depend on a sick, inaccessible mother. The revival of oral conflicts during pregnancy was particularly threatening to Mrs. O because of her history of deprivation.

Although unable to be fully elaborated in this brief treatment, it appeared that another source of deprivation and feminine insult in her childhood was her being in some measure a replacement child for an earlier stillbirth. Not accepted for herself, she became a tomboy to win her parents' affection. In this context, it is possible to understand her identification with the dead, bloody baby in her dreams as the wish to both sacrifice and punish herself, not only for her own dead children, but for the stillborn brother she could not replace. At the same time, her identification with the dead baby is the expression of her own unmet neediness. She becomes the dead, unprotected baby.

Her maternal self-worth, shaken by her perinatal losses, was nourished by caring for her surviving children. The perhaps tactless accusation by her friend that she was selfish in forsaking her responsibility to her living children was an effective confrontation for its element of truth. To the degree that her preoccupation with her loss represented the revived experience of unresolved dependency, it was a self-involvement that prevented the mothering of her surviving children.

Perhaps the paramount factor inhibiting her perinatal mourning was her long-standing inability to tolerate her rage owing to her unconscious conviction that it harmed and ultimately destroyed her mother. The unfortunate emergence of mother's cardiac condition in the midst of her oedipal development probably reinforced the magical thinking in which her rage, fueled by both deprivation and competitiveness, could be held accountable for physical harm. It is not surprising to discover that rage and resulting guilt were displaced and projected onto the "selfish" sister, who was old enough to serve as a maternal substitute. This woman was both hated and held responsible for mother's worsening condition.

Her unresolved guilt over mother's illness and death because of anger at mother can be understood as an important source of her unresolved grief at the death of her last child, James, owing to her ambivalence about this pregnancy. In a manner analogous to her projection of anger and guilt onto her eldest sister, her guilt was externalized in her fury at mothers who purposely "kill" (that is, abort) an unwanted child.

Mrs. O began to mourn her perinatal losses with surprisingly little reluctance. The passage of over fifteen years had not diminished the immediacy and vividness of the deaths. Just as an anniversary may unconsciously revive earlier unresolved losses by a temporal trigger (Hilgard 1969; Pollock 1970), Mrs. O's physical separation from her surviving sons may have precipitated the surfacing of her perinatal losses, enabling the resumption of mourning. Her alcoholism appears overdetermined, as a genetic predisposition with a high loading in her family, social learning of a family style of coping with stress, her own defense against dealing with depression and loss, and an expression of neediness and deprivation (that is, oral yearnings). It was instructive to observe how readily her drinking ceased once she began to mourn her perinatal losses. Coping with her perinatal grief seemed to remove one important motivation for her alcohol abuse.

In the process of working on unresolved perinatal grief, Mrs. O's depressive constellation of earlier losses, history of deprivation, difficulties in maintaining self-esteem, addictive potential, unresolved rage, and self-defeating pattern of relationships were exposed. Although a short-term psychotherapy could not successfully modify these lifelong difficulties, it clarified how unresolved perinatal grief may be a product of, and actively reinforced by, enduring psychopathology. Barry (1981) reported similarly that the successful treatment of unresolved grief in general "uncovered much more severe personality problems upon whose substrate the pathologic or prolonged grief reaction was built" (p. 746). Mrs. O returned for further treatment several years later. Therapeutic gains from resolving her perinatal losses were maintained; she was less preoccupied with these deaths, reporting fewer nightmares and worries about her children, as well as being more able to talk comfortably about these losses. However, her chronic depressive issues and masochistic solutions continued to plague her and proved resistant to further psychotherapy.

Perinatal loss may be particularly difficult to mourn when the unborn child represents an earlier unresolved loss, often a parent who died in childhood. A thirty-seven-year-old woman, consumed with grief and anger, entered psychotherapy eight months after suffering a stillbirth. It quickly became evident that the pregnancy was designed to recover her dead mother, who had died of cancer when the patient was fifteen. She maintained that she had learned her mother's condition was terminal only two weeks before her death.

She was convinced that she would bear a girl (which she did) and had unconsciously timed the delivery to coincide with her mother's birth, having reportedly been unable to conceive for many months prior to this. She regretted not having her daughter's ashes, which she wished to sprinkle on her mother's grave.

Like Mrs. O, this woman benefited considerably from short-term therapy and reported much less depression when she decided to terminate. Despite her sorrow, she did not regret her pregnancy because she had positive memories of loving the daughter alive inside of her. Yet, by her final session, the grieving for her mother and denial of her death continued untouched: lingering doubts remained about whether her mother was actually buried at the grave site because the funeral seemed unreal and she could not recall seeing her mother's body there. She wanted any other children who might die to be buried next to her mother. Although this short-term therapy was able to facilitate her mourning of her stillborn and to forestall a deepening depression, she was unable to resolve her feelings about her mother's death, which this stillbirth signified.

Although it is customary to conceptualize unresolved grief in terms of object loss, there can be strong resistance to mourning narcissistic damage. A forty-seven-year-old woman sought treatment because of intense, frightening, and unacceptable homosexual feelings toward her best friend. The weekly psychotherapy focused on positive oedipal conflicts and her retreat to a negative oedipal, homosexual position. Months into the treatment, while recalling irritation at a physician for treatment of her finger, she revealed for the first time that she had lost a three-day-old son over ten years earlier. He had died of a congenital kidney disease that left him extremely bloated and even difficult to distinguish as a male. Within a week of his death she had a tubal ligation, reportedly on doctor's orders because of her extreme distress and his medical opinion that she should have no further children (she already had a two-year-old son). This mother mourned the object loss of her son for the first time during psychotherapy. Perhaps more important, it became clear that the birth of the malformed child and her subsequent sterilization were severe narcissistic blows to her femininity, which were especially difficult to endure because of long-standing conflicts in sexual orientation and gender identification. Her shame in feeling responsible for her son's deformity represented her own sense of feeling defective as a female; she was often degraded as ugly by her harshly critical mother. Only after she felt her femininity was supported and accepted by her female therapist could she reveal this narcissistic trauma and begin to understand its impact.

Short-term psychotherapy can effectively reduce the chronic repercussions of earlier unresolved perinatal loss. It may also facilitate the resolution of a recent perinatal loss that, because of earlier unresolved losses, would otherwise have gone incompletely mourned. This limited psychotherapy, however, cannot successfully alter the long-standing conflicts and unresolved losses that typically complicate mourning perinatal loss. Perinatal grief may be the more accessible "tip of the iceberg" of a pervasive neurotic, depressive, borderline, or narcissistic character disorder. In planning short-term psychotherapy, both patient and therapist must realize that deep-seated issues that may be activated by pregnancy and perinatal loss and that are almost always involved in unresolved grief will eventually require more intensive treatment.

The Refusal to Grieve: Bolting Psychotherapy

Many women who seek treatment for perinatal loss soon refuse to continue. As many as 25 percent of the women in my sample abruptly ended their psychotherapies within three sessions of formulating the treatment plan. Although this early drop-out rate does not appear especially high for psychotherapy in an outpatient clinic, it may be valuable to consider the factors that are likely to lead to a quick withdrawal from treatment for perinatal loss.

Women who fled therapy just as it was commencing were, without exception, unable to tolerate the helplessness and neediness engendered by the loss. These five women were intensely counterdependent, either characterologically or specifically in reaction to the dependency revived by the loss. For some, the perinatal death revived other unresolved object losses. Recalling the details of the loss and beginning to mourn the death with an empathic therapist foster the bond that will recapitulate the bereavement during treatment and, especially, at termination. By actively inhibiting any overt expression of grief, these women did not allow themselves to reexperience the attachment to and loss of their pregnancies; likewise, they prevented themselves from becoming emotionally engaged in therapy by leaving quickly. Four of these five women demonstrated significant, unresolved separation-individuation from their mothers. In two of these cases, in fact, the pregnancy seemed largely motivated by the wish to provide a sense of autonomy and self-sufficiency that had not yet been achieved intrapsychically. While seeking to identify with a powerful maternal imago, each of these women inevitably became the hungry, deprived infant of her mother, an identification revived in treatment and disavowed by bolting the therapy. In another case, the patient seemed to have achieved a greater degree of psychic independence from her mother, but a miscarriage in the context of her ongoing failure to successfully give birth became a formidable developmental interference to her attaining adult status in parenthood; this resulted in a regression to earlier separation issues with mother. This woman felt compelled to keep her infertility secret from her parents, fearing that discussing the situation with her mother would make her feel that she was a child again, running to "Mommy" with her problems.

These five women were the only patients in my sample who had been infertile for at least two years prior or subsequent to the perinatal loss. Three of these women were childless; one had had a hysterectomy because of cervical cancer five years earlier. Obviously, their infertility distinguished these women as a separate subset of my sample. Their refusal to grieve their losses was probably connected with the greater difficulty of mourning perinatal death when the eventual resolution of producing another child is in doubt or unavailable. Infertility may not only complicate mourning perinatal loss but also intensify preexisting separation-individuation issues, especially if there have been no successful pregnancies. None of these women appeared to be borderline; rather, their unresolved separation difficulties suggested a partial adolescent fixation, perhaps resulting from their infertility as a developmental interference. The only woman among these five whose primary difficulty resulting from her perinatal loss, a miscarriage, was unrelated to separation concerns had two preexisting children.

MRS. S

Mrs. S was a twenty-seven-year-old woman who entered psychotherapy feeling confused and uncertain about the source of her depression. She presented in a rather impulsive, emotional, adolescent fashion. Six months earlier, while in her fifth month of gestation, she had miscarried. After heavy alcohol and marijuana use for the previous two months, recently discontinued at the recommendation of the referring psychiatrist, the miscarriage had just "hit her." The cause was unknown, but she felt it was her fault, because of her being "run-down" and "tired." Although she had been crying, screaming, and vomiting at night since the miscarriage, she was quite vague and unresponsive when asked about feelings and details of the loss. She bitterly recalled a previous miscarriage nine years earlier, which her in-laws had indicated was probably for the best. She wanted to run away now, as she had felt then. She was increasingly critical of her only child, a four-year-old daughter, avoiding her for fear of hitting her for misbehavior. She had been unable to conceive from that birth until this last pregnancy.

Her unhappiness with her husband of ten years preoccupied her. Increasingly she felt something was missing from her marriage. She had had a series of affairs until a year and a half before entering treatment and guiltily confessed that she had begun seeing another man about a month earlier.

This man was portrayed as irresponsible, possessive, and alcoholic, while her husband was described as caring and good to her. She complained that her husband either showed indifference to her or excessively controlled her life by his devotion. Sexual intercourse was infrequent owing to her inability to become aroused by him; she described their relationship as like that of "brother and sister." Despite her therapist's discouraging impulsive decisions, over the course of her six sessions she abruptly left her job as a nurse's aide because of her depression and separated from her husband, fearing that he would be hurt if he discovered her affair.

She reported an unhappy childhood, having to care for three younger brothers. Her father was generally away at work, and her nervous, yelling mother, a "bitch" who was reportedly hypochondriacal, repeatedly went to the hospital for medical problems. She felt controlled by her mother as well, describing how, when she was thirteen, mother had "picked out" her current husband for her to marry four years later because he would be a good provider.

Her therapist reviewed her difficulty in recognizing and grieving her loss, which seemed to intensify previous conflicts regarding intimacy with her husband and earlier conflicts about her feelings of dependency on mother. Although she portrayed herself as in crisis and looked for advice, she could not commit herself even to a twelve-session treatment contract to begin to sort out her behavior and feelings. She agreed to meet session by session.

In the following session, while discussing the recent death of an uncle unfamiliar to her, she claimed she could not have feelings about someone she did not know. After her therapist explained her disavowal of feelings over her miscarriage—someone else she did not know—she described, with more emotion, her ambivalence during this pregnancy. She did not want to bring another child into an unhappy marriage and was afraid of having to care for a sick child, recalling her daughter's frequent illnesses and the serious illnesses (rheumatic fever) of her younger siblings, with whose care she was often entrusted. Her guilty feelings that she was to blame for the miscarriage were interpreted in terms of her conflicts over having a child, of not wanting the burden of caring for a needy infant, which recalled for her the overwhelming duty of nursing her sick siblings. She still was unable to discuss the details of the miscarriage and remembered her mother's encouraging her not to talk about it. This guilty secret appeared to be linked to another guilty secret, her recent affair; her choice of an unsuitable man, jeopardizing her marriage, appeared motivated in part by self-punishment. The next two sessions were cancelled, first because of a scheduling conflict with a conference at her daughter's school and then because of illness.

She used the following two sessions to express her confusion over which man to choose, complaining how each was intruding on her autonomy by pressuring her to stay with him. The therapist pointed out that her own conflicts over being independent seemed to be unconsciously motivating her to be tantalizingly unavailable to these men, thereby provoking their pursuit of her. Her recent cancellations were similarly explored as attempts to provoke her therapist's pursuit of her while preventing the solidification of an attachment that would threaten her precarious sense of autonomy. Her defensive retreat from her earlier discussion about the miscarriage was also noted. She bitterly complained about having had to be a "good girl" in order to be accepted by her parents and was furious that they would reject the man with whom she was having an affair. She protested that her recent pregnancy was planned primarily because of parental pressure. The therapist highlighted how much of her behavior seemed to be designed to defy her mother (that is, abandoning her mother's choice of a partner for her own) or to comply with mother's wishes (that is, not discussing the miscarriage), exemplifying her unsettled independence from mother. Mrs. S cancelled the following session because she had to visit her ill father and, without explanation, did not return for future appointments.

Mrs. S's impulsivity and strong tendency to quickly "act out" her internalized conflicts in provocative and self-defeating behaviors (for example, extramarital affairs, marital separation, therapy cancellations, and bolting) made her a poor candidate for psychotherapy. Had she been able to discuss her miscarriage and begun to grieve this loss, however, I suspect a stronger therapeutic alliance and attachment to the therapist would have been fostered, enabling her to continue in treatment.

As is typical in cases of perinatal loss, there was a close correspondence between the timing of her symptoms and pregnancy. She sought satisfaction of intensified oral yearnings by heavy drug and alcohol use just when she would have given birth had she not miscarried six months earlier. Her loss became real only after she stopped the substance abuse masking her depression. Somatic symptoms simulating pregnancy (for example, vomiting) maintained her denial of the loss.

Unresolved oedipal issues were vividly demonstrated in her ambivalent pursuit of unsuitable men and lack of arousal by her parentally chosen and incestuously tinged husband. It appeared, however, that her difficulty in successfully navigating independence from mother was most critical in preventing her from establishing intimacy with others. Her maternal identity was compromised by her feelings of deprivation by mother and the resulting resentment over giving. Owing to the threat of overwhelming neediness, she was unable to enlist a viable, distinct infantile identification with her unborn child as a part of herself, which could have been mourned. Instead, her child-to-be represented her hated subservience to mother's wishes, which she sought to deny and overthrow and displaced onto the men in her life. Intolerable dependency prevented her from forming an enduring attachment to her husband and developing a positive bond with both her unborn baby and her therapist. In this instance, her guilt over her miscarriage appeared to be based not on the more usual sense of maternal responsibility (that is, omnipotence) in perinatal loss, but on her intense ambivalence toward her mother, experienced as the motive behind this pregnancy. Her guilty reaction to this miscarriage also appeared to be based on her prohibited anger and jealousy over caring for sickly younger siblings, with whom the pregnancy was identified. Once a mother has a child, her subsequent pregnancies, which will produce a sibling, reawaken unconscious memories and conflicts over her own childhood sibling experiences (Abarbanel 1983). Her recent miscarriage seemed to be neither an object nor a narcissistic loss but evoked unresolved separation conflicts with mother associated with her adolescent miscarriage. Once again she defended against another threatening dependency by bolting therapy.

There are many obstacles to resolving a perinatal loss during adolescence. Not only may the pregnancy be a maladaptive attempt to circumvent a more developmentally appropriate process of adolescent separation-individuation, but the additional narcissistic stresses at this time and normal mourning process in intrapsychically detaching from parental objects (Barglow et al. 1973; Kaplan 1986) may make the task of grieving perinatal loss an insurmountable burden. Three of the five cases who left therapy prematurely had suffered a perinatal loss or abortion in late adolescence. The unresolved separation-individuation issues of these women may have been intensified by a partial adolescent fixation resulting from a traumatizing, unresolved perinatal bereavement at this vulnerable time as well as the developmental interference inspired by their subsequent infertility. The fear of once again being overwhelmed by their neediness uncovered in therapy may have precipitated a hasty retreat.

In two cases, quickly ending treatment appeared to be based on the intolerable narcissistic damage ensuing from the loss. Both women presented in a rather brisk, tough manner and had long-standing difficulty accepting their femininity. Perinatal loss (a miscarriage for one and stillbirth for the other) only served to confirm their sense of defectiveness and inferiority. For these women crying was an unacceptable sign of feminine weakness. Rather than grieve and further exacerbate their sense of failure and helplessness as women, they both left treatment precipitously.

The Inability to Grieve: Perinatal Loss and Severe Disturbance

The rigors of resolving perinatal loss may overwhelm the resources of those whose prior emotional impairment is extensive. Because of the dual regressive pull of pregnancy and mourning, the multiple narcissistic assaults of losing one's baby, and the importance of achieving object constancy in order to capably mourn object loss, those with severe personality disorders or psychotic tendencies are unlikely to integrate perinatal loss successfully.

MS. D

Ms. D was a twenty-five-year-old, unmarried, moderately overweight woman who sought help to better understand why she used heroin. Having abstained for about five years, within the past year she had returned to heavy use until the past month, when she began an outpatient methadone program. She presented in a bland and distant manner, although there were moments when her sadness was evident; she was able to accept her therapist's empathic observations. She complained about being shuffled around from one clinic to another to obtain the counseling she was told she needed. Her therapist pointed out her fear that this would happen once again. After wondering if her therapist saw children, she described, with more emotion, her turmoil over her decision six months earlier to have her four-year-old daughter move out to live with the child's father; she was afraid that her increasing anger and impatience would lead her to abuse her daughter physically. She recalled that her own father had often beat her. As the oldest daughter in a sibship of four, she often cared for a baby brother and younger sisters. Although she was unclear exactly why, she had little contact with mother. She began running away and using heroin at thirteen, soon after a grandmother, whom she loved and helped care for, died. She had not gone to the grandmother's funeral, convinced she would be blamed for her death. She could reveal little about her early history except for a half-year commitment to a sanitarium for tuberculars at age six.

She was late for her next session and recognized that she did not want to attend because it was difficult to talk and think about what she had discussed the previous time. She was concerned about how long her insurance would pay for her sessions; the therapist reviewed the possibility of continuing treatment at a reduced fee beyond the ten sessions covered by insurance. She worked part-time for a boyfriend with whom she lived. After her therapist explained that her pattern of running away and heroin abuse seemed designed to avoid depression and related feelings of guilt, she revealed that she had had a stillborn nine months earlier. She had been in an auto accident, reportedly caused by another driver running a stop sign, which led to her water breaking and the baby's death. She felt she could not have any more children—for unspecified reasons. She denied ever feeling blame for the death and could say little more about her loss. She was quite angry and hurt about not being able to pay the sixty dollars necessary to bury her baby, resulting in the child's cremation. Soon after this death she resumed her heroin use and shortly thereafter almost died from a severe bout with influenza.

An open-ended treatment plan was agreed upon to modify her avoidance of mourning major losses, such as the recent stillbirth and her grandmother's death, because of profound guilt and neediness leading to self-destructive behaviors. She was surprised to learn how much her grandmother's death continued to affect her. She arrived at the following session with bandaged arms, describing how she had cut her wrists (although not very seriously) because she felt frustrated about everything bothering her. She had been battling increasingly with her boyfriend, furious that his mother had rejected her. The therapist indicated that she had self-destructively turned the rage and hurt over feeling cast aside by his mother on herself. She recalled several episodes of men hitting her, leading to her becoming violent toward them or herself. Her boyfriend had agreed to pay for the continuation of psychotherapy once her insurance benefits were exhausted.

During the next session, after her therapist announced his vacation plans for the following month, Ms. D became quite angry at her methadone clinic for not giving her much attention. Although she acknowledged not wanting to attend the session that day, she denied any feelings about the upcoming vacation. Her birthday had been the day before, but she would not accept a cake and card from her boyfriend's mother, still feeling rejected by her. Her retaliatory rejection of others and self-denial were discussed. She was late for the following session and claimed not to care about anything, though not appearing overtly depressed. Believing that her boyfriend's mother was pressing him to end the relationship, she decided to leave him. She had returned to using heroin, externalizing blame onto her boyfriend, who she claimed did not care. Her therapist confronted her self-destructive drug abuse and the impossibility of effective psychotherapy unless she abstained.

After missing her next appointment, she returned the following week, explaining that she had forgotten the session because her daughter, who was with her that day, had fallen, splitting her head open. She berated her doctor, boyfriend, and mother for not providing much help. Her heroin abuse increased. The therapist interpreted her repeated pattern of externalizing her guilt by attacking others, noting how bad she must have felt over her daughter's injury. Her self-destructive drug abuse was discussed as a means of expressing her unconscious guilt for events for which she blamed herself, such as this accident, her stillbirth, and her grandmother's death. She was able to associate her increased heroin use with feeling blame for her daughter's injury. Her missed session was understood as both an angry retaliation and avoidance of feelings about the therapist's upcoming vacation, a characteristically masochistic action that prevented her from obtaining the care she craved and needed. The need for inpatient treatment if her drug abuse continued was discussed.

Within a week Ms. D was requesting hospitalization, which was arranged just before her therapist left on vacation.

Ms. D was capable of forming an initial positive attachment to her therapist and of using his empathic communications to begin to deepen her self-awareness. Both of these qualities appeared to make her accessible to psychotherapy despite her addictive history, a poor prognostic indicator for a psychodynamic approach. But it quickly became evident that her massive narcissistic deficits could not be treated successfully in relatively infrequent therapy. Her self-loathing and resulting masochistic behavior would inevitably destroy attempts by others to help her (for example, formulation of a treatment plan followed by a self-destructive suicide gesture) or to acknowledge her importance (rejecting her boyfriend's mother's celebration of her birthday). At the same time, her extremely limited tolerance for feeling disappointed and rejected rendered her unable to mourn. Any significant loss or separation—her grandmother's death, the stillbirth, the transference experience of the therapist's vacation—precipitated rage and neediness; rather than gradually integrating and thereby modulating these feelings by grieving, she resorted to heroin use. This appeared to be a primitive mode of restoring narcissistic equilibrium somatically by withdrawal from the object world experienced as intolerably depriving.

Her profound lack of self-worth prevented her from mourning her stillbirth as a valued part of herself. She was unable to care for his remains, just as she repeatedly became incapable of caring for herself, subjecting her body to self-mutilation, drug abuse, and physical neglect leading to serious illness. Likewise, her maternal identification was dramatically damaged by her stillbirth; she was unable to restore a sense of positive maternity by nurturing her surviving daughter, thus repeating recent and past experiences of being abandoned (for example, by her stillbirth, childhood hospitalization, and early separations from mother) by sending her daughter away. When such major unresolved emotional disturbance and narcissistic deficits are activated by perinatal loss, as with this patient, a short-term, time-limited approach is likely to be ineffective. Unless a longer treatment of sufficient frequency—usually more often than once a week—is planned, the deprivation and rage revived in resolving perinatal loss cannot be constructively contained within the therapy; this usually leads to self-destructive acting-out, which wrecks the treatment.*

Only one other woman in my sample presented with comparably severe emotional disturbance. This extremely depressed thirty-five-year-old woman experienced multiple early separations and repeated sexual abuse as a child and had a long history of uncontrollable extramarital affairs, marijuana abuse, and transient paranoid delusions that others were constantly watching her. Many months into her therapy, it became evident that she had not resolved a miscarriage ten years earlier, because she experienced that loss as punishment for a prior abortion. Guilt over rage at mother enacted in the abortion and profound neediness led to the psychotic delusion during treatment that she was again pregnant, in order to, respectively, undo the earlier loss and care for this imagined girl as she wished to have been loved. Over the course of a year-long weekly psychotherapy, this woman was able to increasingly mourn the losses associated with the miscarriage. Although there was considerable improvement in her functioning and capacity to tolerate depression, frustration, and anger, she left treatment rather abruptly. As I believe is common in more disturbed patients, mourning is often not completed, especially in its most intense form in the here-and-now of the transference in termination.

Although with most patients gains may be enhanced when treatment is conducted soon after the loss, thereby taking

---

*Patients with ongoing substance abuse (such as Ms. D and Mrs. O) who experience perinatal loss present additional technical problems. Although the narcissistic damage resulting from perinatal loss may fuel the addictive pattern, a successful conclusion to mourning is unlikely to occur as long as the alternative of substance abuse is available. The substance abuse will need to be addressed, relinquished, and ultimately mourned before the perinatal loss can be fully resolved (Schafer 1988).

therapeutic advantage of the relative weakening of defenses and heightening of earlier conflicts, with more disturbed patients the exacerbation of their difficulties during pregnancy and its fatal outcome may overwhelm any interpretive attempts to integrate losses during this regressed period. Instead, a supportive psychotherapy that seeks to restore earlier functioning may be the most realistic—and possibly only—treatment then. Perhaps later (as in the second patient briefly discussed) the impact of the earlier perinatal loss can be addressed more extensively as an integral expression of earlier and ongoing disturbance.

Incomplete Grieving: Mixed Results in Psychotherapy

Some patients make significant gains in psychotherapy for perinatal loss, despite unwillingness or inability to finish this work. A major reason for this outcome appears to be the inherent limits in resolving long-term emotional disturbance in short-term psychotherapy, generally the treatment of choice for recent perinatal loss.

MRS. B

Mrs. B* sought help during her fifth month of pregnancy, feeling depressed and fearful of being overwhelmed by the demands of her eighteen-month-old daughter and another child on the way. She was guilty about yelling at her daughter, just as her mother had screamed at her as a child. This twenty-six-year-old woman had been married for eight years to a rather passive but sweet, supportive, nurturing man. During her first appointment with her female therapist she revealed that approximately three years earlier she had suddenly lost a baby, her first pregnancy. Born three months premature, the infant died within two days. No details as to the sex, contact with the child, and fate of the remains were

*The author thanks Carol Barbour, Ph.D., for providing case material on this patient.

given. She did not report much sadness or loss at the time of death.

Mrs. B described an unhappy childhood. Father was alcoholic, unavailable, and irresponsible for much of her childhood. Mother eventually kicked him out of the house when Mrs. B was fifteen; she had not seen him since. Mother was portrayed as cold, unexpressive, and ungiving to the family. She suffered several postpartum depressions. When Mrs. B was seven, mother was hospitalized for depression following the birth of a sibling. Four years later, in her eighth month of another pregnancy, mother attempted suicide but went on to bear her child successfully. Mrs. B recalled feeling depressed with suicidal ideation during her adolescence when the caretaking responsibilities for her younger siblings were placed on her; forced to work to support the family, mother was seldom at home. In her therapy Mrs. B began to understand the feared repetition of this burden with the upcoming birth of her third (but second surviving) child.

Reluctantly, Mrs. B began to explore the extreme guilt she felt over the loss of her first child. She believed she was a bad mother, much too impatient and critical of her toddler. Her therapist pointed out that Mrs. B blamed herself for this death, doubting that she could be a good mother if she had let such a thing happen. Reluctantly, Mrs. B agreed and disclosed a long-standing belief that her adolescent drug use had caused the death of her baby years later. At the session following the emergence of this material, Mrs. B steadfastly maintained that she needed to discontinue her treatment, claiming transportation and babysitting difficulties. The therapist suggested that her fear of being overwhelmed by guilt over her first pregnancy loss was compelling her to leave treatment. She decided to stop but obtained the therapist's reassurance that she could come back should the need arise in the future.

About six months later, Mrs. B returned to this therapist, feeling increasingly depressed and angry at her two-year-old daughter and colicky three-month-old son. Mrs. B refused her therapist's recommendation of intensive psychotherapy, insisting that she could not afford to pay for any treatment once her insurance benefits were exhausted. Instead, a time-limited psychotherapy of fifteen sessions was planned. Mrs. B revealed that she had had a tubal ligation following this delivery, not wanting to suffer through the tremendous fears of losing a baby, as had occurred during her previous pregnancy.

In the early part of her therapy, Mrs. B focused on her guilt over her anger toward her loud, crying son. She was able to meaningfully link her disappointment, frustration, and anger toward this boy with her profound disillusionment about an unavailable father. She guiltily felt she had abandoned her father by not intervening on his behalf when her mother forbade his return. As she gradually separated her unresolved grief over losing father from her feelings about her infant son, her parenting of this child appeared to improve significantly. She began to understand her anger toward her daughter as her own frustrated wish to be mothered, looking to her daughter to take care of her as she wished mother had done. Gains were consolidated as treatment continued, with Mrs. B noting greater patience in caring for her children and increasing happiness in contemplating her recent plans to purchase a house and obtain a part-time job. As termination approached, Mrs. B began to recall the sense of maternal deprivation and neglect she felt as a child. Although the therapist explained that Mrs. B might reexperience these feelings in the upcoming ending of treatment, she could not accept that possibility. She instead emphasized how much therapy had helped her and denied any negative feelings about stopping.

Two sessions before the last one planned, Mrs. B called to cancel an hour before the session, explaining that she had a cold. She assumed that she would not be charged for this session. When it was clarified that she would be billed for this session, as agreed upon in the treatment contract, Mrs. B appeared. For the first time, she was furious at her therapist, convinced that she was being victimized again, as she felt she had been by her parents and others. She claimed that it would have been impossible to pay for the missed appointment because she needed the money for her new house; she felt her therapist was being cruel and unfair. The therapist tried to explain, to no avail, that in approaching the end of treatment she was reexperiencing her rage over feeling deprived, which she had been discussing regarding mother's unavailability and coldness. She was adamant about stopping her therapy that session, impervious to interpretation of her defensive need to leave her therapist before their planned termination.

Mrs. B was unable to modify her identification with a destructive, depriving mother. Witnessing her mother's postpartum depressions—the temporary abandonment of one child owing to psychiatric hospitalization and the threat to an unborn child's life by a suicide attempt near term—intensified the realistic dangers of such a maternal identification for Mrs. B. She abruptly left her first treatment as her increasingly conscious guilt over her view of herself as a dangerous mother began to be explored. She probably feared that her growing awareness of her ambivalence toward her unborn child would destroy him, just as she felt responsible for her first child's death. Her guilt-ridden explanation of adolescent drug use was based on her angry rejection of maternity as a teenager burdened by caring for younger siblings. In this and earlier cases (that is, Mrs. S and Ms. D), angry, sometimes murderous wishes toward younger siblings entrusted to the patient's care during adolescence appeared to be an important obstacle to the resolution of perinatal loss. Ambivalence toward the pregnancy, which represented the hated sibling, can lead to overwhelming unconscious guilt when that unborn child dies. Her fear of potential destructiveness was heightened by the danger that perinatal loss would be repeated cyclically; she fled treatment just at the point in her current pregnancy when the original loss occurred. Her abrupt termination at this time was an attempt not only to save this unborn child from her feared malevolence but to master the earlier, traumatizingly sudden perinatal loss by turning a passive experience into an active undoing. At the same time, her destructive wishes may have been more safely discharged, symbolically, in aborting this first treatment.

Mrs. B's infantile identification as a frightened, needy child whose needs would not be satisfied by a furious, rejecting mother complemented her negative maternal identification. Her intense dependency in approaching termination in her second treatment revived this infantile identification in the transference; the therapist was cast as the dangerous, destructive, and depriving maternal figure from whom she needed to flee. The initially positive maternal identification with her therapist fostered an improvement in her mothering of her two young children. However, this more benign maternal identification could not be consolidated in a short-term treatment for a perinatal loss which exacerbated chronic, unresolved separation-individuation issues with mother. The inaccessibility of a consistently positive maternal identification in the face of her great neediness prevented the completion of mourning her perinatal loss, enacted in the aborted conclusion of her second treatment.

Her more sensitive maternal functioning, enhanced self-esteem, and greater resolution over losing father should not be totally obscured by her inability to resolve more adaptively the separation-individuation issues with mother, involving guilt over rage related to deprivation. The exclusively positive and benign image of her therapist was transformed into that of a malignant persecutor as a result of her wish to violate the payment contract. Her use of splitting, projective identification, and paranoid assaultiveness in her final session demonstrated the activation of borderline dynamics in response to her inability to resolve those earlier issues in brief treatment.

Supportive Psychotherapy for Perinatal Loss

The engine of healing in the psychological treatment of perinatal death is the therapist's empathy with and interpretation of the multifaceted aspects of the bereaved mother's loss. The vehicle of recovery is the fostering and planned dissolution of the therapeutic relationship, simulating the deepening attachment and eventual rupture of the pregnancy bond. Within this framework of psychotherapy, the unresolved psychosexual conflicts, maladaptive identifications, and narcissistic vulnerabilities of childhood that have been intensified during pregnancy may be brought increasingly into the patient's conscious awareness, making possible more flexible, adaptive modes of interpersonal functioning and individual well-being. This kind of psychotherapy is congruent with the nursing model provided by Swanson-Kauffman (1986) in that the therapeutic ingredients of offering insight, empathy, parental nurturance, facilitation of grief, and support of femininity correspond, respectively, to her nursing tasks of knowing, being with, doing for, enabling, and maintaining belief.

In treating perinatal loss, the therapeutic relationship, not the provision of insight, sometimes appears to be the sole beneficial factor. This brand of supportive psychotherapy does not involve a bolstering of defenses and reality-testing in seriously disturbed, usually decompensating individuals. None of the five women in my sample who received supportive psychotherapy appeared to be severely disturbed. Rather, the need for an empathic, nurturant therapist was so critical when they were seeking treatment that the usual psychotherapeutic goal of attaining insight became relatively unimportant. This form of treatment may be the best alternative when the person enters psychotherapy with major stressors after a relatively recent traumatizing perinatal loss (Bourne & Lewis 1984). Many of the women who were successfully treated in supportive psychotherapy were in the midst of a very anxious subsequent pregnancy or had no available supportive figures in their environment, owing to such factors as husband's depression, father's serious illness, and mother's emotional unavailability. Several of these women suffered many recent early-pregnancy losses, making the narcissistic impact devastating. Just as the narcissistically vulnerable victim of any perinatal loss may be unable to accept the additional blow to self-esteem in working on chronic emotional problems in long-term intensive psychotherapy, this subset of narcissistically assaulted women may have found the uncovering of any additional faults too great an insult to bear at that time.

This form of supportive treatment highlights aspects of the therapeutic relationship that occur in more traditional psychotherapy in which the acquisition of insight plays an important role. The woman usually forms an intense, positive transference with her therapist. Her grief and neediness typically elicit a nurturant therapeutic response that bonds them. Despite her profound deprivation and depression, the recently bereaved mother presents herself quite differently from the chronically unhappy and complaining infantile personality or the aloof narcissistic character. The therapist's empathy is usually much more accessible for the bereaved mother than for these more disturbed people. The expression in the relationship of the bereaved mother's infantile identification quite naturally inspires the therapist's active involvement, not unlike the way in which a newborn elicits maternal care. Although some therapists might be moved to offer a concrete expression of their concern, such as a hug, I believe such tokens are more likely to complicate than to improve matters. By communicating an understanding of her grief and a willingness to share it, the therapist satisfies the patient's need to be cared for emotionally (that is, the gratification of oral needs in her infantile identification); this offers a model for maternal identification, regardless of the therapist's gender, which can be increasingly internalized by the patient in healing the damage to her maternal self-esteem.

Certain aspects of this form of supportive psychotherapy for perinatal loss need to be distinguished from more traditional, insight-oriented treatment. Negative transference manifestations are not encouraged and usually not interpreted unless overt. The idealization of the therapist may, on one level, be a resistance to resolving difficulties with maternal ambivalence. Much more important, however, I believe that an idealizing transference is a typical means of restoring the narcissistic equilibrium that has been shattered by the recent perinatal loss. Rather than be interpreted, this idealization must flourish in order to restore the bereaved woman's self-esteem, analogous to the young child's need to idealize his parents in promoting the healthy development of self-worth. In light of the tremendous disappointment after perinatal loss—in the sense of omnipotence invested not only in oneself but in the medical field as well—this idealization of the therapist may be particularly valuable. As a representative of a profession allied with the medical field, the therapist who helps to renew a bereaved woman's self-worth may indirectly revitalize her faith in medical caretakers, an important condition for promoting positive future interactions with medical professionals. Generally, transference manifestations of earlier object relationships are much less noteworthy in these supportive psychotherapies. In fulfilling a narcissistic, developmental role in replenishing self-esteem, the therapist's function as a transference object is much diminished.

The process of termination is typically quite different in these supportive psychotherapies. In a more traditional, interpretive treatment, the termination phase becomes an important recapitulation and additional working through of the original loss. In supportive psychotherapies, however, termination usually seems superfluous. There is an often rapid decathexis of the relationship with the therapist, much like the manner in which the young child gives up the transitional object, without needing to mourn (Winnicott 1953). With the reestablishment of her self-worth on a more secure basis, the bereaved mother has outgrown her need for her therapist. The therapist's function as a temporary, developmentally appropriate self-object has been realized. When final sessions in supportive psychotherapy for perinatal loss are cancelled or termination proceeds with minimal emotional involvement, it should not be assumed that defensive motives against accepting loss and separation are necessarily operating, especially if the treatment appeared to have been successful.

Supportive psychotherapy is specifically warranted when a woman has experienced massive narcissistic assaults and concurrent stressors. Also, a professional may lack the training or technical skill to apply a psychodynamic, interpretive short-term treatment. The value of supportive treatment should not be minimized, even if interpretive psychotherapy is likely to be more advantageous. Many bereaved women are willing to accept such a therapeutic relationship in nonmental health settings (for example, a hospital outreach program) or nontraditional modes (phone counseling), whereas they would be loath to enter psychotherapy in a private practice or outpatient clinic. I suspect that the considerable benefits associated with follow-up contact after perinatal loss are based at least as much on the concern of the caretakers and the kind of relationship established as on the information provided.

MRS. T

Mrs. T* was a slim, attractive, thirty-year-old nurse practitioner. She sought help on the day she broke into tears during an appointment with her obstetrician, who referred her to a private therapist. Her first pregnancy, nine months earlier, was discovered to be ectopic, and her second pregnancy, also ectopic, occurred three months before she sought therapy. She had lost a fallopian tube from the first pregnancy, but her remaining tube was saved from the second. She felt angry after her first tubal pregnancy but increasingly confused and depressed following her second loss.

She was furious at everyone, especially her mother, who always said the "wrong thing." Mrs. T emphasized how "normal" her childhood had been. She had done all the right things—been a cheerleader, gone to college, and gotten married—and did not deserve these losses. It appeared that she was the family caretaker who protected her overly emotional

*The author thanks Judith Adler, A.C.S.W., for providing case material on this patient.

mother. Because of repeated miscarriages, mother had used DES during her pregnancy. The possible jeopardy to Mrs. T's fertility and health caused by this drug, which has been associated with cancer, was never discussed with mother. She felt increasingly jealous of her older sister, who had several children, and had little to say about her younger brothers. She reported feeling more rapport with father than mother.

Mrs. T seemed to take an instant liking to her therapist, whom she felt she could trust, confide in, and identify with. She was increasingly bitter with friends, especially those who were pregnant, over their lack of support and insensitivity. Her weekly sessions seemed to be an opportunity to feel nurtured by her female therapist, who would inquire about her taking care of herself and on occasion compliment her appearance. Mrs. T appreciated this concern about her, which was missing from her current life (and, it appeared, from her preoccupied mother while growing up). Her husband was reportedly supportive, although he seemed to withdraw into his work.

Mrs. T was able to cry over her loss of a much-wanted baby, although her bitterness over the unfairness of her situation seemed paramount. She felt especially distraught over not being "on track"—that is, not having kids like everyone else. She was not accustomed to feeling so different and left out. Although still hoping to bear children, Mrs. T accepted the increasing likelihood that this would not happen. She began attending a support group for infertile couples, although earlier she shunned the idea of being "one of them." As her grief began to subside, Mrs. T was eager to put these feelings behind her. She experienced less turmoil, her diminished sexual life improved, and she became less concerned about what others expected of her. After two months of therapy she began to plan termination. Eventually she cancelled her final sessions, seeming to feel they were unnecessary.

Mrs. T's ectopic pregnancies constituted a major developmental interference, revived unresolved oedipal issues and feelings of deprivation, and dealt a major blow to her self-esteem. However, she was clearly not inclined to work on these issues in the context of her intrapsychic conflicts, emphasizing instead her normalcy (that is, were it not for her current crisis, she insisted, she would not be in psychotherapy). She used the therapeutic relationship as a safe place to begin to grieve her narcissistic losses. This was not accomplished by directly discussing her feelings of being damaged, which no doubt she experienced from the pregnancy losses, multiple surgeries, loss of a fallopian tube, and compromised fertility. Expressing such vulnerability would probably have been too threatening to her self-image of competence and nursing others. Rather, she allowed herself to be consoled and ministered to by another caretaker. This helped to repair not only her sense of being diminished by her perinatal losses but a more chronic deprivation by mother as well, probably intensified by her pregnancies. In this brief, supportive therapy, Mrs. T did not resolve earlier issues exacerbated by her losses or fully grieve the impact of these traumas, which would have required more time. There was sufficient recovery, however, to end treatment. Her abbreviated termination appeared less a defensive avoidance of completing mourning than a symbolic expression of her uncertain pregnancy future. I suspect that she would readily return to this therapist if later difficulties warranted.

CHAPTER 4
PSYCHOTHERAPY FOR PERINATAL SIBLING LOSS

The impact of perinatal loss on the mother is increasingly being studied and understood, but its effects on surviving and subsequent siblings have largely been unexplored. An informal survey of the literature revealed neither systematic research focusing on typical reactions of siblings to perinatal death nor case reports discussing maladaptive responses, except for one adult analysis of a man who had lost a newborn sister at age three (Berman 1978). The best clinical study, published twenty-five years ago, summarizes children's troubled reactions to their mothers' miscarriages (Cain, Erickson, et al. 1964). There are several useful and insightful guides (Hardgrove & Warrick 1974; Moriarty 1978; Weston & Irwin 1963) addressed specifically to parents helping their children cope with perinatal loss rather than to mental health professionals who might treat the survivors of perinatal sibling loss, whether children or adults.

This chapter will examine how perinatal sibling loss may become a destructive, unassimilated childhood stressor, potentially contributing to serious emotional disturbance. Because there are important differences between child and adult survivors of perinatal sibling loss, I shall distinguish between the treatment of these two populations.

Childhood Bereavement

THE CHILD'S CONCEPT OF DEATH

Before a child can mourn, he must acquire a concept of death. A number of empirical quantitative studies indicated that a child's verbal understanding of death became significantly more accurate with cognitive maturation; by age eight to ten, most children were able to describe death as being irreversible (that is, permanent), universal (inevitably occurring to everyone, including oneself), and characterized by nonfunctionality (a total cessation of all bodily functions) (Florian 1985; Hoffman & Strauss 1985; Kane 1979; Koocher 1973; Speece & Brent 1984; Swain 1979; White et al. 1978). Studies differed as to the exact age at which children attained this mature understanding of death and the specific criteria used to define the death concept; however, irreversibility, universality, and nonfunctionality were usually the minimal criteria. Most researchers subscribed to a cognitive-stage paradigm, typically Piagetian, in which the increasingly accurate understanding of death paralleled overall cognitive development, from egocentric, preoperational thinking through concrete operations, and finally to formal reasoning (Florian 1985; Kane 1979; Koocher 1973; Speece & Brent 1984; Sternlicht 1980; White et al. 1978).

It is crucial, however, to distinguish a conscious, verbal conceptualization of death from less conscious and nonverbally mediated understandings. A child may not be able to say what he truly knows and believes. One insightful study (Weininger 1979) demonstrated that a child's doll play portrayed a more accurate understanding of death (for example, its permanence) than his concurrent expressive language indicated. This should not be surprising to either the academic cognitive psychologist or the clinical child psychologist. Piaget (Flavell 1963) often encountered vertical décalage, whereby a child would make a cognitive advance in one mode of expression (for example, the sensorimotor channel) although sometimes require years to attain the same achievement on a higher, more symbolic (for example, verbal) plane. Similarly, play therapy is an effective mode of treatment for children not only because of the child's tendency to concretize fantasies but because of the greater ease with which the child assimilates a therapist's interpretations in play rather than through exclusively verbal explanation. Children with fatal illnesses were significantly more anxious and evidently aware of their terminal condition, according to projective responses on psychological tests, than their chronically but nonfatally ill peers, even when there was no overt discussion of their condition (Spinetta 1974; Spinetta et al. 1973; Waechter 1971).

A child may also disavow, under certain circumstances, what he knows to be true. After having acquired a mature concept of death by late latency, many teenagers regress in their verbal understanding of death (Kane 1979), often denying a total cessation of functioning (McIntire et al. 1972) or irreversibility (Swain 1979). Several studies by Orbach and Glaubman (1978, 1979) suggested that an adolescent's distorted concept of death had less to do with his level of cognitive functioning than with defensive needs; suicidal teens, perhaps needing to deny the permanent implications of their self-destructive intentions, were significantly more likely to have distorted concepts of death than other teens, even though they did not demonstrate cognitive deficits in other areas. Others reported personal bereavement and separation experiences (McIntire et al. 1972; Reilly et al. 1983; Speece & Brent 1984), defensive operations (Orbach et al. 1985), and cultural and religious background (Candy-Gibb et al. 1985) as crucially affecting the formation of the child's death concept independent of cognitive maturation.

The relatively linear acquisition of a verbally mediated *concept* of death paralleling cognitive development must be contrasted, therefore, with a variable, nonlinear *comprehension* of death, which fluctuates on the basis of such factors as the mode in which that understanding is based, personal experiences with death, and defensive needs. In considering a child's capacity to mourn, we are less concerned about the intellectual conceptualization of death as an abstraction than with how that knowledge is transformed into personal conviction or denial in actual encounters with death. In clinical situations, therefore, the research indicating the relative uniformity of the cognitive maturation of the concept of death may be less relevant than individual differences in applying that understanding in reality.

CHILDHOOD MOURNING

The nature and outcomes of childhood mourning continue to be debated. Many psychoanalytic theorists have maintained that children are unable to fully mourn major losses. Nagera (1970) described how the child's proclivity to use denial, inability to tolerate the prolonged painful affects of grieving, greater degree of ambivalence in object relations, and frequently distorted concept of death because of concrete and egocentric thinking all prevent the resolution of mourning childhood losses. Wolfenstein (1966) believed that mourning cannot be concluded until the child's primary tie to parents is itself successfully mourned, during adolescence.

Clearly, certain advances in ego development and object relations must occur before it is possible for a child to mourn. A basic distinction between the object and oneself, an enduring emotional attachment to that person, and a rudimentary understanding of the meaning of death must first be achieved (Furman 1974). In order to mourn a person's death, a child must distinguish that person as a unique individual who is valued in his or her own right (that is, not solely as a source of bodily satisfaction) and must recognize the permanence of the loss. This maturational level is usually achieved by age two to three, by which time the child is increasingly intrapsychically capable of mourning (Bowlby 1980; Furman 1974; Raphael 1983). Each of these investigators and recent clinical studies (Altschul 1988; Muir et al. 1988) emphasized, however, that a child's actual success in mourning is crucially dependent upon environmental guidance and support: he must be provided with accurate information about the death, with direct answers to any questions and clarification of misunderstanding; the family must permit the child to grieve; and the family environment must be secure prior to and after the loss. Although mourning is generally depicted as an *intrapsychic* process, its successful completion in childhood demands a facilitating *interpersonal* context.

Much of a child's unresolved mourning is probably attributable to the failure of his family to assist grieving rather than to an innate inability to mourn. Although parents are able to discuss death with their children in impersonal situations, communication and discussion are dramatically discouraged in a more emotional backdrop (McNeil 1983). A grieving parent will rarely be able to explain the details of a family death accurately to his or her children and to acknowledge (let alone support) their grieving (Becker & Margolin 1967; Bowlby 1980; Raphael 1983). Both survey (Rosen 1985) and interview (Schiff 1977) studies indicate that bereaved parents are usually completely unable to talk about the dead child to the surviving siblings, leaving these children feeling abandoned by unavailable, grieving parents. Perhaps it should not be surprising that children have persistently described death as nonpermanent or represented by a person (Nagy 1948) when their parents have told them that the deceased is now "in heaven with the angels" or to beware of the bogeyman.

This does not mean, of course, that a child's intrapsychic distortions are inconsequential. It is crucial to be sensitive to the child's current developmental level (both psychosexual and cognitive) in anticipating how the child will initially experience and understand a death (Furman 1974). During the second and third years of age, under the influence of both anal-sadistic drives and magical thinking, a child is much more likely to experience a death as resulting directly from his aggressive wishes than would be understood during latency. Adult communication, however, may begin to modify some of these distortions, especially as the child matures and is more receptive to rational explanations. Commonly, parental communication (or lack of it) tends to confirm and exacerbate a child's misunderstandings about death. The scarcity of information available to the child gives freer reign to the child's own cognitive distortions (Nagera 1970). The findings by Bowlby (1980), Furman (1974), and Raphael (1983) that a child as young as two can begin to grasp the essential details of death if provided with concrete but impersonal examples (such as a dead insect or small animal) is based on the sensorimotor acquisition of a death concept before a more symbolic, linguistic understanding is achieved. It is worth speculating and empirically evaluating how much the linguistic distortions about death that are commonly reported by young children may be influenced by verbally mediated and distorted parental communications. Clinicians (Furman 1974, 1976; Salladay & Royal 1981; Schultz 1980; Wessel 1978) and thanatologists (Fulton 1967; Grollman 1967) frequently recommend the bereaved child's attendance at the funeral to make the reality of the loss as concrete as possible, thereby facilitating mourning. Others, however, question this practice (McCown 1984; Schowalter 1976) in light of the common failure of parents to provide the needed support and explanations to their young children during this emotional event.

Psychoanalytic investigators have observed that the death of a parent often became a major developmental interference that prevented both the expectable resolution of childhood conflicts and the availability of needed models for identification at certain critical periods (Furman 1974; Nagera 1970; Pollock 1962). Because most of the literature on childhood mourning involves the death of a parent, it is especially important to distinguish the developmental consequences of losing a parent from mourning that particular loss. Otherwise, much of the enduring negative sequelae of parental death in childhood, which may result from developmental interference, may be erroneously attributed to the child's inability to complete mourning. At the same time, the child's developmental needs to maintain an attachment to the bereaved parent may interfere with the process of decathexis (that is, loosening the libidinal tie to that object-representation), which is a crucial feature of mourning (Furman 1974; Sekaer & Katz 1986). Again, the availability of the other (or substitute) parent may facilitate decathexis without compromising developmental needs for parenting. Recognizing the essential similarity between childhood and adult mourning should not obscure important differences. In addition to children's great reliance on their interpersonal world to provide information, support, and models for grieving, children who mourn look and behave very differently from bereaved adults. The adult mourner's sustained sadness, weeping, and lethargy are strikingly dissimilar from the child's intermittent sadness, much greater denial of the loss (and evident well-being despite it), and tendency to grieve in angry outbursts or expressions of boredom or overactivity.

THE IMPACT OF SIBLING DEATH

The death of a child usually has profound and lasting effects on the surviving and subsequent siblings. In a clinical population, Cain and his colleagues elaborated the intense guilt, death phobias, distorted concepts of death and illness, and sense of being devalued commonly felt by children in the aftermath of a sibling's death (Cain, Fast, et al. 1964). While cognizant of intrapsychic dynamics and conflict (for example, how a child's aggressive and rivalrous wishes toward a sibling who later dies can inspire overwhelming and irrational guilt), they also emphasized the important role of parental mourning and family dynamics. Not only can parental depression resulting from the loss lead to massive emotional deprivation, but the manner in which that death organizes and modifies relationships with their other children (for example, as inferior replacements, blameworthy scapegoats, or endangered survivors) can exert a powerful effect on a child's self-image and character formation. The parent's relationship with surviving children may be so extremely warped as to constitute a developmental interference. The psychological absence of the severely depressed and withdrawn parent dramatically curtails meaningful interaction for long periods of time; the unrelenting vigilance of the overprotective parent deters age-appropriate attempts by a child to become more independent and self-sufficient.

Most studies that examined the impact of a child's death on surviving siblings focused on the resulting symptomatology and psychological disturbance (Binger et al. 1969; Blinder 1972; Cain, Fast, et al. 1964; McCown & Pratt 1985; Pollock 1962; Williams 1981). Anticipatory mourning in preparing for an expected loss may facilitate the resolution of sibling grief (Lascari & Stebbens 1973), just as was found with the parents. However, the evidence is much more sparse with siblings. Although Pollock (1978) described how living in the aftermath of a sibling's death may create "survivor guilt" in a child, inhibiting the prospects of future success, he also has provided vivid examples of how the process of integrating that loss inspired creative works by such writers as James Barrie and Jack Kerouac.

The competitive facet of the sibling relationship has generally been highlighted in focusing on guilt as the most prominent response to a sibling's death. More recently, psychoanalytic investigators have emphasized that siblings relate not only as rivals but as potential playmates, allies, teachers, and friends, fulfilling important object-related roles (as targets of instinctual wishes) and narcissistic needs (in providing empathy and opportunities for idealization) (Colonna & Newman 1983; Provence & Solnit 1983). A sibling rather than a parent may become a primary love-object (Abend 1978), resulting in a major loss upon his or her death. A much younger sibling may be unconsciously experienced as one's oedipally created child, leading to profound grief and guilt if that child dies, owing to both the actual sense of loss and associated conflicts (Ainslie & Solyom 1986). In exploring the impact of sibling death, multiple perspectives must be taken into account—the loving and hating aspects of that bond; the interaction of intrapsychic meanings, parental responses, and family dynamics; and the actual experience of loss against the backdrop of preexisting conflicts.

PERINATAL SIBLING DEATH

Perinatal death is usually an invisible loss for the surviving siblings. Whether the loss occurred because of miscarriage, stillbirth, or neonatal death, the sibling rarely sees the dead baby's body, usually hears very little from the parents about what happened, and is given little opportunity to express his feelings, thoughts, and questions. Nothing is seen, little is heard, and no acknowledgment is given to the child reacting to this powerful family event. Thus, parents' usual neglect in dealing with the effect of perinatal death on their other children parallels the failure of mental health professionals to address this issue in clinical research and practice. Understandably, the child is likely to feel confused, alarmed, and perhaps betrayed over being excluded from this family secret; the child will have to sort out on his own how and why this terrible event occurred. Although perinatal sibling death is often minimized by the family, its impact on surviving children may be enduring, affecting the parent-child relationship, family dynamics, and character formation.

It is not uncommon for a family to cast a shroud of secrecy over family tragedies such as the death (Jensen & Wallace 1967; Krell & Rabkin 1979) or chronic illness (McKeever 1983) of a child. Although open discussion would permit a more adaptive resolution, it would also invite confronting a matrix of painful feelings, including guilt, shame, rage, and sadness. This secrecy is usually heightened with perinatal loss. Not only are the sibling reactions to this event typically denied, but the very reality that the siblings knew of the pregnancy (even if it was openly discussed before the death) is often disputed by parents (Cain, Erickson, et al. 1964; Hardgrove & Warrick 1974). By providing minimal or inaccurate information about the death, parents inadvertently encourage the proliferation of a child's distorted conceptions not only about death but about sexuality as well. Because understanding the facts of perinatal death requires confronting probably two of the greatest taboos within the family—sex and death—it is not surprising that the bereaved child is left to imagine what has occurred. By not acknowledging a child's questions and concerns about this death, a parent denies that child an opportunity to mourn and become reconciled to the loss. Excluding the child from the mourning and understanding of this death may also intensify the child's mistrust of the dissimulating parents and evoke a sense of being unimportant.

Cain and his colleagues reported widely different responses to a mother's miscarriage, from temporary upsets to enduring characterological effects, including a massive inhibition of anger, intense fears of reproduction, and a persistent sense of worthlessness (Cain, Erickson, et al. 1964). In an insightful autobiographical account, Hendrickson (1983) was able to reconstruct the trauma of witnessing mother's stillbirth at age three, an event that was repressed and distorted, leading to his decision to train for the ministry ten years later in order to retreat from overwhelming sexual and death anxieties triggered by mother's pregnancy. This vocational choice solidified sexual inhibitions associated with the earlier perinatal sibling loss. Researchers frequently reported anxiety symptoms (especially death and separation anxieties), anger, depression, and guilt in the immediate aftermath of perinatal sibling death (Cain, Erickson, et al. 1964; Moriarty 1978; Weston & Irwin 1963). A case study (Weiner & Weiner 1984) convincingly demonstrates how, in the context of family secrecy and disharmony, a series of elective abortions could be neurotically misunderstood by the five-year-old sibling as the product of mother's dangerous aggression, thus exacerbating the girl's earlier unresolved conflicts and fears. A parent may facilitate the child's understanding and resolution of perinatal sibling loss by providing accurate information about the death, with a clear-cut explanation that it was not the surviving child's fault; reassuring the child that such a fatality cannot happen to him; including the child in the mourning ceremonies; and sharing parental grief without the expectation that the child should mourn in the same fashion (Hardgrove & Warrick 1974; Moriarty 1978; Panuthos & Romeo 1984; Weston & Irwin 1963).

Perinatal Sibling Loss Treated during Childhood

Nine child and adolescent cases comprise the clinical sample of perinatal sibling loss treated during childhood. Perinatal sibling loss seemed to be a significant factor in the child's or family's disturbance in each of these cases, although none of the parents appeared to recognize this at the outset of the evaluations. In one case, parents sought help during the sibling's infancy; the remaining eight cases were equally divided between latency-age children and adolescents presenting for treatment. Most of the siblings were born relatively soon after or before the deaths: four children were conceived within nine months after the perinatal deaths, and another child was born six years after the loss; two children were less than two years old when the deaths occurred, and the remaining two were over the age of three when their siblings died. Most of the deaths involved full-term losses (three stillbirths, four neonatal deaths, and two miscarriages). All of these children belonged to intact families and had full biological sibship with the deceased. Two-thirds of the sample was middle class and the remaining third was lower class. All but one of the children were boys. Eight of the families were white and one was black. Almost 80 percent of the cases were seen in a private or hospital-based outpatient clinic; one child was treated in private practice, and another was admitted to an inpatient child psychiatric hospital. Eight of these cases continued psychotherapy for at least several months; one adolescent chose not to continue beyond the evaluation sessions. I treated five of these cases; the remaining four were seen by two social workers and two psychiatric residents.

My intrapsychic orientation to interventions has limited these treatments in all but one instance to individual psychotherapy (and parent guidance) in the child sample. In light of the common tendency of families to enforce a "conspiracy of silence" over the circumstances and aftermath of a child's death, it can be especially valuable and effective to use family therapy in some instances. The reader is referred to a growing literature describing the way in which family intervention may challenge family dynamics that maintain unresolved grief (Evans 1976; Jensen & Wallace 1967; Krell & Rabkin 1979), enable the isolated bereaved member to reenter the family system (Rosen 1988), and be integrated with psychoanalytic theory and technique in facilitating mourning (Muir et al. 1988).

As with the maternal bereavement cases, a common protocol was used to collect historical and treatment details as well as to organize clinical hypotheses. The relatively small sample size and the unsuitability of inferential statistical analysis for these data make my conclusions in this area tentative and subject to further investigation.

CONCEPTUALIZING CHILDHOOD PERINATAL
SIBLING LOSS

The child's responses to perinatal sibling loss and its ongoing effects on his development are based on the intrapsychic meanings of this death for the child, the intrapsychic and interpersonal parental reactions to both the deceased and the surviving children, and the consensually shared attributions regarding this death and its aftermath by the entire family.

An intrapsychic model emphasizes how the child constructs personalized meanings about a sibling's death in the context of ongoing developmental trends and conflicts. The four psychoanalytic models used to understand maternal bereavement may be applied in exploring the sibling's responses. Becoming a sibling is generally not understood as a new developmental phase, as is attaining parenthood. Nonetheless, the important roles siblings can play in promoting one another's socialization, in offering avenues to express and master many impulses (including competition, envy, jealousy, aggression, and dependency), and in serving as models for identification and idealization (Colonna & Newman 1983; Provence & Solnit 1983) suggest that siblings typically serve vital developmental purposes that, in their absence, may lead to social-emotional deprivation. A perinatal loss may therefore become a developmental interference for a sibling, though it is usually not in itself as powerful a hindrance to developmental progression as that death is to the parent.

As with the mother, though for very different reasons, perinatal death generally occurs in a regressed state of heightened vulnerability for the sibling. Most children (especially if young) experience the approaching birth of a sibling as a major stressor, intensifying concerns about the availability of maternal supplies, fueling competition and rivalry, and challenging self-esteem in the face of a new object of parental love. It is not uncommon for children to retreat regressively during mother's pregnancy, relinquishing recently attained milestones (achievement of bladder control, mastery of separation anxiety, and so on) both as a response to this additional stress and as an identification with the baby-to-be. This regressive process may not only compromise the child's ability to resolve the additional burden of integrating the sibling's death but cause that death to be experienced in a cognitively more primitive and instinctually more charged intrapsychic atmosphere. The developmental level (both psychosexual and cognitive) to which the sibling has regressed when the death occurs will be a crucial determinant of the intrapsychic meanings and impact of this event. For example, a two or three-year-old child struggling with rage and deprivation over maternal withdrawal during pregnancy may direct intense murderous wishes toward the unborn sibling; owing to cognitive regression to magical thinking, the child is likely to believe that those destructive fantasies killed the sibling. Earlier and harsher superego strictures may inspire severe guilt, less amenable to forgiveness than later forms of conscience would allow.

A somewhat older child may experience the death quite differently. A poignant account of a five-year-old girl mourning the neonatal death of her severely damaged sister described this youngster's intense desire to see her sister—to touch her and admire her soft skin and hair, while tearfully telling her how much she was loved, would be missed, but never forgotten (Scrimshaw & March 1984). This girl's intense grief (and furious envy of other pregnant women) suggested her strong identification as the bereaved mother of her sister/daughter in the oedipal period. The instinctual psychoanalytic model is quite helpful in conceptualizing the intrapsychic response to perinatal sibling loss, although the object and narcissistic perspectives seem less applicable here. Sadness and disappointment can certainly attend perinatal sibling loss, with diminished self-esteem through the child's identification with his deceased sibling. However, this death usually does not constitute in itself as powerful an object loss or blow to self-worth for the sibling as it does for the grieving parent.

The impact of perinatal sibling loss may be felt indirectly, but no less powerfully, through the parental, especially maternal, reactions to the death. As already discussed, childhood mourning crucially depends on parental facilitation in providing information, a secure environment, and permission to mourn. Any grief a child may feel over a perinatal sibling death is likely to go unexpressed and unresolved because of the usual parental tendency to deny surviving children's reactions or to be too overwhelmed by their own feelings to attend to their children. In addition, the shrapnel of parental grief—rage, guilt, anxiety, and depression—may barrage a child's home environment for a prolonged time. This second factor does not include parents' direct responses to surviving children but concerns the effect of their mourning on the overall quality of their parenting. The emotional absence and depletion of a grieving parent can constitute a developmental interference for the surviving children, especially if the death occurs during important developmental phases of the children that require parental participation for adaptive resolution.

The child's experience of both object loss and narcissistic damage is often mediated by the parental reaction to the death. The child's image of the deceased sibling and especially the intensity of the loss may be greatly colored by the degree of parental attachment to and capacity to mourn the

unborn child. The narcissistic wound inflicted during pregnancy by the mother's investment in another child may become a scar when the surviving child witnesses profound
maternal grief.

Finally, perinatal sibling death may affect how a parent
regards and interacts with surviving children. Not uncom-
monly, a surviving child will become intertwined with parental intrapsychic dynamics designed to manage the loss.
An unconsciously guilt-ridden mother may scapegoat a child
with whom she identifies, thereby freeing herself from conscious, overwhelming self-blame; a narcissistically devastated
mother may require perfection in another (replacement) child
in order to replenish her own self-esteem. Perinatal sibling
death may exert lasting influences on surviving children,
therefore, through the capacity of parents to assist their children in resolving the loss, parental reactions to the loss itself,
and changes in parental relationships.

In addition to the children's and parents' intrapsychic responses to the perinatal loss, commonly shared understandings about the death may be constructed by the family as a
unit. The "family myth" is a useful theory to describe certain
consensually attributed beliefs and roles that may unconsciously motivate family members' attitudes and interpersonal relationships in order to preserve equilibrium within
the family (Ferreira 1963; Glick & Kessler 1980). Although
family therapy as an intervention was used in only one of
my clinical sample cases, defining the underlying family
myth may help explain the organization of family interactions
around the meanings of and proposed resolutions for the
death.

The most complete understanding of the impact of perinatal sibling death on the developing child can be achieved
by integrating these three perspectives as conceptually distinct but mutually interacting factors. A child's response to
perinatal sibling death is rooted in his intrapsychic interpretation of the event, determined by the instinctual, defensive,
and cognitive functions operating at the developmental level
of regression. This intrapsychic understanding is not a static

entity constructed independent of parental reactions and family-wide role and belief systems; parental and family pressures may correct distorted intrapsychic understandings or, alternatively, undo potentially adaptive intrapsychic resolutions. *A child's erroneous interpretation of the event may be as much a product of accurately understanding and literally believing parental misrepresentations and unconscious family myths as of the child's own intrapsychic cognitive distortions.* The family myth may become a potent organizer of adult depressive and psychotic anniversary reactions to childhood bereavement through the transmission of distorted memories and covert expectations for the child (Hilgard 1969). Conversely, family myths may be predicated on the defensive, intrapsychic needs of the family members.

When evaluating perinatal sibling loss, therefore, it is important to take into account the child's intrapsychic structure in the context of parental intrapsychic and interpersonal responses. The way in which the death is embedded in the general family mythology and the particular attributions regarding the death must also be considered. A child's guilty feelings of having caused the death may be the result not only of equating jealous, aggressive wishes with murder, owing to the egocentrism and magical thinking of childhood, but also of parental scapegoating based on intrapsychic, defensive operations to reduce guilt or family myths requiring a blameworthy culprit for any and all misfortunes. A child's fear of dying in the aftermath of perinatal sibling death may be rooted in earlier separation fears and infantile dependency. This fear may be powerfully compounded by the absence of parental communication about the causes of perinatal death, intense parental anxiety about the safety of surviving children, and family myths impugning the age-appropriate acquisition of increased separation and self-sufficiency by children as a divisive and destructive attack upon family cohesion. A child may act as a replacement for a deceased sibling in an attempt to secure parental love. This may also be encouraged by parental idealization of the deceased, parental inability to relinquish that attachment, and family myths discouraging mourning as placing stresses on members labeled vulnerable. Blaming parents for a perinatal death may be anchored in the child's view of parental omnipotence and the projection of hostility toward the deceased baby onto the parents. It may also result when the child takes quite literally the guilt and sense of responsibility that bereaved parents may unconsciously feel. The associated family myth may be the unspeakable and unknowable secret belief that the deceased child was the victim of parental infanticide.

Sibling responses to perinatal death will be discussed using four child cases, each of which highlights a distinct constellation with particular intrapsychic, parental, family, affective, and symptomatic expressions. These four modes of experiencing and reacting to perinatal loss are not necessarily mutually exclusive and do not exhaust the range of potential reactions. Rather, they are intended to illustrate how the child's intrapsychic structure, parental dynamics and behavior, and family mythology may organize a mutually reinforcing system of unconscious conflicts, interpersonal interactions, and consensually shared beliefs among family members. There can be a wide range of disturbances within each constellation, from a relatively mild misunderstanding that may be modified by empathic parental communication to a major pathogenic issue around which future character development, child-parent interaction, and family dynamics revolve.

The Scapegoated Child

Major unresolved difficulties in the ownership and expression of guilt and rage by the child, parents, and family as a unit typically underlie the constellation of a scapegoated child. The younger the child, the more his understanding of reality will be distorted by egocentrism and magical thinking, a confusion between thought and action. The world is construed in relation to oneself; one's wishes and powerful feelings are equated with actions and real events; cause and consequence may be turned on their heads. Thus, even when a perinatal death is totally beyond the control of a sibling, it can be experienced as the direct result of his anger over a forthcoming rival for parental love and attention. The child's feelings of anger and deprivation during the pregnancy, resulting in powerful death wishes directed toward the unborn child, may produce profound guilt in the event of perinatal death. Such a misunderstanding can be corrected (or indirectly confirmed) by parental willingness to provide accurate information about the death.

Parents will often scapegoat a child who comes to represent the hated aspects of themselves that, defensively, need to be disavowed (Tooley 1975). The intolerable maternal guilt and rage engendered by perinatal death may catalyze this process. In these cases the mother usually experiences no conscious guilt over the death (an atypical reaction to perinatal loss in general), which becomes externalized in blistering animosity toward the surviving child (with whom she identifies). Scapegoating not only may serve this intrapsychic defensive purpose of guarding against the eruption of intolerable parental guilt but also may displace serious marital tensions (Vogel & Bell 1967) and ensure the continued functioning of the family unit (Bermann 1973). In some families, the predominant response to loss and mode of handling guilt is rage and scapegoating others (Bowlby 1980; Raphael 1983). When a child's own distorted sense of culpability is confirmed and buttressed by parental blame, the child's conviction of his guilt can become quite resistant to change. A self-perpetuating intrapsychic and interpersonal cycle is established in which the child's misbehavior (in part provoked by parental expectations) elicits punishment satisfying his conscience and sense of badness; this further reinforces the parental sense of legitimacy in attributing blame. The low self-esteem and compromised functioning of the child within and outside the family confirms a profound sense of parental worthlessness. While the overt symptomatology and presenting problems in this constellation are usually defined in oppositional, provocative behavior, considerable depression and low self-esteem are ultimately more significant. The parents view the child as "bad" and warranting punishment. This encourages the child to comply by displaying few direct manifestations of guilt (at first), which might elicit parental empathy.

BOBBY

There was pervasive disappointment and fury as the parents of eight-year-old Bobby described their frustration with their oppositional son. He was disobedient at home, quarrelsome, and refused to do household chores. He lied and was mistrustful. The parents complained that he was self-centered and demanding, "only interested in himself and nobody else." An escalating cycle of misbehavior and punishment had occurred at home, leading to frequent spankings and restrictions. His parents often felt that Bobby did not want to be a part of the family and, in their hurt and frustration, increasingly excluded him from family activities and threatened to send him away. School reports portrayed him as inattentive and withdrawn, a sad, "passive thing." Although he was bright, he did poorly in school and frequently daydreamed. Weekly individual psychotherapy and parent guidance were planned.

Bobby was the firstborn; his birth had been preceded by a miscarriage two years earlier, after which the mother had difficulty conceiving. Bobby's birth was unremarkable, but mother was very disappointed when she had to discontinue nursing after one month because of mastitis. She complained that Bobby was uncuddly as an infant, that he did not want to be held. His oppositionality intensified after she gave birth to a stillborn girl, Amy, when Bobby was eighteen months old. Mother never saw her daughter. She remembered this as a difficult time but felt she could not wallow in self-pity and returned to work in several days. She derided bereaved mothers who "fell apart" after a perinatal loss as self-indulgent. Both parents felt Bobby was too young to understand or be affected by the death of his sister. They hardly ever talked to him about it. Not long after the death of her daughter, mother consulted a psychological center about Bobby's oppositionality. When she was told that her son was normal and her recent loss a source of stress, she angrily decided not to return, feeling that she was being blamed for Bobby's difficulties. She soon attempted another pregnancy, which resulted in another miscarriage, followed, several years later, by the birth of a baby girl. Despite feeling very burdened with her son, she still wished to have another daughter.

Mother was unable to mourn and resolve her daughter's death. When she was encouraged to talk about that loss, she quickly changed the subject, feeling it was "over and done," with nothing more to say about it. Although mother's self-doubts as a parent predated the stillbirth, that death appeared to powerfully reinforce her unconscious sense of failure. Her feeling of being rejected by her son and her rage at him served to bolster her view of herself as an unloving mother. Her guilt over her sense of inadequacy as a mother was intolerable; she indirectly expressed this guilt in the form of feeling attacked by others and angrily attacking her child with whom she identified. Much like her son, she saw herself as stubborn and willful; she vaguely recalled similar battles with her mother as a child.

During much of his individual psychotherapy, Bobby needed to exert almost complete control over the interaction. He would enact episodes of the television show "Knight Rider," in which his car, with ever-increasing magical powers, would invariably triumph over the therapist's weaker vehicle. In competitive games, he would often change the rules just in time to ensure his victory. The therapist increasingly felt bullied, controlled, and pushed around, an indication of how Bobby often felt he was treated by his punitive and controlling parents. The omnipotence Bobby sought to evoke in sessions masked the helplessness and multiple fears he had outside the sessions.

Paramount among his fears was the danger of dying, expressed as separation anxiety. At bedtime, he was often quite frightened and insecure, sometimes waking up with nightmares of being killed. He was terrified that his bed sheets would cover his head and resorted to a ritualistic manner of tucking himself in to ensure safety. He still relied on an old blanket to comfort himself in times of stress, much like a younger child with a transitional object. He strenuously tried to protect himself from experiencing any separation anxiety between sessions. It was imperative that one session begin right where the last one ended. Sessions before and after interruptions in treatment were marked by intense anxiety and indirect expressions of anger at the therapist. With the fear of separation was the danger of abandonment. At the beginning of each session a battle typically ensued between him and his mother. He demanded that she keep his jacket while he was with the therapist, a symbolic way of staying with mother as well as a practical means of ensuring that she would not leave him.

Bobby's separation fears occurred in the context of parents who powerfully rejected their child. His fears of dying coincided with parental fears that he would one day die by accident. Father believed that owing to sickness and accidents only 50 percent of children survived to the age of ten. Similarly, Bobby's association of death wishes with murder closely corresponded to his parents' beliefs. Both parents became visibly upset when Bobby's hostile feelings were discussed. Although their son had no significant problems in impulse control, they were concerned that his verbalizing anger would be more likely to lead to the expression than to the mastery of aggression.

Bobby's internal sense of badness was reinforced by being the family scapegoat. His parents appeared unconsciously to blame him for other family misfortunes in addition to the death of his sister. After father returned home from an emergency appendectomy, Bobby's behavior became increasingly intolerable, leading to several spankings. Having been told little of his father's medical condition, Bobby's misbehavior seemed to express both his anxiety and guilt. He was berated for adding to his father's stress and warned to watch what he ate lest he become similarly ill. Again, the distorted view of his culpability was evoked with the talion threat of his having the same fate. Bobby's devaluation by his parents was particularly highlighted by their joyful appreciation of their adorable two-year-old daughter.

When the therapist broached the subject of his sister's death, Bobby had many unanswered questions that he was reluctant to ask. How had she died? When was she named? Where was she now? Not having had clear explanations, he had formulated some of his own. Perhaps she had been stabbed by a knife or strangled. The jealousy over a competitor for parental attention fueled his anger about his sister's impending birth. Through the distorting lens of magical thinking, he viewed her death as caused by his hating, murderous feelings. His guilty conscience demanded punishment in kind. In a particularly frightening dream, his mother was trying to stab him with a knife. His sense of guilt was enormous: he said he felt the devil was in him. His feeling of being devalued in comparison to his idealized deceased sister was quite acute, evidenced by his verselike chant during this time, "First is worst and second is president."

When Bobby was able to talk to his mother about his sister's death—to ask questions and receive clear answers—there was improved communication and understanding between them. His mother began to understand his mistrust of her. Perhaps, she reasoned, when she had told him she would bring home a new baby brother or sister and then did not, he felt she had lied. It was clear that this loss—how it happened and what it meant to him and his parents—was still on his mind six years after the event. Most nights he checked his two-year-old sister to make sure she was all right.

Bobby's separation difficulties closely paralleled those of his parents. Parental frustration and anger with the therapist mounted as his three-week vacation approached. Although the parents earlier had reported a better understanding of and closer relationship with their son, they now began to believe nothing had changed. When the therapist wondered if they might not be feeling angry and hurt by his impending vacation, they claimed it would be a relief not to attend sessions for a while. Upon the therapist's return, they continued to disclaim any feelings about not having met during the past month. As that session was to end, they abruptly announced their decision to stop treatment, after about one year. They felt hopeless that their son would ever change and refused to discuss the decision further.

Many of Bobby's difficulties could be understood in the intrapsychic terms of a child who felt like a murderer and provoked parental punishment as confirmation of his sense of badness and worthlessness. The unfortunate occurrence of his sister's death when Bobby was struggling developmentally with intense ambivalence during rapprochement (Mahler et al. 1975) would have made a successful integration of this death very difficult then. At the same time, it seems doubtful that the conviction underlying these beliefs would have been so intense were it not for its continuous reinforcement by parental attitudes and behaviors. Bobby's massive guilt and pervasive sense of worthlessness seemed to both provoke and be reinforced by parental scapegoating.

Bobby's separation fears, magical thinking in equating angry feelings with destructive actions, and tendency to split his object world into consummately good or evil figures mirrored identical parental proclivities with which he may have identified. Parental idealization of his live and dead sisters, contrasted with their devaluation of Bobby, demonstrated their defensive use of splitting within the family. Splitting interfered with their mourning of their dead daughter and forming a positive attachment to their live son. Mother's first pregnancy loss by miscarriage, followed by infertility for more than a year before Bobby was conceived, may have established an early foundation of maternal inadequacy, intensified by the disappointments in nursing and melding with Bobby in the postpartum period. Against this backdrop of experienced maternal failure, it is readily understandable that a subsequent stillbirth would present an intolerable burden of guilt. This perinatal death—a fresh narcissistic assault—may have consolidated earlier tendencies to scapegoat Bobby as a means of defending against her unconscious guilt and sense of inadequacy. Mother's inability to tolerate her guilt and her tendency toward externalization appeared in her feeling blamed by a therapist soon after the stillbirth. Bobby had always been seen as a demanding, ungiving child, a view that only hardened after the stillbirth.

Although it did not appear that scapegoating Bobby deflected marital tensions, clearly all family members subscribed to Bobby's incorrigible, innate badness as a family myth that organized parental alliance against him and favoritism toward their daughter. Though not a passive figure at home or in treatment, father clearly followed his wife's lead. It also seemed that the second child was unconsciously designed to compensate for disappointment with Bobby. Perhaps the underlying family myth was that it should have been Bobby who died and not Amy; this would have provided additional fuel for his being scapegoated and ambivalent concern about his safety.

The earlier traumatizing abandonment the parents felt by their daughter's death was reevoked by the therapist's vacation. They defended against this by bolting treatment—their attempt to turn "passive into active" through a projective identification in which they sought to unconsciously provoke in their therapist their masked hurt, anger, loss, and confusion by their sudden departure.

A Child's Fantasy of Infanticide

A sibling who feels guilty about murderous wishes toward the unborn child may project that blame onto the parents. This defense, combined with the young child's tendency to view the parents as omnipotent, can reinforce the child's suspicion that the parents, especially the mother, caused the death of the unborn child. Such a cognitive distortion may be indirectly confirmed by the usual parental guilt after perinatal loss. A depressed parent's withdrawal from the surviving children may reinforce the children's feelings of deprivation and anger. The common parental denial of the death may suggest to the confused child that the parents are trying to mask their terrible deed. Families that prohibit mourning may externalize their grief and guilt in paranoid defenses of feeling blamed and accused by others. This constellation may be more common among younger children, for whom the sense of parental omnipotence holds greater sway. Angry outbursts at parents (which may at times be displaced onto others) and fear of parents or parental substitutes are common symptoms. There may be intense anxiety over body damage; children may feel that their own safety is in jeopardy if they believe the parents killed a sibling.

STEVE

Steve was ten years old when he returned to psychotherapy because of persistent behavior problems in school. His grades were declining, and he was increasingly fighting with peers. He had been in psychotherapy with another therapist for six months the previous year with the same presenting problems. His parents abruptly decided to discontinue treatment when his school problems were alleviated and a change in insurance coverage would not pay for further sessions.

At first both parents blamed others for their child's difficulties, maintaining that there were no problems at home. Father was convinced it was Steve's teachers' fault that they were unable to control and discipline him. Although they felt their son's functioning had improved during earlier treatment, the parents criticized his first therapist because they were told nothing of their son's problems. Mother said she felt Steve was too demanding and always wanted attention. She roundly criticized her husband for spending little time with the family and being too preoccupied with his home project of building an airplane. Mother believed that father's shame and anxiety over having a younger brother who was homosexual accounted for his distancing himself from his sons. She felt that he feared a similar outcome if he was more affectionate to them. Mother came across as bitter, hostile, and hurt; father sought to keep a safe distance from his disparaging wife.

Steve's developmental history was unremarkable, except for surgery at age three to correct an undescended testicle, which was still much higher than the other. The parents denied that Steve had much reaction to the surgery or to the appearance of his genitals. However, this period had been stressful for the entire family because for ten months father was away during the week owing to a job transfer before the family relocated to join him. In father's absence, Steve often cried for him.

In his first therapy session, Steve began talking about a stillborn brother who had died six years prior to his own birth. He had no idea how his brother had died but wished he were alive, believing that he would be an ally against his twelve-year-old brother, Jim, who continuously teased him. Both death and birth preoccupied him during his sessions. Steve began to worry more about his parents dying. His father, a security guard, might be killed in a shoot-out, he fantasized, or his mother, a bank teller, might be shot in a robbery. Although Steve had sustained several injuries in minor accidents, he denied any anxiety about his own safety. He felt he had to show others (especially father, it seemed) how tough he was, lest he be viewed as a "wimp." Steve complained that others "picked" on him. He wanted to have a baby sibling and anticipated with pleasure the Cabbage Patch doll he was about to receive.

His identification with his dead brother became increasingly clear. Several years earlier he had used the brother's name on school papers. He believed he resembled a snapshot of him that his parents carefully preserved. In his attempts to understand his brother's death, he was struggling unconsciously with the possibility that his mother had murdered this child. In one session he told the therapist that a mother bird will kill her chick if the nest is handled by humans. In another session he talked at length about a science fiction movie in which an alien, disguised as a human, gave birth to twins, a lizardlike creature that died (having been poisoned) and a human who survived. The lizardlike creature reminded him of the picture he had seen of his dead brother.

He anxiously wanted his therapist to ask his mother about his dead brother. He thought about this brother daily and said, "He is in my heart."

In a parent guidance session, mother had difficulty saying much about the stillbirth, and father dismissed its significance. When the therapist met with mother alone, she angrily attacked her husband's family, who had never acknowledged or discussed the death with her. She became angry about discussing it with the therapist, convinced that he would not understand. Reluctantly, she said that she had been toxemic and that her physician had told her the stillbirth was caused by the placenta separating owing to her frequent sneezing brought on by hay fever. The therapist questioned this dubious explanation and wondered aloud if she might erroneously hold herself responsible for the death. She denied ever feeling any guilt but soon became anxious and then angrily stormed out of the session a few minutes before it was to end. The next day she discontinued treatment, less than two months after beginning, steadfastly convinced that the therapist was blaming her for the death of her son.

Mother protected herself against the tremendous guilt she unconsciously felt over her son's death by externalizing the source of the blame from her conscience to her therapist. Paranoia may defend against depression (Zigler & Glick 1988), which, in this instance, appeared to be her intolerable conviction that she had killed her son. The unconscious self-blame for her stillbirth probably reinforced or inspired Steve's unconscious suspicions that his mother was a murderer. This paranoid distortion may have been a family myth maintained by all family members.

This case provides striking evidence of how much perinatal sibling loss can be mediated by parental, especially maternal, unresolved grief. Steve's powerful sense of having lost a real-life brother, an object loss, was based not on any fantasies and disappointment prior to the loss (which occurred years before his own birth) but on mother's incomplete mourning for her stillborn. It was unclear whether the family exerted pressure on Steve to serve as a replacement child to temper mother's grief or whether his identification with his dead brother was internally motivated to win approval from a depressed mother.

Steve was clearly struggling with other neurotic difficulties, especially feminine identifications, which his aggressive tendencies sought to disavow. These negative oedipal conflicts were probably exacerbated by his genital surgery, intensifying castration anxiety, as well as by longings for father fueled by paternal absence at age three and by father's distancing himself from his son because of his own homosexual anxieties. Although pregnancy fantasies embodied in Steve's interest in dolls are an expectable feature of negative oedipal dynamics (that is, in wishes to be impregnated by father), it is possible that such feminine identifications were intensified by mother's perinatal loss. Steve's pregnancy wishes may have been an attempt to undo maternal object loss by producing a replacement baby or to reduce parental narcissistic damage by successfully delivering a child.

Paranoid elements were evident within the family system, Steve, and mother. Parental externalization of rage took the form of blaming outsiders for Steve's problems and then feeling attacked by them. Steve similarly externalized his anger by unconsciously believing that his mother was responsible for his brother's death and viewing himself as the victim of others' provocation. The degree of hostility among family members was limited and family cohesion heightened by locating belligerent agents and causes of family problems outside the family, against whom the family needed to unite.

Perceived Vulnerability

The shock of unexpected perinatal death can powerfully evince the fragility of life. The child may wonder, "If this can happen to a baby, why not me?" In its earliest manifestation in the first year, separation anxiety represents the child's sense of helplessness and dread without the comforting and protective presence of parents. A child's dependency on parents, enduring to some degree throughout youth, provides the psychological foundation upon which fears of dying can be built. The child's fears about his own well-being may be compounded considerably by overprotective parents. Instead of receiving parental reassurance of physical safety, the child confronts parental anxiety and, perhaps, compulsive rituals to guarantee the child's security. The terrible burden of responsibility that parents often suffer after perinatal death may shake their sense of adequacy in caring for their remaining children. The parents' underlying anxiety over their child's vulnerability and doubts about their own caretaking ability may be covertly communicated to the child, confirming the legitimacy of his insecurities. Anxiety will typically be a major symptomatic expression, whether in phobic responses or in a resurgence of separation anxiety. Fears of illness or dying may be somatically manifested, although outside the child's conscious awareness of the underlying causes. The psychosomatic abdominal pain of a six-year-old, for example, was discovered to be closely related to the mother's anxiety over an earlier, unmourned stillbirth that this sibling did not know about (Jolly 1976).

TERRY

A seventeen-year-old boy, Terry, began psychotherapy with a vague malaise and many worries about his future. He was graduating from high school and preparing to go to an excellent university. But instead of expressing exuberance, pride, and optimism about his future, he was depressed about leaving high school. He viewed going to college as the first in a series of steps in growing up, each bringing him closer to death. In the second session, he casually mentioned that when he was a year old, a three-day-old brother had died of congenital heart defects. His father had visited his brother's grave every other month for many years as Terry was growing up, but his anxious mother was too upset to accompany her husband. Mother had become increasingly overprotective as the time for Terry to leave for college approached. She constantly demanded to know where he was going and worried about something happening to him.

In a separate meeting with the parents, it became clear that the perinatal death remained a very powerful and unresolved loss for mother—an event too painful to discuss. She recalled that her own mother's death the year after the loss of her son made that period particularly difficult. She became pregnant again within six months of the perinatal loss and proceeded to have two additional successful pregnancies less than six months after each birth. Mother continued to struggle with transient anxiety attacks, occurring usually on vacation, which she managed with tranquilizers. She resisted the recommendation of her son's therapist that she enter individual psychotherapy to resolve her difficulties with loss and separation. Both parents were apprehensive about Terry's leaving home for college because they felt he was too young and immature. They complained that he was irresponsible and "let things slide," but it became evident that they gave him little opportunity to face the consequences of his actions (or inactions), readily "bailing him out" of his mishaps. The family secret of which all the children were supposedly unaware was that Terry was conceived out of wedlock, an upsetting circumstance for his practicing Catholic parents-to-be, who quickly married. Owing to the centrality of Terry's unresolved separation-individuation issues, meetings with his parents were discontinued after several evaluation sessions. As one of the many signs of marital tension, mother criticized her husband's strictness with the children and lack of warmth toward her.

Terry missed or cancelled several of his first appointments until the therapist made it clear that he would be charged for cancelling without twenty-four-hour notice. Subsequently he missed only one session, for which he paid. An important focus of Terry's short-term therapy was his anxiety about wanting to end his relationship with his high school girlfriend. He was frightened by her dependency on him, afraid that she would not be able to cope without him and might even attempt to harm herself. Bitterly, he wondered if he would have to remain tied to her out of a sense of responsibility and guilt. Although Terry's concerns about his girlfriend had a basis in reality—she had a history of instability—it soon became clear that they represented his fears for his mother. He felt guilty about mother's insomnia and troubled by her encouragement for him to live at home when attending college. Although he recognized his mother's need for help, Terry was ambivalent about her entering psychotherapy, fantasizing that the therapist might recommend his not leaving home for his mother's sake.

During his final sessions, Terry reported much less anxiety about going to college, leaving home, and ending the relationship with his girlfriend. He was able to distinguish some of his own anxieties and worries from his mother's fears. Several months after Terry had left for college, his mother decided to enter psychotherapy to resolve her difficulties about loss and separation.

Both the intrapsychic and the family sources of the separation-individuation issues were examined in therapy. The therapist explored Terry's *own* anxieties about dependency and being on his own, which he had projected onto his mother and girlfriend. At the same time, the external pressures on Terry not to leave home, stemming from maternal anxiety and vulnerability, also needed to be recognized. In the family mythology, separation seemed to be equated with death and had to be avoided at all costs. Now that her oldest son was leaving home, mother was reexperiencing her fears and feelings about her earlier loss. As he entered a new developmental phase of separation in becoming an adult, the original separation in the birth and death of her second child was being repeated for her. Mother's overprotection, rooted in the perceived vulnerability of her son, appeared to be a projection of her own feared neediness revived by the neonatal death, which was significantly associated with her mother's death.

Terry's imminent departure for college may have also been experienced as a threat to marital stability, because they decided to wed as a result of his conception. Perhaps his leaving evoked the fear that their rationale for marrying would be gone. Although not documented within the treatment, one might expect that the subsequent neonatal death would have been experienced by these practicing Catholics as a punishment for their sexual transgression of conceiving out of wedlock, impeding the resolution of this loss.

Replacement Dynamics

When parents have another baby to replace a child who has died, there is an unwillingness to accept and mourn that loss. Although the dynamics of the replacement child have usually been elaborated for the death of older children (Cain & Cain 1964; Legg & Sherick 1976; Poznanski 1972), it is applicable as well to the unresolved mourning of perinatal death (Lewis & Page 1978). In both instances, an overprotective, anxious attitude often dominates parental interactions with the replacement child, because of a feared repetition of the death as well as underlying disappointment and anger that this child cannot undo the original loss. The common pattern of idealizing the dead child (Cain & Cain 1964; Poznanski 1972) testifies to the profound narcissistic injury and attempted restitution resulting from the death of one's child. Legg and Sherick (1976) have observed that the psychological insertion of the dead child's identity into early interactions with the replacement child often resulted in a major developmental interference with the usual acquisition of such important narcissistic functions as positive bodily cathexis, establishment of a self-soothing capacity, and the early formation of identity.

Seeking to replace a perinatal loss through a subsequent pregnancy may be fueled by factors unique to this loss. Having minimal or no interaction with the deceased may increase the tendency for parents to displace feelings from the dead child onto the next infant, because concrete characteristics and memories that could distinguish the two are not available. Positive fantasies about the unborn child during pregnancy may cause idealization after death to be even more pronounced and difficult to relinquish than with later loss, for there is no realistic image that could modulate the idealization.

As an aftermath to perinatal death, the replacement child syndrome can be dissected into several distinct patterns. The object hunger caused by the loss of a real, unborn, or newly born baby may ignite a powerful wish for a replacement child. However, this motive of denying the object loss by replacing it is more commonly encountered after the death of an older child, in which the depth of the loss is generally more profound than in perinatal death. When replacing object loss is the primary motive in a subsequent pregnancy, it is likely that an earlier object loss, especially the death of a parent, has become associated with the perinatal death.

Repairing narcissistic injuries is a more typical aim in replacement dynamics after perinatal death. A replacement pregnancy, or series of pregnancies in quick succession, may be designed to restore the mother's view of her femininity, damaged through her failure to produce a healthy baby. Because a successful delivery, as opposed to mothering a child, may be her principal unconscious goal, such a woman may be quite unprepared, at least initially, to care for the child who results. The usual narcissistic function that one's children serve—that of replenishing self-esteem as an auxiliary ego ideal—helps explain the piercing deflation of self-worth commonly experienced after perinatal death. A replacement child may be sought primarily as a narcissistic reparation for mother with her great, usually unrealistic expectations of the child, based on her need to undo the earlier narcissistic wound and restore her self-esteem. Replacement dynamics designed to recover an object loss or restore narcissistic equilibrium, disturbed by assaults on either her femininity or her ego ideal, suggest that mourning the original object or narcissistic loss is incomplete and that the subsequent child cannot be loved in his own right.

The likelihood of replacement dynamics infiltrating a subsequent pregnancy increases when there is little delay (less than one year) in attempting pregnancy again. Even if the next pregnancy is not unconsciously intended to circumvent mourning, the possible incompatibility of grieving and forming an attachment simultaneously may impede both the resolution of mourning and the process of bonding during pregnancy if insufficient time has elapsed between the two events. At the same time, guidelines must be flexible to accommodate individual differences. Mourning does not follow an unvarying schedule. Some mothers for whom perinatal loss (especially early miscarriage) was not devastating may experience a subsequent pregnancy within six months as part of the healing process through the formation of a new attachment. Yet other mothers who conceive many years after an unresolved perinatal loss may still inflict replacement dynamics on that pregnancy.

The clinical literature (Cain & Cain 1964; Legg & Sherick 1976; Poznanski 1972) has tended to focus on the severe disturbances resulting from being a replacement child, but a recent study (Johnson 1984) suggests the conscious wish for a replacement child may be growth-promoting when experienced as a reaffirmation of life. In light of the hasty decision to produce a replacement child in this sample (that is, within a year of the death), without evidence of the profound grief typically accompanying the death of a child, and the absence of follow-up data on these children, this conclusion does not appear convincing. Producing a replacement child again appears to be a maneuver designed to inhibit mourning rather than the inferred adaptive outcome of bereavement. Although replacement dynamics have been typically related to unresolved parental grief, the child's active participation in becoming a replacement must not be overlooked. As a reparative wish to relieve parental grief or as an attempt to secure parental love by modeling oneself after the idealized image of the deceased child, the subsequent sibling may eagerly adopt this replacement status. Replacement dynamics may readily become organized into the family mythology of unspoken beliefs that inform a child's identity within the family; for example, a replacement child may be viewed as a sorry substitute for the earlier loss who cannot be, but must be, replaced.

One's sense of individuality and self-esteem can be shattered by feeling that one must be someone else in order to be appreciated and loved. Because the replacement child is inevitably a poor second compared to the predecessor, he may disengage from life pursuits because of the futility of competing with an idealized figure. Finally, profound guilt may haunt the replacement child for having survived the deceased sibling (Legg & Sherick 1976). In a very real sense, the replacement child conceived soon after a perinatal loss owes his very existence to that death.

JOSEPH

Parents sought help with their two-year-old son, Joseph,* who for the past year had been regressing (ceasing to talk) and displaying autistic symptoms including social withdrawal from the parents, head banging, hitting, and staring into space. Other than his having to remain in the hospital for two weeks following his birth because of hypoglycemia and a mild infection, no early developmental problems were reported. Mother felt disappointed that her diabetes made her unable to nurse Joseph. Only two months after his birth, mother again became pregnant; she uneventfully delivered an adorable girl before Joseph's first birthday. This exuberant daughter was the delight of both parents.

Joseph was born less than one year after the death of his brother James. The doctors had congratulated the parents on the birth of a "beautiful, healthy," son, but within a day James died of a serious infection associated with mother's gestational diabetes. Both parents felt shocked and furious at the doctors who were unable to save their child.

The family was of lower-middle-class status. Although mother had a college degree in early childhood education and

*The author thanks Jean Twomey, A.C.S.W., for providing case material on this patient.

had worked in a nursery school for several years, she became disillusioned with her job and left it to work in a laundry, during which time she met her husband. They had married four years earlier, when she was thirty. Father was a custodian during the day and attended night classes to earn his college degree. Frequently absent from home, he was passive in relating to his wife, who was six years his senior. Eight years earlier, at the age of twenty, he had been devastated by the sudden death of his eighteen-year-old sister (and only sibling) in an auto accident.

Father's mother had been the source of considerable marital tension because of her overinvolvement with his family, especially Joseph. She visited daily, devoting herself to and infantilizing her grandson, who stayed with her several days a week. Grandmother reportedly rocked Joseph, bottlefed him in a high chair, and slept in the same bed, just as she had done with her son until he was five. Grandfather was an aloof, often absent figure in the household. Grandmother had never recovered from the death of her daughter, whose bedroom she had converted into a shrine. Idealized after her death, this daughter had frequently been criticized by her mother when she was alive, much as grandmother currently berated her daughter-in-law.

Assessed in a hospital-based early intervention program, Joseph was diagnosed as having a mild seizure disorder, although nonspecific, diffuse EEG abnormalities at age two could not definitely confirm seizure activity. A serious disruption in the maternal-child relationship, leading to dramatic regression and social withdrawal, was also noted. Psychiatric recommendations included prescribing medication for the probable seizures, reducing contacts with grandmother, and beginning parent guidance with a social worker in order to improve the mother-child relationship. Joseph began to attend an early remedial program to compensate for language deficits.

In conjoint parent guidance, mother and father were unable to share their grief over James's death. Although saddened and disappointed by the loss of his son, father felt guilty because he was much more affected by his sister's death. Mother blamed herself for James's death; because she had carried the child, she reasoned that she must have done something to make him die, despite her doctors' reassurances that she had done nothing wrong. She felt profoundly inadequate as a mother, and her sense of failure and shame was magnified by Joseph's difficulties. She recalled her anxiety at his birth, fearing that he too would quickly die of infection, repeating the trauma of death in the family.

The weekly parent guidance helped to enhance the mother's self-esteem by exposing her irrational feelings of guilt and shame. Initially mother was guarded, revealing little, until it emerged that she saw herself as being singled out to meet with a social worker because of her incompetency. This feeling was exacerbated by the fact that she had been trained in early childhood education. She was quite relieved to learn that all parents whose children had difficulties received parent guidance. By developing her interactive skills in engaging an avoidant and insecurely attached child, mother was able to experience herself as a more effective parent who could enjoy relating to her son. After four months of meetings, mother felt considerable progress had been made and was ready to end parent guidance, having stated that "we're getting there."

Mother's pregnancy with Joseph was shrouded by the profound narcissistic blow to her maternal self-worth that she had recently suffered from the death of James, her firstborn. There were, consequently, multiple interferences to her establishing a solid, positive attachment to Joseph. Maladaptive anticipatory grief, the expectation that this son would die too, and the early separation caused by his two-week hospitalization prevented the usual deepening of the bond with her neonate. Her inability to nurse this child, perhaps a desperately needed experience for this mother because of her attenuated symbiosis during pregnancy, compounded her sense of failure and emotional distance from her son. Having an atypical child became an additional narcissistic burden and precipitant of grief in her longing for a normal son; her maternal capacity was further taxed by the demands of interacting with such a child. Finally, grandmother intrusively usurped the maternal role while inappropriately interacting with Joseph in a manner inviting his further regression.

As a replacement for James, Joseph embodied the sense of maternal worthlessness evoked by the death of her firstborn. By rushing into another pregnancy and giving birth to a daughter before Joseph was one, she unconsciously abandoned her devalued son, both repeating and reversing the sense of loss experienced when her first son left her by dying. By splitting off her degraded sense of maternity and deflecting it to her relationship with Joseph, she was able to restore her maternal self-worth in a more satisfying relationship with her daughter (although distorted, it would seem, by idealization). Maintaining no relationship with a detached and emotionally absent son may have become a substitute for an inevitably frozen and incomplete mourning; by the replacement of the deceased James with the psychologically deadened Joseph, the dead child was never relinquished whereas the live child was never truly allowed to exist. Although the completion of grieving for James and the acquisition of insight into replacement dynamics were not achieved in treatment, the amelioration of mother's narcissistic injury by an empathic therapeutic relationship and increased skills in interacting with her child enabled her to better relate to her son as a distinct person providing pleasure instead of narcissistic mortification.

Replacement dynamics reverberated across three generations in this family. Grandmother was unable to resolve her daughter's death because of her unbearable ambivalence and resulting guilt, defensively managed by splitting: although Joseph was idealized by grandmother, his mother became the target of grandmother's attacks, much as grandmother's daughter had been before her death. Devalued by his mother and idealized by his grandmother, Joseph became a replacement child for two generations of mothers maladaptively managing their children's deaths. Child loss evoked profound narcissistic damage for both mothers. Joseph's mother experienced diminished self-worth in the psychological abandonment of her son, which compromised his functioning, thereby confirming her sense of maternal incompetence; grandmother projectively defended against feelings of maternal inadequacy by harshly condemning her daughter-in-law's mothering. In this family mythology, men assumed figurehead status as passive, detached figures who were idealized for narcissistic purposes.

Women typically attempt a replacement pregnancy within months of the perinatal loss; frequently that birth is quickly followed by one or more additional pregnancies. This rapid succession of pregnancies often represents desperate maneuvers to undo the narcissistic wound through restitution, exemplifying the aim of mastering a trauma in the repetition compulsion (Freud 1920). This pattern may also indicate the special meanings of the replacement child. The parents' non-relationship with the replacement child as a substitution for mourning may enable them to form warmer attachments to subsequent children. In fact, in many of these cases the replacement child appeared to be considerably more disturbed than subsequent offspring. This pattern may also be the mother's unconscious wish to abandon the replacement child as she herself felt deserted by the perinatal death.

The mother's narcissistic injury may be handled by splitting, by means of which feelings of worthlessness are defended against by being deflected onto a devalued child, who, in another realm, may be idealized to restore maternal self-esteem. In the case of a severely depressed replacement child who needed to be hospitalized, the mother magnified her son's disturbance, believing that he was schizophrenic, while maintaining her unrealistically high expectations for his academic achievement.

Psychotherapy for Adult Survivors of Perinatal Sibling Loss

This clinical sample is composed of eleven adults—eight women and three men—whose perinatal sibling loss during childhood appeared to be a significant factor in their emotional problems. Eight of these people sought psychotherapy between their mid-twenties and mid-thirties; one eighteen-year-old sought help as did two individuals of about forty. All of their mothers suffered multiple (in nearly 75 percent of the group) and/or late-term losses; for most of this population, therefore, perinatal losses became a recurrent feature of their development. In four cases the siblings died before the patients were born; three experienced perinatal sibling deaths between the ages of one and four; and another three experienced losses both before and after their own births. All of these patients were white, about equally divided between middle and lower classes. Six were married when they sought help, three were divorced, and the remaining two were single. Eight entered therapy in outpatient clinics, and the remaining three were seen in private practice. All of the patients were seen by clinical psychologists, seven by myself. As with the other samples, a protocol was used to organize historical information, treatment details, and clinical hypotheses. Again, the unsuitability of inferential statistical analysis for these data makes my conclusions tentative and subject to further research.

In their initial presentation none of these patients showed any awareness of the important role childhood perinatal sibling losses played in their emotional problems. There was a common disbelief that such an event (or series of losses) could have had much impact on them. They could provide only scant details regarding medical information on what had occurred, parental responses to the deaths, and how the event might have affected parental interaction with them. It was not atypical for patients to first reveal these losses, quite matter-of-factly, many months into their treatment. The use of repression helps explain the absence of memories and feelings about these disturbing events and their symbolic expression in dreams and symptoms. Repression is significantly reinforced by the virtually universal tendency of these patients' parents to regard (or more accurately disregard) these losses with dread, anxiety, guilt, and anger. These patients' withholding of information, minimization of impact, and lack of knowledge about these losses are the logical outcomes of family secrecy and suppression surrounding these deaths. They needed to talk to surviving parents decades after these losses occurred in order to learn the most basic details. A striking difference between child and adult survivors of perinatal sibling loss is that while the child often readily acknowledged the death, sometimes with much feeling, viewing the loss as the death of a brother or sister, the adult acted as if it never occurred (that is, as if no one had died). The perinatal sibling loss becomes truly invisible, unintegrated, and unresolved for the adult survivor.

No family history is complete unless one has carefully inquired about perinatal losses. Large gaps in sibling births (during which time such losses may have occurred) or a quick succession of births (often immediately after an unresolved loss) should alert the clinician to explore the possibility of perinatal deaths. The convincing proclivity of patients to minimize the importance of these deaths may deter the clinician from appreciating their actual effects. This may account for, at least in part, why this has been overlooked as a major potential trauma in the mental health literature. In fact, in reviewing Arlow's (1972) paper on "The Only Child," it is possible to argue that many of the dynamics he associated with sibling absence may be based on unresolved perinatal sibling loss. Three of the four cases Arlow presented involved perinatal or later sibling loss. Many of the issues Arlow's patients demonstrated, including "survivor guilt," hypochondriacal and psychosomatic complaints, and narcissistic vulnerability, are commonly encountered in patients who were not only children but experienced unresolved perinatal sibling loss in childhood. Arlow described the virtually universal fantasy among only children of having orally devoured in utero the imagined sibling competitor, with intense guilt and fears of retribution. Perhaps this fantasy is predicated on the actual loss of the unborn sibling during or immediately following pregnancy, seemingly providing greater confirmation of the child's magical thinking, confusing his mur-

derous wishes with the unborn sibling's death. The prominence of the sibling's cannibalistic wishes may be fueled by
the usual unavailability of the depressed, withdrawn, bereaved mother, frustrating the child's oral needs. It is crucial,
I believe, to consider the genesis of these fantasies and dynamics in the familial context of parental grief and resulting
deprivation.

Because so much of the impact of perinatal loss is mediated
by parental responses and family myth disavowing this invisible loss, it may often be impossible to directly link the
intrapsychic repercussions to the death itself. Overt discussion of these deaths and their connection with later disturbance may occur rarely, if at all, even in extended intensive
psychotherapy. However, the therapist's understanding of
the emotional aftermath of perinatal bereavement for the
mother and entire family and its effect on the patient's development (especially in the areas of guilt, stability of self-
esteem, and expression of anger) may be a vital aid in empathizing with a patient's conflicts and anguish. In fact, those
patients for whom perinatal sibling loss has been a significant
factor in their disturbance present some strikingly similar intrapsychic features and difficulties.

In all but one or two of these cases, oedipal conflicts
seemed to play a secondary role to earlier difficulties with
aggression and guilt. In psychoanalytic, instinctual terms, it
appeared that the regression from oedipal issues to the anal-
fixation point was caused less by heterosexual conflicts than
by the difficulty of modulating sadistic impulses and toler-
ating overwhelming guilt. The object relationships of most of
these patients, both within and outside treatment, were negotiated in the sado-masochistic currency of inflicting suffering on themselves or others. Many of these patients struggled
with profound, often unconscious guilt, propelling them toward self-destructive actions to satisfy their need to be punished. This caused some to destroy their therapies through
negative therapeutic reactions that precluded happier ad-
justments. (See Berman's [1978] case report for an excellent,
richly detailed illustration of these dynamics.) Almost half of

my sample ended treatment prematurely, typically after gaining some symptomatic relief but before a more lasting resolution of their difficulties could be achieved. This frequent intrapsychic pattern can be best appreciated in the context of the guilt-inducing circumstances in which they often grew up (that of parental scapegoating and the survivor dynamics of being a replacement child), combined with the absence of parental support and information that could have facilitated their understanding of these deaths in a more realistic, less egocentric, less self-blaming manner.

All of these patients experienced significant narcissistic problems, ranging from narrowly circumscribed areas of low self-esteem to pervasive difficulty maintaining self-worth which led to poor impulse control, addictive behavior, and an exploitation of others to satisfy narcissistic needs. Profound guilt and narcissistic problems often united in the consolidation of depressive and masochistic character formation. Although replacement dynamics may be most closely associated with these problems, even those children who escaped being born under that shadow were often parented by depleted, depressed, angry individuals who viewed their offspring as frustrating burdens and were unable to give them the nurturance these parents themselves craved. The emerging picture of their parenting often appeared wildly inconsistent, ranging from cruel, critical, and at times abusive assaults to overprotective indulgence. Such parenting would interfere with the establishment of both a secure sense of positive self-esteem and adequate impulse control capable of coping with narcissistic frustration and disappointment.

Finally, a majority of these patients displayed major psychosomatic ailments, including gynecologic symptoms, headaches, and, especially, obesity (with the associated medical hazards, such as heart disease and diabetes). For these patients, a contributing influence to the development of psychosomatic disease may be the original association of all perinatal loss with bodily dysfunction. Psychosomatic illness may become a means of expressing both narcissistic deficits and self-punitive tendencies as one's body is slowly destroyed by flagrant neglect and self-destructive abuse (for example, overeating and smoking). Many dynamics may be involved in the development of obesity in these patients, most of whom were not overweight as children. Obesity may become an attempted identification with the pregnant mother as a means of undoing the loss or recovering infantile closeness with and dependency on mother.

The Internalization of Scapegoating and Replacement Dynamics

Although scapegoating and mobilizing replacement dynamics were viewed as distinct family constellations in responding to perinatal sibling loss during childhood, these patterns may coexist and become mutually reinforcing. Disappointment in the replacement child who is not able to compensate for the recent loss may become the psychological rationale for scapegoating this child, as well as the usual dynamic of externalizing parental guilt. The loss associated with the perinatal death is displaced onto the narcissistic hurt of having a disappointing replacement child, which then substitutes for mourning.

MRS. M

Mrs. M* entered psychotherapy in her mid-thirties, with the same therapist who was completing a two-year treatment of her seven-year-old daughter. Mrs. M suffered from longstanding characterological problems, especially masochism. Although she had an IQ of over 150 and a college education, she had held only low-paying jobs requiring little education. Her husband, legally blind since childhood, was both bitter and angry. In addition to her job working ten hours a day as a proofreader, she had all the household responsibilities because of her husband's handicap. Her only pleasure in life

*The author thanks William Schafer, Ph.D., for providing case material on this patient.

was her severe exercise regimen, particularly her training in karate, in which she held a black belt. She struggled against multiple fears (for example, of rape, burglary, and driving), which threatened to restrict her life even further.

Mrs. M was the oldest surviving child of six. The year prior to her birth, a three-day-old baby boy had died. Shortly thereafter mother conceived again. She could recall little information or discussion about her brother's death. Throughout her childhood, Mrs. M remembered being physically assaulted by mother without warning or reason. Her arms became black and blue trying to ward off mother's blows. While mother heaped verbal abuse on her other children as well, they were not physically abused. As a child and later as an adult, Mrs. M was subjected to mother's unending complaints that she could never do anything right and was not making mother's life better. Father was a meek, aloof university professor whom mother dominated.

Mrs. M's first child, Donald, died of Sudden Infant Death Syndrome at eight months. Both parents experienced him as a terrible, unsatisfying burden while he lived. Father had a vasectomy when Donald was three months old to ensure no further children. Neither parent mentioned or mourned Donald for some time after his death. Not long after her son's death, Mrs. M again conceived through artificial insemination. Although she had desperately wanted another child after her son's death, father still opposed having any more children. The circumstances of this child's conception were a closely guarded family secret that only the parents and therapist knew.

When this child, Susan, was five years old, she entered psychotherapy because of her anxious and provocative behavior. Her parents were concerned about Susan's physical and mental development and were convinced that she would be emotionally damaged. Mother's lack of any physical contact with her daughter appeared to be a protective defense against maternal rage. Susan courted the therapist's rejection and anger by constant badgering. She felt herself to be a worthless, bad, empty nothing compared to the ideal person represented by her dead brother Donald. She thought he had died because God wanted Donald close to Him. Her idealization of Donald was reportedly based not on any overt parental idealization of their son but simply on his treasured place on the mantel in a baby photograph.

Only after one year of individual therapy (already over eight years after her son's death) could Mrs. M begin to share her feelings of depression and fear over Donald's death. Afraid to look at the autopsy report, she finally asked her therapist to read it to her. Mourning her son's death became an important part of her treatment. By confronting her aggression more directly, she was able to stop karate, resulting in her becoming more overtly depressed for a time. As Mrs. M neared the end of her therapy, she was less masochistic and more able to enjoy a better job and a new house.

Perhaps the most remarkable aspect of this case was the bequeathal of the dynamics of perinatal loss to the following generation. Susan's profound narcissistic insult mirrored Mrs. M's intense devaluation and scapegoating by her own mother as an inadequate replacement child for a perinatal loss. Mrs. M's unresolved grief over her son's death and her indirect infliction of those narcissistic wounds on Susan seemed to repeat unconsciously her own mother's failure to mourn a neonatal loss. The enormous maternal rejection Mrs. M experienced as a child dramatically impaired her ability to give to her daughter emotionally. The mother who is left bereft by perinatal loss fosters deprivation in her other children, who in turn pass it on to the next generation. Mrs. M's own rage appeared to be based on an identification with her furious mother as well as on a response to mother's denigration of her. The consolidation of her masochistic dynamics seemed rooted in both the internalization of her relationship with her critical, abusing mother and her inwardly directed rage. Her devotion to karate appeared to be an attempt to at once express, control, and protect against her fury. The circumstances of Susan's birth and the secrecy in which it was shrouded appeared to mirror closely Mrs. M's own birth as a replacement child for a "ghost" whose effects were potently felt, but who was never openly discussed.

In another case, a strikingly attractive thirty-year-old woman had been the self-professed black sheep of her family. Her birth was immediately preceded by four late-term pregnancy losses (who were all male) in as many years and followed by the birth of a sister before she herself was one year old. Exhibiting obvious phallic identification, she aggressively functioned as an industrial plant manager in a male-dominated field. This phallic behavior and a lifelong wish (and sometimes deception) to be several years older than she actually was seemed to be motivated by her replacement dynamics of seeking to become the deceased male children who preceded her. Actively scapegoated by a masochistic mother who was brutalized by her alcoholic father, this patient strenuously defended against her masochistic identification, both as mother and in her relationship with mother, by sadistically entering and discarding extramarital affairs, which boosted her flagging self-esteem.

Magical Thinking and the Conviction of Guilt

Among another group of patients, profound and usually unconscious guilt did not appear to be rooted in either replacement dynamics or scapegoating. Rather, these patients unconsciously felt that they had murdered their siblings. This belief seemed to be due not to the family's attribution of blame but to the prominence of magical thinking in their unconscious conceptualization of the perinatal death. Not surprisingly, many of them experienced multiple perinatal sibling losses, typically at a young age, when confusion between thought and action, cause and consequence, is cognitively normal.

MS. J

Ms. J* entered psychotherapy when she was thirty, three years after her divorce. Initially she claimed to "not know

*The author thanks Martha Diamond, Ph.D., for providing case material on this patient.

why I am here," having been referred by her nine-year-old son's therapist just after the child began therapy for behavior problems at school. She presented pervasive, characterological isolation of affect and inhibition of pleasure, and described long-standing physical complaints including chest and pelvic pains, often without organic cause.

Her mother had suffered multiple pregnancy losses when she was growing up, although Ms. J could recall little about why and when most of them occurred. Mother reportedly had had thirteen miscarriages in addition to the neonatal death of a baby boy because of congenital defects when Ms. J was eight. Her three surviving siblings were two sisters nine years older and four years younger and a brother ten years younger. Four years before Ms. J's birth, a month-old sister had died in an accident. The family rarely mentioned these deaths. During her seven years of intensive psychotherapy, Ms. J also rarely discussed these deaths.

She portrayed mother as controlling, infantile, and effusive. Ms. J had always had difficulty standing up to mother, feeling she would have to capitulate to her demands or face being criticized as an unloving, terrible daughter. Mother was frequently bedridden for numerous physical ailments during Ms. J's childhood years; many of the household responsibilities fell on the children. Father was a traveling salesman who was seldom at home. Her parents divorced when she was seventeen. Lately, mother's health had been poor; she was diabetic and seventy pounds overweight.

As a child, Ms. J had frequent nosebleeds and was enuretic until the age of eight. During her teenage years, she was unable to separate from her mother to go to a friend's house overnight, too afraid of something terrible happening to either of them.

Her massive inhibition of anger had been a central issue in her treatment. Rather than directly express anger toward her therapist, Ms. J would frequently miss appointments. This appeared to be less a passive-aggressive mode of expression than a wish to protect her therapist from her angry feelings, which she felt would be destructive. Although her ego functions were intact, magical thinking prevailed in this area.

In her sixth year of treatment, her rage over separation and abandonment became evident. Not long before her therapist's month-long vacation, she was able to recall a traumatic separation when she was thirteen to twenty months old. Following father's involvement in a serious car accident out-of-town, Ms. J was sent to another state to stay with an aunt while mother left to care for father. She tearfully recalled wanting to stomp her feet in protest. She became terrified of her anger, which felt like a volcano about to explode. Soon after working on this difficult material about loss, she was finally able to quit smoking after many unsuccessful attempts to stop.

Ms. J had two sons but wished to have a baby girl. She felt her older sister, Cathy, who died before she was born, was special. She thought that having a baby girl would make her feel special. She admired her female therapist, whom she experienced as her idealized dead sister.

Only as termination approached did the importance of her brother's death at age eight become clearer. In the second year of therapy during her therapist's vacation, Ms. J had an abortion. She had not wanted to give up the excellent position she had recently obtained working with high-risk infants in a hospital emergency unit in order to have another child. Her guilt was enormous; she felt like a murderer. During her last month of treatment, she described her thoughts of wanting to name her aborted child (if a boy) after her dead brother. Her difficulty in remarrying after a long-standing relationship with a man and anxiety over hostility toward men appeared related to her view of herself as a murderer and castrater of males.

Sometime before her abortion, she reported dreaming of fourteen faceless heads, tiny hands, and many body parts. She thought of her mother's thirteen miscarriages, associating the tiny hands with fetuses and linking the dismembered body parts with Nazi torture and the Holocaust. She wondered if she felt responsible for her mother's miscarriages.

For many years Ms. J pursued a specialty in pediatric nursing, which kept her in contact with dangerously ill babies. Instead of remembering a childhood traumatized by multiple perinatal losses, her choice of profession in a high-risk pediatric hospital required her to repeat those childhood experiences on a daily basis in an attempt to repair and undo the harm she believed her anger had inflicted in causing the perinatal deaths of so many siblings. Her professional preoccupation with death can be contrasted with her personal detachment from it. She disclaimed having any feelings upon learning that her younger sister had uterine cancer. Over the course of therapy, Ms. J decided to leave the medical field for an unrelated line of work.

Growing up with multiple perinatal sibling deaths contributed to Ms. J's major conflicts with anger. Those losses increased mother's unavailability and rejection of her, thereby fueling her rage. At the same time the expression of that rage became dangerous owing to her repeated exposure to death, leading to the misconception that her anger was a deadly force, capable of destroying others as she felt it had killed her siblings. When magical thinking was "confirmed" by reality and not corrected by more accurate explanations her parents failed to provide, it became more difficult to relinquish. It is not surprising that by growing up in an environment marked by mother's bloody miscarriages, her own perceived bodily vulnerability became translated into psychosomatic symptomatology and preoccupation. Her metaphorical description of herself as a volcano about to explode appeared to capture both the perceived dangerousness of a destructive, violent womb and the way in which that rage can be turned upon oneself in the form of self-destructive smoking.

Another patient who suffered the neonatal sibling deaths of two sisters when she was two and three years old presented remarkably similar dynamics. This woman persistently used reaction-formation to guard against her anger; she was terrified of having any hostile thoughts for fear of their coming true, needing to immediately suppress fantasies of others dying. In a particularly upsetting dream, she had forgotten to rescue her two daughters from a building doomed to collapse—apparently a symbolic expression of her repressed guilt and resulting punishment for the deaths of her two sisters who were rarely discussed in her therapy. A teenage pregnancy (and subsequent relinquishment in adoption) as well as a later, planned high-risk pregnancy against medical advice (because of high blood pressure) appeared to be attempts to undo the sibling deaths she unconsciously felt she had caused. At the same time, these pregnancies exacted talion punishment in losing her child to adoption in the first instance and endangering her life in the second. Death anxiety was manifested in her claustrophobic avoidance of enclosed places, suggesting her identification with the imperiled unborn child in utero; she probably feared retaliation based on her unconscious guilt over believing she had murdered her sisters.

In these cases, there is profound unconscious guilt based on the conviction, through the distorting lens of magical thinking, that one has murdered one's sibling(s). Any aggressive expression is often harshly suppressed and, through reaction-formation, disavowed, while self-punishment is exacted by negative therapeutic reactions (Berman 1978), psychosomatic symptoms, or self-destructive actions endangering one's own life or threatening the loss of loved ones.

The Dangers of Overprotective Indulgence

Some patients who suffered perinatal sibling death in childhood sought psychotherapy as adults for rather severe depression that appeared to be based much less on unconscious guilt over aggression than on intense neediness and frustrated demands for nurturance. Displaying, in instinctual terms, a profound oral fixation, they presented themselves in an infantile manner, desperately unable to grow up and become self-sufficient, despite sometimes considerable intellectual abilities. Green and Solnit (1964) have observed that parental exaggeration of a child's vulnerability because of serious illness or, sometimes, perinatal losses may result in overpermissive parenting. The regressive effects of indul-

gence may be an important factor in shaping character. Many
of these patients demonstrated impaired ego functions (especially in the development of impulse control and frustration and affect tolerance) as well as superego deficits (commonly ending treatment and leaving outstanding bills unpaid).
In some instances, this overprotection may represent the unconscious maternal wish to keep her child perpetually as an
infant, thereby undoing the previous death as a form of replacement dynamics.

MR. R

This obese thirty-nine-year-old man plaintively sought help
for depression, reportedly feeling anxious and helpless and
suffering uncontrollable crying spells for the past two months.
There was no clear precipitant or evident anniversary reaction. He described outbursts of temper, furious over having
to wait for a stockboy on the job and a waiter at a restaurant.
His self-destructive behavior jeopardized his health; he was
careless about his diet and medications for his diabetes, and
he had recently resumed smoking. He reported feeling depressed for much of his life but had never sought treatment.
Although scoring the second highest on aptitude tests in college, he obtained mediocre grades and dropped out as a senior. He had been a salesman in a department store for fifteen
years.

Mr. R could say almost nothing about his childhood, explaining that it was "average." Having few friends, he was
a loner. His brother, nine years older, seemed to serve as a
paternal figure, as his father had died of a heart attack when
he was seventeen. He knew his mother had had many miscarriages before his birth, but he could provide no details as
to how many or the cause. His parents were ready to adopt
a child when he was born.

Unable to consciously recall much about his relationship
with his mother, Mr. R appeared to unconsciously repeat it
with his wife. Much of the time he criticized her for either
being too permissive with their two sons or for not being

available enough for them or himself. Not having had sexual intercourse with her for several years based on mutual decision, he masturbated about twice daily.

An open-ended psychotherapy was planned, in conjunction with a regimen of antidepressant medication. Mr. R was quite passive yet demanding in treatment, wishing to be told what to discuss and complaining of not having more time; because of financial difficulties therapy was limited to one session a week. Mr. R clearly longed for his parents, especially mother, who had died three years earlier of cancer. He tearfully described how he had cried at their graves and how alone he felt. However, when his therapist pointed out how much he missed them, he steadfastly denied having much feeling. His mother was portrayed as increasingly depressed during his adolescence following the death of her sister when he was fourteen and his father's death three years later. She visited the cemetery daily and withdrew from interactions. But Mr. R could not be engaged in any discussion of what this might have meant to him.

He had difficulty disciplining his six-year-old son and covertly encouraged the boy's aggressive behavior in school, believing it was normal for someone his age. He recalled having "accidentally" burned down his house at the same age while playing with matches. His parents had not reprimanded him, fearing he would be traumatized. When Mr. R felt lonely and rejected by his wife, he sometimes invited his son into his bed to cuddle him. He ignored his therapist's warning that this was overstimulating the boy, who, not surprisingly, was enuretic.

After visiting with his older brother, a successful professional who was supportive and offered to help him pay his debts, his mood brightened noticeably. Feeling increasingly less depressed over several sessions, his need for therapy waned, and he became indifferent to his chronic difficulties. After several cancellations, he decided to discontinue treatment.

Mr. R's infantile personality—considerable demandingness,

limited frustration tolerance, helplessness, and passivity—
appeared to be associated to a large degree with parenting
that did not foster the acquisition of age-appropriate self-
control of his impulses and delay-gratification. There was a
striking discrepancy between his superior ego endowment
and his inability to actualize that potential in either career
achievements or developing mature interpersonal relationships. Parental indulgence could not be linked conclusively
to mother's multiple miscarriages, although his older brother's adaptive functioning suggested that there may have been
important differences in parenting the two boys, probably
because of the intervening perinatal losses. Although unconscious guilt and unresolved homosexual conflicts contributing to his passive orientation were clearly additional conflicts
for Mr. R, they were not highlighted in this presentation in
order to focus on the disruptive effects inadequate parenting
can have on ego development. Mother's depressive tendencies probably resulted in inconsistent parenting that fluc-
tuated between neglect (caused by withdrawal) and overper-
missiveness, the identical criticisms Mr. R directed at his
wife's mothering.

A thirty-year-old, obese man suffering from serious heart
disease similarly presented with severe depression. This patient was the sole survivor of a sibship of five. Four younger
siblings had died immediately after birth because of RH incompatibility. Plagued by feelings of responsibility for his
siblings' deaths, he unconsciously punished himself through
a series of debilitating accidents and by failing to lose the
massive weight he had acquired as an adult, seriously endangering his life. When RH incompatibility is the cause of
subsequent sibling losses, the surviving child's guilt can be
profound, since his birth is linked in fact to the siblings'
deaths. In addition to experiencing himself as the murderer
of his siblings, this patient had a profound oral fixation, having been a heavy drinker before he became obese. He described his mother as overprotective and hypochondriacal
during his childhood. In a seeming repetition compulsion,
she endlessly repeated the traumatic cycle of forming and

breaking the bonds of attachment to her offspring by becoming a foster mother.

Another patient said his parents had "spoiled" him by "giving me everything I wanted." Mother especially worried about something happening to him and whether he would "make it to the next day." His mother had three miscarriages prior to his birth and one after he was born. He sought treatment for anxiety attacks, which seemed related to oedipal conflicts. This patient demonstrated serious narcissistic problems, readily missing appointments and calling his therapist after hours. His sense of entitlement in doing things on his schedule created considerable difficulty on his job and eventually became an insurmountable obstacle in his treatment.

The Resolution of Perinatal Sibling Loss

The adult clinical sample clearly demonstrated that unresolved childhood perinatal sibling loss can lead to serious character disturbance requiring long-term intensive psychotherapy. Many later difficulties can be linked to and were probably exacerbated by the maladaptive effects of the earlier perinatal sibling deaths. This clinical sample, however, should not be viewed as representative of those who experience perinatal sibling loss. The parents' psychological disturbances and destructive family dynamics probably existed prior to these losses.

The individual's intrapsychic conflicts, deficits, and distortions can be understood most meaningfully in the context of family dynamics. A child's tendency toward magical thinking, egocentrism, and blurring of fantasy and reality is encouraged by the absence of clear, objective information and the proliferation of conscious and unconscious parental distortion of the facts. Fantasies more readily become convictions when supported by parental views. Self and object representations become anchored in the pattern of family interactions and mythology. Bobby's guilt and provocation of punishment complemented his role as the family scapegoat. Steve's unconscious belief that his mother murdered his brother was supported by her own unconscious guilt. Terry's adolescent separation fears mirrored his mother's anxiety over his well-being if apart from her. Joseph's deadened detachment from others and Mrs. M's profound sense of worthlessness reflected, in part, their mothers' overt rejection of them as ungratifying replacement children. Ms. J's massive inhibition of anger became understandable in light of a childhood marred by repeated sibling loss without benefit of parental attempts to explain those deaths in realistic and empathic terms, which could have tempered the force of magical thinking. Mr. R's poor frustration tolerance and impulse control appeared to be not the product of constitutional ego weakness but that of indulgent parents who, scarred by multiple perinatal losses, were unable to promote age-appropriate forms of self-control.

The family plays a crucial role in mediating the child's experience of death and resolution of mourning. John Bowlby's (1980) extensive investigation of bereavement led him to conclude that "nothing has impressed me more deeply than the evidence showing the pervasive influence at all ages of the pattern of a human being's family life on the way he responds to loss" (p. 439). Cain and his colleagues (Cain and Cain 1964; Cain, Erickson, et al. 1964; Cain, Fast et al. 1964) observed that a child's reaction to sibling death is inextricably interwoven with family dynamics, structure, and communications. Several case reports involving sibling death (Evans 1976; Jensen & Wallace 1967; Krell & Rabkin 1979) demonstrated that individual psychotherapy with the surviving child needs to be supplemented by family treatment in order to address the family's unresolved grief, which continued to impede the child's mourning and functioning.

My clinical experience with both child and adult survivors of perinatal sibling loss powerfully confirms the vital roles that parental responses and family dynamics play in the resolution of this loss. Every family in this sample shared three features that impeded the resolution of perinatal sibling loss. Accurate and complete information was never given to the child. In no instance were both parents able to mourn and resolve their perinatal losses. In *every* case pathogenic family interaction involving the child occurred in which the task of helping the child to resolve the death was sacrificed for maintaining the family's unresolved grief.

Just as parental disturbance inevitably instigates or intensifies the child's difficulties, nurturant and effective parenting becomes a healing influence for both parent and child. Erna Furman (1978) wisely recognized that the most effective means of repairing the injury to parental self-esteem resulting from perinatal death is to care for the remaining children and help them deal with the loss. The inability of the parents in these cases to respond empathically to their children's needs contributed to these children's difficulties, confirming their sense of failure as parents. Parental complaints that their children were too demanding may have reflected their own depressed self-preoccupation. Perhaps parents felt their children wanted so much because they themselves had so little to give. A child who was portrayed by parents as self-centered may have been responding to inadequate parenting and attempting to draw a parent out of depression.

When these children of deficient parenting became parents themselves, they encountered more difficulty. Having children revived their own childhood conflicts and identifications with ineffective parents and, in so doing, propagated the legacy of parental inadequacy from their own mothers and fathers. The sense of failure born of perinatal death may endure through resulting parenting deficiencies passed down, psychologically, to subsequent generations.

CHAPTER 5
FUTURE RESEARCH

Methodological Considerations

Although this book is clinically oriented to the psychotherapist treating the survivors of perinatal loss, empirical research serves a crucial function by furthering our understanding of both the impact of this death and the efficacy of different interventions. Unfortunately, most of the research in this area has been poorly designed or haphazardly executed (Kirkley-Best & Kellner 1982). Reviewing these major pitfalls may be useful for those planning future projects, who must also recognize that practical limitations may thwart the actualization of the ideal research design.

The time at which data is collected powerfully affects and potentially distorts the results. Retrospective studies in which most survivors are interviewed a year or more after the loss (for example, Feeley & Gottlieb 1988; Lockwood & Lewis 1980; Peppers & Knapp 1980a; Rowe et al. 1978; Smith & Borgers 1988; Stringham et al. 1982) are susceptible to distortion of recall. If the follow-up assessment of parental bereavement is done too early—that is, within several months after the loss (for example, Benfield et al. 1978; Clarke & Williams 1979; Clyman et al. 1980; Kennell et al. 1970; LaRoche et al. 1982)—it will not be possible to determine if intense grief indicates an inappropriate reaction or severe but not necessarily maladaptive mourning. Frequently there is no follow-up to determine the resolution of mourning (for example, Giles, 1970; Seibel & Graves 1980). Rather than evaluate parental grief at only one or two points (as do most studies), it is necessary to trace the course of mourning over a period of at least two years. Grieving does not follow a rigid pattern as first believed but is subject to considerable individual variation.

The researcher should pay careful attention to sample selection. A self-selected sample responding to a researcher's invitation to be interviewed (for example, Lockwood & Lewis 1980; Peppers & Knapp 1980a; Stringham et al. 1982) is not likely to be representative of all bereaved parents. If the sample comprises a variety of losses including miscarriage, stillbirth, neonatal death, and SIDS, it becomes impossible to distinguish the effects of the particular kind of loss.* Most studies omit a comparison control group of mothers with healthy births (for example, Cullberg 1972; Kennell et al. 1970; LaRoche et al. 1982), thereby preventing any inferences regarding significantly more disturbance following perinatal loss than during uneventful motherhood. Sample size is typically very small (for example, Helmrath & Steinitz 1978; Wilson et al. 1982), often owing to the attenuation of sample size (for example, Jensen & Zahourek 1972), which makes the detection of statistically significant findings much more unlikely.

The accuracy of one's assumptions and the construction of appropriate variables are also important in research design. Some investigators assume a much more precise distinction between normal and maladaptive grief reactions in the midst of mourning (for example, LaRoche et al. 1982)† than appears warranted. Crucial variables that may be difficult to assess (for example, previous emotional disturbance) were generally absent in research design, making it impossible to evaluate the independent and interactive effects of earlier emotional dysfunction and perinatal death on the eventual outcome.

Finally, the interpretation of results sometimes blatantly

---

*In one especially poorly designed study (Horowitz 1978), perinatal losses were not distinguished from elective abortions.
†In fact, their follow-up study (LaRoche et al. 1984) reported that unresolved maternal grief one to two years after a perinatal loss could not always be anticipated by maternal functioning three months after the death.

contradicts the reported data. Peppers (1987) infers that the "grief associated with elective abortion was found to be symptomatically similar to grief experienced following involuntary fetal/infant loss" (p. 1), disregarding the statistically significant decrease in grieving from the time the decision was made to the postabortion scoring (that is, that the grief response was actually quite brief and readily resolved as found by other abortion studies). Cavenar and his colleagues (1979) caution against the possible harmful impact of an abortion on the surviving siblings by reporting a single case of a five-year-old boy's evident aggressive reactions, minimizing such early trauma as mother's postpartum psychosis after his birth, his own hospitalization for pneumonia at age two, and the recent death of mother's father with her resulting depression during the time of the abortion. It is not surprising that both these exaggerations of disturbance occur in the abortion literature, in which it is especially important to not have one's moral and political beliefs impede an impartial interpretation of the data.

Certain assumptions are universally regarded as true with little or no empirical confirmation. Although clinical impressions have persuaded virtually all workers in this field to encourage parents to view and interact with the deceased baby in the belief that this facilitates the resolution of grief, no study has provided statistically significant evidence of this.* Research reporting unexpected results tends to be ignored.† Similarly, the purported value of widely recom-

---

*LaRoche and her colleagues (1984) discovered a statistically significant association between depression and not seeing or touching one's baby. However, because the entire sample was given the opportunity to have contact with their babies (that is, there was not random assignment to contact and noncontact groups), it is not possible to infer the causal direction of this correlation. It may be that less depressed women are better able to tolerate the emotional intensity of contact with their dead babies, or that such contact reduces depression by facilitating the resolution of grief.

†There have been few citations of Cooper's (1980) descriptive study of seventeen British couples recovering from stillbirths. Although no child was named or buried and few couples chose to view the stillborns, the nature and duration of grief appeared quite similar to those of couples who had contact with, named, and buried their children.

mended crisis intervention by the medical team in preventing unresolved grief has not yet been conclusively established. These convictions were not, in fact, borne out by my clinical sample, in which viewing the dead baby and the responsiveness of medical caretakers did not appear to be strongly associated with either the nature or the outcome of parental bereavement. I believe, nonetheless, that these interventions can be effective in promoting a more benign outcome. Further research is necessary, however, to determine the circumstances in which such approaches are most useful and those in which they will not be sufficient.

Ideally, a longitudinal, prospective study would be designed to assess parents as early as possible during pregnancy so that the outcome of those who experience perinaal loss could be compared with previous functioning as well as with controls. This could be accomplished as part of a large-scale pregnancy study in which obstetric patients at a university-based medical center with access to research support were routinely administered questionnaires with brief interviews during pregnancy visits. Objective scales (of depression, for example) would complement clinical interviews in constructing a range of independent variables indexing strengths and liabilities on both the intrapsychic (ego functioning, conflicts, parental identifications and object representations, level and stability of self-esteem, and so on) and the interpersonal (marital relationship, informal sources of support, community involvement, and so on) level. Followup assessments should be done on a regular basis (about every three to six months) for at least two years postbereavement. A particularly important outcome measure would be the mother's response to her next pregnancy and birth. Comparisons should be available among groups who had crisis intervention, supportive counseling, or psychotherapy and those who received no professional assistance. Unless there was random assignment into these different groups, it would not be possible to compare relative efficacy because the treatment populations might vary by self-selection. Ultimately, the relationship among independent intrapsychic, interpersonal, circumstantial, and treatment variables with dependent outcome measures would begin to indicate which factors and interventions are conducive to adaptive resolutions.

These guidelines are oriented toward exploring parental (especially maternal) bereavement. There is, however, no quantitative, empirical research investigating the impact of perinatal loss on siblings. Although such research is sorely needed, clinical studies (which are also quite scarce) may be better suited to assess the long-range effects of perinatal loss and the interaction of intrapsychic, parental, and family dynamics.

Clinical investigations may complement more quantitative, empirical studies in a naturalistic setting. The protocols used in organizing my clinical case data may be adapted for either clinical or research-oriented samples. Clinical samples may tap a more disturbed population, although the discontinuity between treated and nontreated samples may not be as great as one might imagine; seeking psychotherapy is probably based more on help-seeking variables than on degree of disturbance. However, my clinical sample should not be generalized to represent the typical outcomes to perinatal bereavement. Because the purpose of this book has been to elaborate disturbed reactions to perinatal loss and to discuss treatment, maladaptive response was a crucial factor to include in my sample. It would be very valuable to understand which features promote an adaptive outcome to perinatal loss.

Selected Observations and Questions

Perinatal death is often a traumatizing event for mothers—creating developmental obstacles to fulfilling lifelong goals of parenthood, exacerbating earlier internalized conflicts revived during pregnancy, and exposing narcissistic vulnerabilities in maintaining positive self-esteem. This death can evoke multiple bereavements including the loss of a distinct person (one's unique child), the revived loss of an earlier deceased loved one who was linked with that child, the loss of a part of oneself who was that child, and the loss of one's sense of perfection, personified by that child. There may also be the loss of one's omnipotence normally associated with the act of creation and the all-powerful mother, the loss of one's immortality in the continuity of one's blood line, the loss of one's proud bodily affirmation in failing to fulfill one's reproductive function, and the loss of one's sense of adequacy as a parent. By providing insight into intensified conflicts, encouraging the expression of grief over these manifold losses, and offering empathy as a form of narcissistic sustenance, psychotherapy may facilitate both the resolution of this crisis and related underlying issues. A subsequent pregnancy may complete the resolution of this loss if sufficient mourning and time have occurred to allow a psychological separation between the earlier death and upcoming birth as distinct lives.

Most therapies with bereaved women uncovered primarily negative, dissatisfying relationships with their own mothers. Further exploration is needed to determine if a childhood history of feeling deprived and ambivalent toward mother is a particularly important factor aggravating the impact of perinatal loss. Conversely, is it possible that reports of unhappy maternal relationships are a product of the loss itself, that is, a selective activation of needy, unfulfilled experiences of being parented that complement one's current failed attempts to mother? Bereaved women who had struggled with infertility for several years were especially inaccessible to treatment, typically leaving within a few sessions. Perhaps the combined burdens of ongoing infertility and recent perinatal loss were overwhelming, making any introspective therapy unsuitable at the time. More effective interventions need to be developed for this especially vulnerable group.

The enduring impact of perinatal sibling loss is mediated by parental reactions and family dynamics. In every instance of child and adult disturbance, parents failed to provide adequate information and facilitation of their children's grief and were unable to mourn the losses themselves. Profound, unconscious, and lifelong guilt was sometimes rooted in the magnified potency of murderous wishes through magical thinking, especially with losses occurring in the early years. The often severe narcissistic deficits and conflicts with aggression commonly found in sibling survivors of perinatal loss appeared powerfully determined by the corrosive family climates of scapegoating, parental depression with indifference or indulgence, and the shadow of the deceased cast on the immediately subsequent birth. The legacy of perinatal death continued in successive generations, who struggled with wounded self-worth and inadequate parenting.

Perinatal loss, if unattended, can leave scars that impair one's own well-being as well as afflict one's offspring. When this occurs, the parental bond transfers a psychological heritage that rends the best part of oneself from one's child. A more promising outcome may be achieved if the rendering of understanding and expression of grief can occur in the formation and dissolution of a therapeutic relationship that enables a reparative revision of this loss.

APPENDIX

Clinical Protocols for Perinatal Loss

Maternal Cases

I. Background: age; marital status; race; ethnic membership; occupation; religion.

II. Circumstances of loss

A. Nature of loss: time elapsed since occurrence; whether planned pregnancy; kind of loss; how far along in pregnancy; medical complications; causality; suddenness or anticipation of loss; visible abnormalities; viability of fetus; concurrent stressors.

B. Prior history: infertility problems; fate of all other conceptions; months attempting this conception; family history of pregnancy losses and related difficulties; medical history (especially obstetric-gynecologic problems).

C. Involvement with the baby: knowledge of sex; contact (whether saw, touched, held); whether named; memorabilia (e.g., photographs, finger- or footprints); funeral or memorial service; fate of body.

D. Future planning: likelihood of recurrence; impact on future fertility; plans for future pregnancy (if felt as urgent); interval until next pregnancy.

III. Interpersonal reactions

A. Medical: reported quality and sensitivity of medical care; grieving suppressed or encouraged; information and advice provided; hospital procedures; any follow-up after discharge; change in relationship to medical caretakers.

B. Spouse: background information (age, occupation, and so on); how involved with wife and unborn child during pregnancy; meaning of loss; course of grief; general personality and dynamics; availability to wife after loss; empathy with wife's grief; impact of loss on communication; closeness and sexual relations in marriage; prior and subsequent marital problems.

C. Family (children, parents, siblings): tolerance of maternal grief; quality of prior relationship; ability of parents to facilitate resolution of other children's grief (i.e., provide information, answer questions, support mourning, and empathize with feelings); expression of unresolved grief with children (e.g., overprotective, scapegoating, replacement dynamics); change in valuing of parental role and children.

D. Friends: tolerance of maternal grief; quality of prior relationship; impact of loss on relationship; change in empathy with others facing losses and hardships.

E. Community: availability of and participation in support groups; knowledge and sensitivity about perinatal loss on part of ministers and teachers; any change in religious identification; any change in job.

IV. Intrapsychic responses

A. History: prior deaths and unresolved losses; individual and family history of traumas; prior psychotherapy; relevant developmental history (personal, parental, sexual).

B. Psychodynamics: symptoms; central dynamic issues and conflicts; character structure (with favored defenses); extent and tolerance of depression; gender identification; narcissistic deficits (stability of self-esteem and ego ideal); susceptibility to regression or decompensation; superego functioning; pregnancy dynamics (nature of prenatal attachment, conscious and unconscious wishes, conflicts over baby and motherhood, nature of infantile and maternal identifications).

C. Reactions to loss: nature of loss (narcissistic versus object); patterning of grief; defenses against mourning; meanings of loss.

V. Psychotherapy

A. Treatment particulars: referral source; contract (length and frequency of recommended and actual plans); orientation of treatment; source of payment.

B. Course of therapy: presenting problems (manifest description and latent association with loss); anniversary effects; focus of therapeutic work (facilitating mourning, providing insight, restoring narcissistic equilibrium); role of therapist; importance of transference; reactions to separations and interruptions in treatment; memorable material (sessions, dreams, and fantasies); termination (planned or abrupt, any acting-out, intensity of feelings over ending, interpretation and resolution of termination issues).

C. Role of perinatal loss: source of new disturbance; revival of earlier problems; stimulus to adaptation or growth.

D. Outcome: resolution of perinatal loss and unrelated issues; comparison with preloss functioning; comparison with functioning upon entering treatment; unresolved disturbance and symptoms.

Sibling Cases

I. Background: same as maternal but applied to child. Add: age at loss; siblings; grade.

II. Circumstances: same, except for:
C. Involvement with baby: distinguish parental from sibling experiences.

III. Interpersonal reactions: same, except for:
B. Parents: background information on parents; omit involvement in pregnancy, meaning of loss, course of grief, and general dynamics.
C. Grandparents' response: tolerance of parental grief and quality of prior relationship.
D. Friends (of both parents and siblings).

IV. Intrapsychic responses: same, except applies to child instead of mother. Add:
A. History: school functioning; other significant events.
B. Psychodynamics: psychosexual phase dominance; nature of cognitive functioning (defenses, deficits, lapses in reality-testing, use of magical thinking); brief dynamic formulation of each parent; pregnancy dynamics distinguished for parents and child.
C. Reactions to loss: conscious understanding of loss; preconscious beliefs about loss; unconscious meanings of loss; expression of grief; defenses against grief and degree of resolution of grief (all distinguished for parents and child).

V. Psychotherapy: same, with additional review of parent guidance.

VI. Family relationships
A. Prior relationships: with mother, father, siblings; family role.
B. Impact of loss: on parent-child relationship; children's family roles and family system; expression of unresolved parental grief with children (overprotective, scapegoating, replacement dynamics).
C. Parenting: ability to facilitate resolution of siblings' grief (provide information, answer questions, support mourning, empathize with feelings); effects on quality of parenting; change in valuing of parental role and children.

REFERENCES

Abarbanel, A., & Bach, G. (1959). Group psychotherapy for the infertile couple. *International Journal of Fertility, 6,* 151–160.

Abarbanel, J. (1983). The revival of the sibling experience during the mother's pregnancy. In *The psychoanalytic study of the child* (vol. 38, pp. 353–379). New Haven: Yale University Press.

Abend, S. (1978). Sibling love and object choice. (Notes from meeting of the New York Psychoanalytic Society, Nov. 12, 1977.) *Psychoanalytic Quarterly, 47,* 660–661.

Abraham, K. (1924/1968). A short study of the development of the libido, viewed in the light of mental disorders. In D. Bryan & A. Strachey (ed. and trans.), *Selected papers of Karl Abraham* (pp. 418–501). New York: Basic Books.

Adolf, A., & Patt, R. (1980). Neonatal death: The family is the patient. *Journal of Family Practice, 10,* 317–321.

Affleck, G., McGrade, B., Allen, D., & McQueeney, M. (1985). Mothers' beliefs about behavioral causes for their developmentally disabled infant's condition: What do they signify? *Journal of Pediatric Psychology, 10,* 293–303.

Ainslie, R., & Solyom, A. (1986). The replacement of the fantasized Oedipal child: A disruptive effect of sibling loss on the mother-infant relationship. *Psychoanalytic Psychology, 3,* 257–268.

Ainsworth, M. D. S. (1973). Development of infant-mother attachment. *Review of Child Development Research, 3,* 1–94.

Altschul, S. (ed.) (1988). *Childhood bereavement and its aftermath.* Madison, Conn.: International Universities Press.

Arlow, J. (1972). The only child. *Psychoanalytic Quarterly, 41,* 507–536.

Aruffo, R. (1971). Lactation as a denial of separation. *Psychoanalytic Quarterly, 40,* 100–122.

Baetson, K., Rankin, R., Fuller, G., & Stack, J. (1985). A comparative MMPI study of abortion-seeking women and those who intend to carry their pregnancies to term. *Family Practice Research Journal, 4,* 199–207.

Ballou, J. (1978). The significance of reconciliative themes in the psychology of pregnancy. *Bulletin of the Menninger Clinic, 42,* 383–413.

Barglow, P., Istiphan, I., Bedger, J., & Welbourne, C. (1973). Response of unmarried adolescent mothers to infant or fetal death. In S. Feinstein & P. Giovacchini (eds.), *Adolescent psychiatry* (vol. 2, pp. 285–304). New York: Basic Books.

Barnes, A., Cohen, E., Stoeckle, J., & McGuire, M. (1971). Therapeutic abortion: Medical and social sequels. *Annals of Internal Medicine, 75,* 881–886.

Barry, M. (1981). Therapeutic experience with patients referred for "prolonged grief reaction": Some second thoughts. *Mayo Clinic Proceedings, 56,* 744–748.

Beard, R., Beckley, J., Black, D., Brewer, C., Craig, Y., Hill, A., et al. (1978). Help for parents after stillbirth. *British Medical Journal, 1,* 172–173.

Becker, D., & Margolin, F. (1967). How surviving parents handled their young children's adaptation to the crisis of loss. *American Journal of Orthopsychiatry, 37,* 753–757.

Becker, E. (1973). *The denial of death.* New York: Free Press.

Behrman, R., & Vaughan, V., III (eds.) (1983). *Nelson textbook of pediatrics* (13th ed.). Philadelphia: W. B. Saunders.

Bell, J. (1981). Psychological problems among patients attending an infertility clinic. *Journal of Psychosomatic Research, 25,* 1–3.

Benedek, T. (1937). Adaptation to reality in early infancy. *Psychoanalytic Quarterly, 7,* 200–214.

——— (1949). The psychosomatic implications of the primary unit: Mother-child. *American Journal of Orthopsychiatry, 19,* 642–654.

——— (1952). Infertility as a psychosomatic defense. *Fertility and Sterility, 3,* 527–541.

——— (1955). Psychobiological aspects of mothering. *American Journal of Orthopsychiatry, 26,* 272–278.

——— (1956/1973). Toward the biology of the depressive constellation. In *Psychoanalytic investigations* (pp. 356–376). New York: Quadrangle.

——— (1959). Parenthood as a developmental phase. *Journal of the American Psychoanalytic Association, 7,* 389–417.

——— (1960). The organization of the reproductive drive. *International Journal of Psycho-Analysis, 41,* 1–15.

——— (1970). The psychobiology of pregnancy. In E. J. Anthony and T. Benedek (eds.), *Parenthood: Its psychology and psychopathology* (pp. 137–155). Boston: Little, Brown & Co.

Benedek, T., & Rubenstein, B. (1942). *The sexual cycle in women.* Washington, D.C.: National Research Council.

Benfield, D. G., Leib, S., & Vollman, J. (1978). Grief response of parents to neonatal death and parent participation in deciding care. *Pediatrics, 62,* 171–177.

Benfield, D. G., & Nichols, J. (1984). Attitudes and practice of funeral directors toward newborn death. *Death Education, 8,* 155–167.

Benson, R., & Pryor, D. (1973). When friends fall out: Developmental interference with the function of some imaginary companions. *Journal of the American Psychoanalytic Association, 21,* 457–473.

Bentovim, A. (1972). Emotional disturbances of handicapped pre-school children and their families: Attitudes to the child. *British Medical Journal, 3,* 579–581.

Berezin, N. (1982). *After a loss in pregnancy.* New York: Simon & Schuster.

Berger, D. (1977). The role of the psychiatrist in a reproductive biology clinic. *Fertility and Sterility, 28,* 141–145.

Bergman, A. (1974). Psychological aspects of sudden unexpected death in infants and children. *Pediatric Clinics of North America, 21,* 115–121.

Berman, L. (1978). Sibling loss as an organizer of unconscious guilt: A case study. *Psychoanalytic Quarterly, 47,* 568–587.

Bermann, E. (1973). *Scapegoat.* Ann Arbor: The University of Michigan Press.

Bibring, G. (1959). Some consideration of the psychological processes in pregnancy. In *The psychoanalytic study of the child* (vol. 14, pp. 113–121). New York: International Universities Press.

Bibring, G., Dwyer, T., Huntington, D., & Valenstein, A. (1961a). A study of the psychological processes in pregnancy and of the earliest mother-child relationship: 1. Some propositions and comments. In *The psychoanalytic study of the child* (vol. 16, pp. 9–24). New York: International Universities Press.

——— (1961b). A study of the psychological processes in pregnancy and of the earliest mother-child relationship: 2. Methodological considerations. In *The psychoanalytic study of the child* (vol. 16, pp. 25–72). New York: International Universities Press.

Bibring, G., & Valenstein, A. (1976). Psychological aspects of pregnancy. *Clinical Obstetrics and Gynecology, 19,* 357–371.

Binger, C., Ablin, A., Feurstein, R., Kushner, J., Zoger, S., & Mikkelsen, C. (1969). Childhood leukemia: Emotional impact on patient and family. *New England Journal of Medicine, 280,* 414–418.

Blinder, B. (1972). Sibling death in childhood. *Child Psychiatry and Human Development, 2,* 169–175.

Blitzer, J., & Murray, J. (1964). On the transformation of narcissism during pregnancy. *International Journal of Psycho-Analysis, 45,* 89–97.

Blos, P. (1962). *On adolescence.* New York: Free Press.

Bluglass, K. (1981). Psychosocial aspects of the sudden infant death syndrome. *Journal of Child Psychology and Psychiatry, 22,* 411–421.

Blumberg, B., Golbus, M., & Hanson, K. (1975). The psychological sequelae of abortion performed for a genetic indication. *American Journal of Obstetrics and Gynecology, 122,* 799–808.

Blumenfeld, M. (1978). Psychological factors involved in request for elective abortion. *Journal of Clinical Psychiatry, 39,* 17–25.

Borg, S., & Lasker, J. (1981). *When pregnancy fails*. Boston: Beacon Press.

Bos, C., & Cleghorn, R. (1958). Psychogenic sterility. *Fertility and Sterility, 9*, 84–98.

Bourke, M. (1984). The continuum of pre and post bereavement grieving. *British Journal of Medical Psychology, 57*, 121–125.

Bourne, S. (1968). The psychological effects of stillbirths on women and their doctors. *Journal of the Royal College of General Practitioners, 16*, 103–112.

——— (1977). Stillbirth, grief, and medical education. *British Medical Journal, 1*, 1157.

Bourne, S., & Lewis, E. (1984). Pregnancy after stillbirth or neonatal death. *Lancet, 2*, 31–33.

Bowlby, J. (1969). *Attachment and loss*. Vol. 1, *Attachment*. New York: Basic Books.

——— (1973). *Attachment and loss*. Vol. 2, *Separation*. New York: Basic Books.

——— (1980). *Attachment and loss*. Vol. 3, *Loss*. New York: Basic Books.

Bozeman, M., Orbach, C., & Sutherland, A. (1955). Psychological impact of cancer and its treatment. *Cancer, 8*, 1–19.

Brazelton, T. B., Koslowski, B., & Main, M. (1974). The origins of reciprocity: The early mother-infant interaction. In M. Lews & L. Rosenblum (eds.), *The effect of the infant on its caregiver* (pp. 49–76). New York: Wiley.

Bresnick, E., & Taymor, M. (1979). The role of counseling in infertility. *Fertility and Sterility, 32*, 154–156.

Bruce, S. (1962). Reactions of nurses and mothers to stillbirths. *Nursing Outlook, 10*, 88–91.

Brunswick, R. M. (1940). The preoedipal phase of the libido development. *Psychoanalytic Quarterly, 9*, 293–319.

Burden, R. (1980). Measuring the effects of stress on the mothers of handicapped infants: Must depression always follow? *Child: Care, Health, and Development, 6*, 111–125.

Bydlowski, M., & Dayan-Lintzer, M. (1988). A psycho-medical approach to infertility: "Suffering from sterility." *Journal of Psychosomatic Obstetrics and Gynaecology, 9*, 139–151.

Byrne, E., & Cunningham, C. (1985). The effects of mentally handicapped children on families: A conceptual review. *Journal of Child Psychology and Psychiatry and Allied Disciplines, 26*, 847–864.

Cain, A., & Cain, B. (1964). On replacing a child. *Journal of the American Academy of Child Psychiatry, 3*, 443–456.

Cain, A., Erickson, M., Fast, I., & Vaughan, R. (1964). Children's disturbed reactions to their mother's miscarriage. *Psychosomatic Medicine, 26*, 58–66.

Cain, A., Fast, I., & Erickson, M. (1964). Children's disturbed reactions to the death of a sibling. *American Journal of Orthopsychiatry, 34*, 741–752.

Calef, V. (1972). The hostility of parents to children: Some notes on infertility, child abuse and abortion. *International Journal of Psychoanalytic Psychotherapy, 1*, 76–96.

Candy-Gibb, S., Sharp, K., & Petrun, C. (1985). The effects of age, object, and cultural/religious background on children's concepts of death. *Omega, 15,* 329–345.

Carr, D., & Knupp, S. (1985). Grief and perinatal loss: A community hospital approach to support. *Journal of Obstetric, Gynecologic & Neonatal Nursing, 14,* 130–139.

Case, R. (1978). When birth is also a funeral. *Journal of Pastoral Care, 32,* 6–21.

Cavenar, J., Maltbie, A., & Sullivan, J. (1978). Aftermath of abortion: Anniversary depression and abdominal pain. *Bulletin of the Menninger Clinic, 42,* 433–444.

Cavenar, J., Spaulding, J., & Sullivan, J. (1979). Child's reaction to mother's abortion. *Military Medicine, 144,* 412–413.

Chasseguet-Smirgel, J. (1984). The femininity of the analyst in professional practice. *International Journal of Psycho-Analysis, 65,* 169–178.

Chodoff, P., Friedman, S., & Hamburg, D. (1964). Stress, defenses, and coping behavior: Observations in parents of children with malignant disease. *American Journal of Psychiatry, 120,* 743–749.

Clarke, M., & Williams, A. (1979). Depression in women after perinatal death. *Lancet, 1,* 916–917.

Clyman, R., Green, C., Mikkelsen, C., Rowe, J., & Ataide, L. (1979). Do parents utilize physician follow-up after the death of their newborn? *Pediatrics, 64,* 665–667.

Clyman, R., Green, C., Rowe, J., Mikkelsen, C., & Ataide, L. (1980). Issues concerning parents after the death of their newborn. *Critical Care Medicine, 8,* 215–218.

Cohen, L., Zilkha, S., Middleton, J., & O'Donnohue, N. (1978). Perinatal mortality: Assisting parental affirmation. *American Journal of Orthopsychiatry, 48,* 727–731.

Coleman, R., Kris, E., & Provence, S. (1953). The study of variations of early parental attitudes. In *The psychoanalytic study of the child* (vol. 8, pp. 20–47). New York: International Universities Press.

Colman, A. (1969). Psychological state during first pregnancy. *American Journal of Orthopsychiatry, 39,* 788–797.

Colonna, A., & Newman, L. (1983). The psychoanalytic literature on siblings. In *The psychoanalytic study of the child* (vol. 38, pp. 285–309). New Haven: Yale University Press.

Condon, J. (1985). The parental-foetal relationship: A comparison of male and female expectant parents. *Journal of Psychosomatic Obstetrics and Gynaecology, 4,* 271–284.

——— (1986). Management of established pathological grief reaction after stillbirth. *American Journal of Psychiatry, 143,* 987–992.

Conn, J. (1947). Children's awareness of the origins of babies. *Journal of Child Psychiatry, 1,* 140–176.

Conway, P., & Valentine, D. (1987). Reproductive losses and grieving. *Journal of Social Work and Human Sexuality, 6,* 43–64.

Cooper, B., & Ekstein, R. (1978). Concerning parental vulnerability: Issues around child and infant loss. In E. J. Anthony, C. Koupernik, & C. Chiland (eds.), *The child in his family* (vol. 4, pp. 219–230). New York: Wiley.

Cooper, J. (1980). Parental reactions to stillbirth. *British Journal of Social Work, 10,* 55–69.

Cooper, J. E., Bledin, K., Brice, B., & Mackenzie, S. (1985). Effects of female sterilization: One year follow-up in a prospective controlled study of psychological and psychiatric outcome. *Journal of Psychosomatic Research, 29,* 13–22.

Cooper, P., Gath, D., Rose, N., & Fieldsend, R. (1982). Psychological sequelae to elective sterilisation: A prospective study. *British Medical Journal, 284,* 461–464.

Cordell, A., & Apolito, R. (1981). Family support in infant death. *Journal of Obstetric, Gynecologic & Neonatal Nursing, 10,* 281–285.

Corney, R., & Horton, F. (1974). Pathological grief following spontaneous abortion. *American Journal of Psychotherapy, 131,* 825–827.

Cornwell, J., Nurcombe, B., & Stevens, L. (1977). Family response to loss of a child by sudden infant death syndrome. *The Medical Journal of Australia, 1,* 656–658.

Cranley, M. (1981). Development of a tool for the measurement of maternal attachment during pregnancy. *Nursing Research, 30,* 281–284.

Crawford, K., & Schuman, M. (1988). Helping families with miscarriage and newborn loss: How to start and maintain a community support system. Lamaze Childbirth Preparation Association of Ann Arbor, Inc., 3060 Packard, Suite F, Ann Arbor, Michigan 48108.

Cullberg, J. (1972). Mental reactions of women to perinatal death. In N. Morris (ed.), *Psychosomatic medicine in obstetrics and gynaecology* (pp. 326–329). Basel: Karger.

Cummings, S. T. (1976). The impact of the child's deficiency on the father: A study of mentally retarded and of chronically ill children. *American Journal of Orthopsychiatry, 46,* 246–255.

D'Arcy, E. (1968). Congenital defects: Mothers' reactions to first information. *British Medical Journal, 3,* 796–798.

Davanloo, H. (1980). A method of short-term dynamic psychotherapy. In H. Davanloo (ed.), *Short-term dynamic psychotherapy* (pp. 43–71). New York: Aronson.

Davidson, G. (1977). Death and the wished-for child: A case study. *Death Education, 1,* 265–275.

Defrain, J., & Ernst, L. (1978). The psychological effects of sudden infant death syndrome on surviving family members. *Journal of Family Practice, 6,* 985–989.

Deutsch, H. (1945). *The psychology of women.* Vol. 2, *Motherhood.* New York: Grune & Stratton.

Deykin, E., Campbell, L., & Patti, P. (1984). The postadoptive experience of surrendering parents. *American Journal of Orthopsychiatry, 54,* 271–280.

Donnai, P., Charles, N., & Harris, R. (1981). Attitudes of patients after "genetic" termination of pregnancy. *British Medical Journal, 282,* 621–622.

Dorner, S. (1975). The relationship of physical handicap to stress in families with an adolescent with spina bifida. *Developmental Medicine and Child Neurology, 17,* 765–776.

Dorner, S., & Atwell, J. D. (1985). Family adjustment to the early loss of a baby born with spina bifida. *Developmental Medicine and Child Neurology, 27,* 461–466.

Drotar, D., Baskiewicz, A., Irvin, N., Kennell, J., & Klaus, M. (1975). The adaptation of parents to the birth of an infant with a congenital malformation: A hypothetical model. *Pediatrics, 56,* 710–717.

Duff, R., & Campbell, A. (1973). Moral and ethical dilemmas in the special-care nursery. *New England Journal of Medicine, 289,* 890–894.

Dunlop, J. (1979). Bereavement reaction following stillbirth. *Practitioner, 222,* 115–118.

Durfee, R. (1987). Obstetric complications of pregnancy. In M. Pernoll & R. Benson (eds.), *Current obstetric and gynecologic diagnosis and treatment* (6th ed., pp. 255–278). Norwalk, Conn.: Appleton & Lange.

Easson, W. (1972). The family of the dying child. *Pediatric Clinics of North America, 19,* 1157–1165.

Edelstein, L. (1984). *Maternal bereavement: Coping with the unexpected death of a child.* New York: Praeger.

Ekblad, M. (1955). Induced abortion on psychiatric grounds. A follow-up study of 479 women. *Acta Psychiatrica et Neurologica Scandinavica, 99* (suppl.), 1–237.

Elliott, B. (1978). Neonatal death: Reflections for parents. *Pediatrics, 62,* 100–102.

Elliott, B., & Hein, H. (1978). Neonatal death: Reflections for physicians. *Pediatrics, 62,* 96–99.

Elstein, M. (1975). Effect of infertility on psychosexual function. *British Medical Journal, 2,* 296–299.

Engel, G. (1964). Grief and grieving. *American Journal of Nursing, 64,* 93–98.

Erikson, E. (1963). *Childhood and Society* (2d ed.). New York: Norton.

Estok, P., & Lehman, A. (1983). Perinatal death: Grief and support for families. *Birth, 10,* 17–25.

Evans, N. (1976). Mourning as a family secret. *Journal of the American Academy of Child Psychiatry, 15,* 502–509.

Ewy, D., & Ewy, R. (1984). *Death of a dream.* New York: Dutton.

Fajardo, B. (1987). Parenting a damaged child: Mourning, regression, and disappointment. *Psychoanalytic Review, 74,* 20–43.

Falik, L. (1984). Psychosexual aspects of infertility. *Medical Aspects of Human Sexuality, 18,* 82–92.

Fast, I. (1984). *Gender identity: A differentiation model.* Hillsdale, N.J.: Analytic Press.

—— (1985). *Event theory: A Piaget-Freud integration.* Hillsdale, N.J.: Lawrence Erlbaum.

Feeley, N., & Gottlieb, L. (1988). Parents' coping and communication following their infant's death. *Omega, 19,* 51–67.

Ferreira, A. J. (1963). Family myths and homeostasis. *Archives of General Psychiatry, 9,* 457–463.

Fischhoff, J., & O'Brien, N. (1976). After the child dies. *Journal of Pediatrics, 88,* 140–146.

Fisher, S., & Scharf, K. (1980). Teenage pregnancy: An anthropological, sociological and psychological overview. In S. Feinstein, P. Giovacchini, J. Looney, A. Schwartzberg, & A. Sorosky (eds.), *Adolescent psychiatry* (vol. 8, pp. 393–403). Chicago: University of Chicago Press.

Flavell, J. (1963). *The developmental psychology of Jean Piaget.* New York: Van Nostrand.

Florian, V. (1985). Children's concept of death: An empirical study of a cognitive and environmental approach. *Death Studies, 9,* 133–141.

Ford, C., Castelnuovo-Tedesco, P., & Long, K. (1971). Abortion: Is it a therapeutic procedure in psychiatry? *Journal of the American Medical Association, 218,* 1173–1178.

Ford, E., Forman, I., Willson, J., Char, W., Mixson, W., & Scholz, C. (1953). A psychodynamic approach to the study of infertility. *Fertility and Sterility, 4,* 456–466.

Forrest, G., Standish, E., & Baum, J. (1982). Support after perinatal death: A study of support and counselling after perinatal bereavement. *British Medical Journal, 285,* 1475–1479.

Fost, N. (1981). Counseling families who have a child with a severe congenital anomaly. *Pediatrics, 67,* 321–324.

Frankel, R. (1985). The stolen child: A fantasy, a wish, a source of countertransference. *International Review of Psycho-Analysis, 12,* 417–430.

Freitag-Koontz, M. J. (1988). Parents' grief reaction to the diagnosis of their infant's severe neurologic impairment and static encephalopathy. *Journal of Perinatal and Neonatal Nursing, 2,* 45–57.

Freud, S. (1915/1957). Thoughts for the times on war and death. In J. Strachey (ed. and trans.), *The standard edition of the complete psychological works of Sigmund Freud* (vol. 14, pp. 273–300). London: Hogarth Press.

—— (1917a/1957). On transformations of instinct as exemplified in anal erotism. In J. Strachey (ed. and trans.), *The standard edition of the complete psychological works of Sigmund Freud* (vol. 17, pp. 126–133). London: Hogarth Press.

—— (1917b/1957). Mourning and melancholia. In J. Strachey (ed. and trans.), *The standard edition of the complete psychological works of Sigmund Freud* (vol. 14, pp. 239–258). London: Hogarth Press.

—— (1920/1957). Beyond the pleasure principle. In J. Strachey (ed. and trans.), *The standard edition of the complete psychological works of Sigmund Freud* (vol. 18, pp. 3–64). London: Hogarth Press.

Frias, A., & Wilson, S. (1985). When biological childlessness is inevitable. *Medical Aspects of Human Sexuality, 19,* 43–51.

Friedman, R., & Gladstein, B. (1982). *Surviving pregnancy loss.* Boston: Little, Brown & Co.

Friedman, S. (1967). Care of the family of the child with cancer. *Pediatrics, 40,* 498–504.

—— (1974). Psychological aspects of sudden unexpected death in infants and children. *Pediatric Clinics of North America, 21,* 103–111.

Friedman, S., Chodoff, P., Mason, J., & Hamburg, D. (1963). Behavioral observations on parents anticipating the death of a child. *Pediatrics, 32,* 610–625.

Fulton, R. (1967). On the dying of death. In E. Grollman (ed.), *Explaining death to children* (pp. 32–47). Boston: Beacon Press.

Furlong, R., & Hobbins, J. (1983). Grief in the perinatal period. *Obstetrics and Gynecology, 61,* 497–500.

Furman, E. (1974). *A child's parent dies.* New Haven: Yale University Press.

—— (1976). Commentary. *Journal of Pediatrics, 89,* 143–145.

—— (1978). The death of the newborn: Care of the parents. *Birth and the Family Journal, 5,* 214–218.

Gardner, R. (1969). The guilt reaction of parents of children with severe physical disease. *American Journal of Psychiatry, 126,* 636–644.

Gedo, J. (1965). Unmarried motherhood. *International Journal of Psycho-Analysis, 46,* 352–357.

Geller, J. (1985). The long-term outcome of unresolved grief: An example. *Psychiatric Quarterly, 57,* 142–146.

Giles, P. F. (1970). Reactions of women to perinatal death. *The Australian and New Zealand Journal of Obstetrics and Gynecology, 10,* 207–210.

Glick, I., & Kessler, D. (1980). *Marital and family therapy* (2d ed.). New York: Grune & Stratton.

Gorer, G. (1965). *Death, grief, and mourning.* Garden City, N.Y.: Doubleday.

Green, M., & Solnit, A. (1964). Reactions to the threatened loss of a child: A vulnerable child syndrome. *Pediatrics, 34,* 58–66.

Greenfeld, D., Diamond, M., & DeCherney, A. (1988). Grief reactions following in-vitro fertilization treatment. *Journal of Psychosomatic Obstetrics and Gynaecology, 8,* 169–174.

Greenley, J., & Mechanic, D. (1976). Social selection in seeking help for psychological problems. *Journal of Health and Social Behavior, 17,* 249–262.

Greer, H., Lal, S., Lewis, S., Belsey, E., & Beard, R. (1976). Psychosocial consequences of therapeutic abortion. *British Journal of Psychiatry, 128,* 74–79.

Grollman, E. (1967). Explaining death to children. In E. Grollman (ed.), *Explaining death to children* (pp. 3–27). Boston: Beacon Press.

Grubb, C. (1976a). Is the baby alive or dead: Psychological work of a woman with an intrauterine fetal death. *Maternal-Child Nursing Journal, 5,* 25–37.

———— (1976b). Body image concerns of a multipara in the situation of intrauterine fetal death. *Maternal-Child Nursing Journal, 5,* 93–116.

Hagan, J. (1974). Infant death: Nursing interaction and intervention with grieving families. *Nursing Forum, 13,* 371–385.

Hallet, E. (1974). Birth and grief. *Birth and the Family Journal, 1,* 18–22.

Halpern, W. (1972). Some psychiatric sequelae to crib death. *American Journal of Psychiatry, 129,* 398–402.

Hardgrove, C., & Warrick, L. (1974). How shall we tell the children? *American Journal of Nursing, 74,* 448–450.

Harmon, R., Glicken, A., & Siegel, R. (1984). Neonatal loss in the intensive care nursery: Effects of maternal grieving and a program for intervention. *Journal of the American Academy of Child Psychiatry, 23,* 68–71.

Harris, B. G. (1986). Induced abortion. In T. Rando (ed.), *Parental loss of a child* (pp. 241–256). Champaign, Ill.: Research Press.

Helmrath, T., & Steinitz, E. (1978). Death of an infant: Parental grieving and the failure of social support. *Journal of Family Practice, 6,* 785–790.

Helström, L., & Victor, A. (1987). Information and emotional support for women after miscarriage. *Journal of Psychosomatic Obstetrics and Gynecology, 7,* 93–98.

Hendrickson, P. (1983). *Seminary: A search.* New York: Summit.

Herz, E. (1984). Psychological repercussions of pregnancy loss. *Psychiatric Annals, 14,* 454–457.

Hilgard, J. (1969). Depressive and psychotic states as anniversaries to sibling death in childhood. *International Psychiatry Clinics, 6* (2), 197–211.

Hochstaedt, B., & Langer, G. (1959). Psychoendocrine factors in sterility. *International Journal of Fertility, 4,* 253–258.

Hoffman, S. I., & Strauss, S. (1985). The development of children's concepts of death. *Death Studies, 9,* 469–482.

Horowitz, M., Marmar, C., Weiss, D., DeWitt, K., & Rosenbaum, R. (1984). Brief psychotherapy of bereavement reactions. *Archives of General Psychiatry, 41,* 438–448.

Horowitz, N. (1978). Adolescent mourning reactions to infant and fetal loss. *Social Casework, 59,* 551–559.

Ilse, S., & Furrh, C. B. (1988). Development of a comprehensive follow-up care program after perinatal and neonatal loss. *Journal of Perinatal and Neonatal Nursing, 2,* 23–33.

Jackel, M. (1966). Interruptions during psychoanalytic treatment and the wish for a child. *Journal of the American Psychoanalytic Association, 14,* 730–735.

Jacobson, E. (1968). On the development of a girl's wish for a child. *Psychoanalytic Quarterly, 37,* 523–538.

Janoff-Bulman, R. (1979). Characterological versus behavioral self-blame: Inquiries into depression and rape. *Journal of Personality and Social Psychology, 37,* 1798–1809.

Jensen, G., & Wallace, J. (1967). Family mourning process. *Family Process, 6,* 56–66.

Jensen, J., & Zahourek, R. (1972). Depression in mothers who have lost a newborn. *Rocky Mountain Medical Journal, 69,* 61–63.

Jessner, L., Weigert, E., & Foy, J. (1970). The development of parental attitudes during pregnancy. In E. J. Anthony & T. Benedek (eds.), *Parenthood: Its psychology and psychopathology* (pp. 209–244). Boston: Little, Brown & Co.

Johnson, S. (1984). Sexual intimacy and replacement children after the death of a child. *Omega, 15,* 109–118.

Jolly, H. (1976). Family reactions to stillbirth. *Proceedings of the Royal Society of Medicine, 69,* 835–837.

———— (1978). Loss of a baby. *Australian Paediatric Journal, 14,* 3–5.

Jörgensen, C., Uddenberg, N., & Ursing, I. (1985). Ultrasound diagnosis of fetal malformation in the second trimester: The psychological reactions of the women. *Journal of Psychosomatic Obstetrics and Gynecology, 4,* 31–40.

Kadushin, C. (1969). *Why people go to psychiatrists.* New York: Atherton.

Kaij, L., Malmquist, A., & Nilsson, A. (1969). Psychiatric aspects of spontaneous abortion. *Journal of Psychosomatic Research, 13,* 53–59.

Kane, B. (1979). Children's concepts of death. *The Journal of Genetic Psychology, 134,* 141–153.

Kaplan, L. (1986). *Adolescence: The farewell to childhood.* New York: Aronson.

Karahasanaglu, A., Barglow, P., & Growe, G. (1972). Psychological aspects of infertility. *Journal of Reproductive Medicine, 9,* 241–247.

Kellner, K., Donnelly, W., & Gould, S. (1984). Parental behavior after perinatal death: Lack of predictive demographic and obstetric variables. *Obstetrics and Gynecology, 63,* 809–814.

Kellner, K., Kirkley-Best, E., Chesborough, S., Donnelly, W., & Green, M. (1981). Perinatal mortality counseling program for families who experience a stillbirth. *Death Education, 5,* 29–35.

Kennell, J., Slyter, H., & Klaus, M. (1970). The mourning response of parents to the death of a newborn infant. *New England Journal of Medicine, 283,* 344–349.

Kestenberg, J. (1956). On the development of maternal feelings in early childhood. In *The psychoanalytic study of the child* (vol. 11, pp. 257–291). New York: International Universities Press.

———— (1976). Regression and reintegration in pregnancy. *Journal of the American Psychoanalytic Association, 24* (suppl.), 213–250.

Kirkley-Best, E., & Kellner, K. (1982). The forgotten grief: A review of the psychology of stillbirth. *American Journal of Orthopsychiatry, 52,* 420–429.

Kirkley-Best, E., Kellner, K., & LaDue, T. (1985). Attitudes toward stillbirth and death threat level in a sample of obstetricians. *Omega, 15,* 317–327.

Klass, D. (1985). Bereaved parents and the compassionate friends: Affiliation and healing. *Omega, 15,* 353–373.

Klass, D., & Marwit, S. (1988). Toward a model of parental grief. *Omega, 19,* 31–50.

Klass, D., & Shinners, B. (1983). Professional roles in a self-help group for the bereaved. *Omega, 13,* 361–375.

Klaus, M., & Kennell, J. (1982). *Parent-infant bonding* (2d ed.). St. Louis: C. V. Mosby.

Klemer, R., Rutherford, R., Banks, A., & Coburn, W. (1966). Marriage counseling with the infertile couple. *Fertility and Sterility, 17,* 104–109.

Knapp, R. (1986). *Beyond endurance: When a child dies.* New York: Schocken Books.

Knapp, R., & Peppers, L. (1979). Doctor-patient relationships in fetal/infant death encounters. *Journal of Medical Education, 54,* 775–780.

Kohut, H. (1971). *The analysis of the self.* New York: International Universities Press.

Koocher, G. (1973). Childhood, death, and cognitive development. *Developmental Psychology, 9,* 369–375.

Kowalski, K. (1980). Managing perinatal loss. *Clinical Obstetrics and Gynecology, 23,* 1113–1123.

Kowalski, K., & Osborn, M. R. (1977). Helping mothers of stillborn infants to grieve. *American Journal of Maternal-Child Nursing, 2,* 29–32.

Kraft, A., Palombo, J., Mitchell, D., Dean, C., Meyers, S., & Schmidt, A. (1980). The psychological dimensions of infertility. *American Journal of Orthopsychiatry, 50,* 618–628.

Krell, R., & Rabkin, L. (1979). The effects of sibling death on the surviving child: A family perspective. *Family Process, 18,* 471–477.

Kroger, W. (1952). Evaluation of personality factors in the treatment of infertility. *Fertility and Sterility, 3,* 542–553.

Krone, C., & Harris, C. (1988). The importance of infant gender and family resemblance within parents' perinatal bereavement process: Establishing personhood. *The Journal of Perinatal and Neonatal Nursing, 2,* 1–11.

Kubler-Ross, E. (1969). *On death and dying.* New York: Macmillan.

Kummer, J. (1963). Post-abortion psychiatric illness: A myth? *American Journal of Psychiatry, 119,* 980–983.

LaFerla, J., & Good, R. (1985). Helping patients cope with pregnancy loss. *Contemporary OB/GYN, 25,* 107–115.

Lake, M., Knuppel, R., Murphy, J., & Johnson, T. (1983). The role of a grief support team following stillbirth. *American Journal of Obstetrics and Gynecology, 146,* 877–881.

Lalos, A., Lalos, O., Jacobsson, L., & Schoultz, B. (1985). A psychosocial characterization of infertile couples before surgical treatment of the female. *Journal of Psychosomatic Obstetrics and Gynaecology, 4,* 83–93.

Lamb, J. M. (1986). SHARE. In T. Rando (ed.), *Parental loss of a child* (pp. 499–507). Champaign, Ill.: Research Press.

LaRoche, C., Lalinec-Michaud, M., Engelsmann, F., Fuller, N., Copp, M., McQuade-Soldatos, L., & Azima, R. (1984). Grief reactions to perinatal death: A follow-up study. *Canadian Journal of Psychiatry, 29,* 14–19.

LaRoche, C., Lalinec-Michaud, M., Engelsmann, F., Fuller, N., Copp, M.,

& Vasilevsky, K. (1982). Grief reactions to perinatal death: An exploratory study. *Psychosomatics, 23,* 510–518.

Lascari, A., & Stebbens, J. (1973). The reactions of families to childhood leukemia. *Clinical Pediatrics, 12,* 211–214.

Lask, B. (1975). Short-term psychiatric sequelae to therapeutic termination of pregnancy. *British Journal of Psychiatry, 126,* 173–177.

Lax, R. (1972). Some aspects of the interaction between mother and impaired child: Mother's narcissistic trauma. *International Journal of Psycho-Analysis, 53,* 339–344.

Legg, C., & Sherick, I. (1976). The replacement child: A developmental tragedy. *Child Psychiatry and Human Development, 7,* 113–125.

Lehman, D., Wortman, C., & Williams, A. (1987). Long-term effects of losing a spouse or child in a motor vehicle crash. *Journal of Personality and Social Psychology, 52,* 218–231.

Leifer, M. (1977). Psychological changes accompanying pregnancy and motherhood. *Genetic Psychology Monographs, 95,* 55–96.

Leon, I. (1983). *The decision to seek mental health care: Multivariate analysis of a national survey.* Ph.D. dissertation, University of Michigan.

Leppert, P., & Pahlka, B. (1984). Grieving characteristics after spontaneous abortion: A management approach. *Obstetrics and Gynecology, 64,* 119–122.

Lester, E., & Notman, M. (1986). Pregnancy, developmental crisis, and object relations: Psychoanalytic considerations. *International Journal of Psycho-Analysis, 67,* 357–366.

Lewis, E. (1976). The management of stillbirth: Coping with an unreality. *Lancet, 2,* 619–620.

——— (1979a). Mourning by the family after a stillbirth or neonatal death. *Archives of Disease in Childhood, 54,* 303–306.

——— (1979b). Inhibition of mourning by pregnancy: Psychopathology and management. *British Medical Journal, 2,* 27–28.

Lewis, E., & Page, A. (1978). Failure to mourn a stillbirth: An overlooked catastrophe. *British Journal of Medical Psychology, 51,* 237–241.

Lewis, T. (1975). A culturally patterned depression in a mother after loss of a child. *Psychiatry, 38,* 92–95.

Limerick, L. (1976). Support and counselling needs of families following a cot death bereavement. *Proceedings of the Royal Society of Medicine, 69,* 839–842.

Lindemann, E. (1944). Symptomatology and management of acute grief. *American Journal of Psychiatry, 101,* 141–148.

Lloyd, J., & Laurence, K. (1985). Sequelae and support after termination of pregnancy for fetal malformation. *British Medical Journal, 290,* 907–909.

Lockwood, S., & Lewis, I. (1980). Management of grieving after stillbirth. *Medical Journal of Australia, 2,* 308–311.

Loewald, E. (1982). The baby in mother's therapy. In *The psychoanalytic study of the child* (vol. 37, pp. 381–404). New Haven: Yale University Press.

Lovell, A. (1983). Some questions of identity: Late miscarriage, stillbirth and perinatal loss. *Social Science and Medicine, 17,* 755–761.

Lumley, J. (1980). The image of the fetus in the first trimester. *Birth and the Family Journal, 7,* 5–14.

—— (1982). Attitudes to the fetus among primigravidae. *Australian Paediatric Journal, 18,* 106–109.

Lundin, T. (1984). Morbidity following sudden and unexpected bereavement. *British Journal of Psychiatry, 144,* 84–88.

McCown, D. (1984). Funeral attendance, cremation, and young siblings. *Death Education, 8,* 349–363.

McCown, D., & Pratt, C. (1985). Impact of sibling death on children's behavior. *Death Studies, 9,* 323–335.

McGuire, L. (1975). Psychologic management of infertile women. *Postgraduate Medicine, 57,* 173–177.

McIntire, M., Angle, C., & Struempler, L. (1972). The concept of death in midwestern children and youth. *American Journal of Diseases of Children, 123,* 527–532.

McKeever, P. (1983). Siblings of chronically ill children: A literature review with implications for research and practice. *American Journal of Orthopsychiatry, 53,* 209–218.

MacKeith, R. (1973). The feelings and behaviour of parents of handicapped children. *Developmental Medicine and Child Neurology, 15,* 524–527.

McNeil, J. (1983). Young mothers' communications about death with their children. *Death Education, 6,* 323–339.

Maguire, D., & Skoolicas, S. (1988). Developing a bereavement follow-up program. *Journal of Perinatal and Neonatal Nursing, 2,* 67–77.

Mahan, C., & Schreiner, R. (1981). Management of perinatal death: Role of the social worker in the newborn ICU. *Social Work in Health Care, 6,* 69–76.

Mahler, M., Pine, F., & Bergman, A. (1975). *The psychological birth of the human infant.* New York: Basic Books.

Mai, F., Munday, R., & Rump, E. (1972). Psychiatric interview comparisons between infertile and fertile couples. *Psychosomatic Medicine, 34,* 431–440.

Malan, D. (1976). *The frontier of brief psychotherapy.* New York: Plenum.

Mandell, F., McAnulty, E., & Reece, R. (1980). Observations of paternal response to sudden unanticipated infant death. *Pediatrics, 65,* 221–225.

Mann, J. (1973). *Time-limited psychotherapy.* Cambridge: Harvard University Press.

Martin, H., Lawrie, J., & Wilkinson, A. (1968). The family of the fatally burned child. *Lancet, 2,* 628–629.

Menning, B. E. (1980). Emotional needs of infertile couples. *Fertility and Sterility, 34,* 313–319.

Miles, M., & Demi, A. (1984). Toward the development of a theory of bereavement guilt: Sources of guilt in bereaved parents. *Omega, 14,* 299–314.

Millen, L., & Roll, S. (1985). Solomon's mothers: A special case of patholog- ical bereavement. *American Journal of Orthopsychiatry, 55*, 411–418.

Mintzer, D., Als, H., Tronick, E., & Brazelton, T. B. (1984). Parenting an infant with a birth defect: The regulation of self-esteem. In *The psycho- analytic study of the child* (vol. 39, pp. 561–589). New Haven: Yale Uni- versity Press.

Moriarty, I. (1978). Mourning the death of an infant: The sibling's story. *Journal of Pastoral Care, 32*, 22–33.

Morris, D. (1976). Parental reactions to perinatal death. *Proceedings of the Royal Society of Medicine, 69*, 837–838.

Morse, C., & Van Hall, E. (1987). Psychosocial aspects of infertility: A review of current concepts. *Journal of Psychosomatic Obstetrics and Gynecology, 6*, 157–164.

Mozley, P. (1976). Psychophysiologic infertility: An overview. *Clinical Ob- stetrics and Gynecology, 19*, 407–417.

Muir, E., Speiss, A., & Todd, G. (1988). Family intervention and parental involvement in the facilitation of mourning in a 4-year-old boy. In *The psychoanalytic study of the child* (vol. 43, pp. 367–383). New Haven: Yale University Press.

Mulhern, R., Lauer, M., & Hoffman, R. (1983). Death of a child at home or in the hospital: Subsequent psychological adjustment of the family. *Pe- diatrics, 71*, 743–747.

Nagera, H. (1970). Children's reactions to the death of important objects. In *The psychoanalytic study of the child* (vol. 25, pp. 360–400). New York: International Universities Press.

Nagy, M. (1948). The child's theories concerning death. *The Journal of Genetic Psychology, 73*, 3–27.

Naylor, A. (1982). Premature mourning and failure to mourn: Their rela- tionship to conflict between mothers and intellectually normal children. *American Journal of Orthopsychiatry, 52*, 679–687.

Newton, M., & Newton, E. (1988). *Complications of Gynecologic and Obstetric Management* (6th ed.). Philadelphia: W. B. Saunders.

Niswander, K., & Patterson, R. (1967). Psychologic reactions to therapeutic abortion. *Obstetrics and Gynecology, 29*, 702–706.

Olshansky, S. (1962). Chronic sorrow: A response to having a mentally de- fective child. *Social Casework, 43*, 190–193.

Olson, L. (1980). Social and psychological correlates of pregnancy resolution among adolescent women: A review. *American Journal of Orthopsychiatry, 50*, 432–445.

Orbach, C. (1959). The multiple meanings of the loss of a child. *American Journal of Psychotherapy, 13*, 906–915.

Orbach, I., & Glaubman, H. (1978). Suicidal, aggressive, and normal chil- dren's perception of personal and impersonal death. *Journal of Clinical Psychology, 34*, 850–857.

——— (1979). Children's perception of death as a defensive process. *Journal of Abnormal Psychology, 88*, 671–674.

Orbach, I., Gross, Y., Glaubman, H., & Berman, D. (1985). Children's perception of death in humans and animals as a function of age, anxiety, and cognitive ability. *Journal of Child Psychology and Psychiatry, 26,* 453–463.

Osofsky, H. (1982). Expectant and new fatherhood as a developmental crisis. *Bulletin of the Menninger Clinic, 46,* 209–230.

Osofsky, J., & Osofsky, H. (1972). The psychological reaction of patients to legalized abortion. *American Journal of Orthopsychiatry, 42,* 48–60.

Osterweis, M., Solomon, F., & Green, M. (eds.) (1984). *Bereavement: Reactions, consequences and care.* Washington, D.C.: National Academy Press.

Outerbridge, E., Chance, G., Beaudry, M., McMurray, S., & Shea, D. (1983). Support for parents experiencing perinatal loss. *Canadian Medical Association Journal, 129,* 335–339.

Palmer, C. E., & Noble, D. (1986). Premature death: Dilemmas of infant mortality. *Social Casework, 67,* 332–339.

Panuthos, C., & Romeo, C. (1984). *Ended beginnings: Healing childbearing losses.* South Hadley, Mass.: Bergin & Garvey.

Pare, C., & Raven, H. (1970). Follow-up of patients referred for termination of pregnancy. *Lancet, 1,* 635–638.

Parkes, C. M. (1980). Bereavement counselling: Does it work? *British Medical Journal, 281,* 3–6.

——— (1985). Bereavement. *British Journal of Psychiatry, 146,* 11–17.

——— (1988). Research: Bereavement. *Omega, 18,* 365–377.

Parrish, S. (1980). Letting go. *The Canadian Nurse, 76,* 34–37.

Patt, S., Rappaport, R., & Barglow, P. (1969). Follow-up of therapeutic abortion. *Archives of General Psychiatry, 20,* 408–414.

Peck, A., & Marcus, H. (1966). Psychiatric sequelae of therapeutic interruption of pregnancy. *Journal of Nervous and Mental Disease, 143,* 417–425.

Peppers, L. (1987). Grief and elective abortion: Breaking the emotional bond? *Omega, 18,* 1–12.

Peppers, L., & Knapp, R. (1980a). *Motherhood and mourning: Perinatal death.* New York: Praeger.

——— (1980b). Maternal reactions to involuntary fetal/infant death. *Psychiatry, 43,* 155–159.

Perez-Reyes, M., & Falk, R. (1973). Follow-up after therapeutic abortion in early adolescence. *Archives of General Psychiatry, 28,* 120–126.

Phipps, S. (1981). Mourning response and intervention in stillbirth: An alternative genetic counseling approach. *Social Biology, 28,* 1–13.

——— (1985). The subsequent pregnancy after stillbirth: Anticipatory parenthood in the face of uncertainty. *The International Journal of Psychiatry in Medicine, 15,* 243–264.

Pine, V., & Brauer, C. (1986). Parental grief: A synthesis of theory, research, and intervention. In T. Rando (ed.), *Parental loss of a child* (pp. 59–96). Champaign, Ill.: Research Press.

Pines, D. (1972). Pregnancy and motherhood: Interaction between fantasy and reality. *British Journal of Medical Psychology, 45,* 333–343.

—— (1982). The relevance of early psychic development to pregnancy and abortion. *International Journal of Psycho-Analysis, 63,* 311–319.

Pizer, H., & Palinski, C. O. (1980). *Coping with a miscarriage.* New York: Dial Press.

Platt, J., Ficher, I., & Silver, M. (1973). Infertile couples: Personality traits and self-ideal concept discrepancies. *Fertility and Sterility, 24,* 972–976.

Pollock, G. (1962). Childhood parent and sibling loss in adult patients. *Archives of General Psychiatry, 7,* 295–305.

—— (1970). Anniversary reactions, trauma, and mourning. *Psychoanalytic Quarterly, 39,* 347–371.

—— (1978). On siblings, childhood sibling loss, and creativity. *The Annual of Psychoanalysis, 6,* 443–481.

Poznanski, E. (1972). The "replacement" child: A saga of unresolved parental grief. *Journal of Pediatrics, 81,* 1190–1193.

Provence, S., & Solnit, A. (1983). Development-promoting aspects of the sibling experience: Vicarious mastery. In *The psychoanalytic study of the child* (vol. 38, pp. 337–351). New Haven: Yale University Press.

Rando, T. (1983). An investigation of grief and adaptation in parents whose children have died of cancer. *Journal of Pediatric Psychology, 8,* 3–20.

—— (ed.) (1986a). *Loss and anticipatory grief.* Lexington, Mass.: Lexington Books.

—— (1986b). The unique issues and impact of the death of a child. In T. Rando (ed.), *Parental loss of a child* (pp. 5–43). Champaign, Ill.: Research Press.

Raphael, B. (1975). The management of pathological grief. *Australian and New Zealand Journal of Psychiatry, 9,* 173–180.

—— (1977). Preventative intervention with the recently bereaved. *Archives of General Psychiatry, 34,* 1450–1454.

—— (1978). Mourning and the prevention of melancholia. *British Journal of Medical Psychology, 51,* 303–310.

—— (1983). *The anatomy of bereavement.* New York: Basic Books.

Raphael-Leff, J. (1983). Facilitators and regulators: Two approaches to mothering. *British Journal of Medical Psychology, 56,* 379–390.

—— (1986). Facilitators and regulators: Conscious and unconscious processes in pregnancy and early motherhood. *British Journal of Medical Psychology, 59,* 43–55.

Rappaport, C. (1981). Helping parents when their newborn infants die: Social work implications. *Social Work in Health Care, 6,* 57–67.

Reilly, T., Hasazi, J., & Bond, L. (1983). Children's conceptions of death and personal mortality. *Journal of Pediatric Psychology, 8,* 21–30.

Rosen, E. (1988). Family therapy in cases of interminable grief for the loss of a child. *Omega, 19,* 187–202.

Rosen, H. (1985). Prohibitions against mourning in childhood sibling loss. *Omega, 15*, 307–316.

Rosenfeld, D., & Mitchell, E. (1979). Treating the emotional aspects of infertility: Counseling services in an infertility clinic. *American Journal of Obstetrics and Gynecology, 135*, 177–180.

Ross, J. M. (1975). The development of paternal identity: A critical review of the literature of nurturance and generativity in boys and men. *Journal of the American Psychoanalytic Association, 23*, 783–817.

Rowe, J., Clyman, R., Green, C., Mikkelsen, C., Haight, J., & Ataide, L. (1978). Follow-up of families who experience a perinatal death. *Pediatrics, 62*, 166–170.

Rubin, R. (1975). Maternal tasks in pregnancy. *Maternal-Child Nursing Journal, 4*, 143–53.

Rubin, S. (1981). A two-track model of bereavement: Theory and application in research. *American Journal of Orthopsychiatry, 51*, 101–109.

—— (1984). Mourning distinct from melancholia: The resolution of bereavement. *British Journal of Medical Psychology, 57*, 339–345.

—— (1985). Maternal attachment and child death: On adjustment, relationship, and resolution. *Omega, 15*, 347–352.

Russell, W. (1975). My baby's dead. *Journal of Pastoral Care, 29*, 196–201.

Rynearson, E. (1982). Relinquishment and its maternal complications: A preliminary study. *American Journal of Psychiatry, 139*, 338–340.

Salladay, S. A., & Royal, M. (1981). Children and death: Guidelines for grief work. *Child Psychiatry and Human Development, 11*, 203–212.

Sanders, C. (1980). A comparison of adult bereavement in the death of a spouse, child, and parent. *Omega, 10*, 303–321.

Sandler, A. M. (1988). Aspects of the analysis of a neurotic patient. *International Journal of Psycho-Analysis, 69*, 317–326.

Saylor, D. (1977). Nursing response to mothers of stillborn babies. *Journal of Obstetric, Gynecologic, and Neonatal Nursing, 6*, 39–42.

Schafer, W. (1988). Personal communication.

Schiff, H. S. (1977). *The bereaved parent.* New York: Crown.

Schneider, J. (1973). Repeated pregnancy loss. *Clinical Obstetrics and Gynecology, 16* (1), 120–133.

Schowalter, J. (1976). How do children and funerals mix? *Journal of Pediatrics, 89*, 139–142.

Schreiner, R., Gresham, E., & Green, M. (1979). Physician's responsibility to parents after death of an infant. *American Journal of Diseases of Children, 133*, 723–726.

Schultz, C. (1980). Grieving children. *Journal of Emergency Nursing, 6*, 30–36.

Sciarra, J. J. (ed.) (1983). *Gynecology and obstetrics.* New York: Harper & Row.

Scrimshaw, S., & March, D. (1984). "I had a baby sister but she only lasted one day." *Journal of the American Medical Association, 251*, 732–733.

Scupholme, A. (1978). Who helps? Coping with the unexpected outcomes of pregnancy. *Journal of Obstetric, Gynecologic, and Neonatal Nursing, 7,* 36–39.

Seibel, M., & Graves, W. (1980). The psychological implications of spontaneous abortion. *Journal of Reproductive Medicine, 25,* 161–165.

Seibel, M., & Taymor, M. (1982). Emotional aspects of infertility. *Fertility and Sterility, 37,* 137–145.

Seitz, P., & Warrick, L. (1974). Perinatal death: The grieving mother. *American Journal of Nursing, 74,* 2028–2033.

Sekaer, C., & Katz, S. (1986). On the concept of mourning in childhood: Reactions of a 2 1/2-year-old girl to the death of her father. In *The psychoanalytic study of the child* (vol. 41, pp. 287–314). New Haven: Yale University Press.

Senay, E. (1970). Therapeutic abortion: Clinical aspects. *Archives of General Psychiatry, 23,* 408–415.

Seward, G., Wagner, P., Heinrich, J., Bloch, S., & Myerhoff, H. L. (1965). The question of psychophysiologic infertility: Some negative answers. *Psychosomatic Medicine, 27,* 533–545.

Shapiro, C. H. (1986). Is pregnancy after infertility a dubious joy? *Social Casework, 67,* 306–313.

——— (1988). *Infertility and pregnancy loss.* San Francisco: Jossey-Bass.

Shectman, K. W. (1980). Motherhood as an adult developmental stage. *American Journal of Psychoanalysis, 40,* 273–281.

Simon, N., Rothman, D., Goff, J., & Senturia, A. (1969). Psychological factors related to spontaneous and therapeutic abortion. *American Journal of Obstetrics and Gynecology, 104,* 799–808.

Simon, N., Senturia, A., & Rothman, D. (1967). Psychiatric illness following therapeutic abortion. *American Journal of Psychiatry, 124,* 59–65.

Siögren, B., & Uddenberg, N. (1988). Prenatal diagnosis and maternal attachment to the child-to-be. *Journal of Psychosomatic Obstetrics and Gynecology, 9,* 73–87.

Smith, A. (1979). Psychiatric aspects of sterilization: A prospective survey. *British Journal of Psychiatry, 135,* 304–309.

Smith, A., & Borgers, S. (1988). Parental grief response to perinatal death. *Omega, 19,* 203–214.

Smith, E. (1973). A follow-up study of women who request abortion. *American Journal of Orthopsychiatry, 43,* 574–585.

Solnit, A., & Green, M. (1959). Psychologic considerations in the management of deaths on pediatric hospital services. *Pediatrics, 24,* 106–112.

Solnit, A., & Stark, M. (1961). Mourning and the birth of the defective child. In *The psychoanalytic study of the child* (vol. 16, pp. 523–537). New York: International Universities Press.

Soricelli, B., & Utech, C. (1985). Mourning the death of a child. *Social Work, 30,* 429–434.

Speck, W. (1978). Commentary: The tragedy of stillbirth. *Journal of Pediatrics, 93,* 869–870.

Speece, M., & Brent, S. (1984). Children's understanding of death: A review of three components of a death concept. *Child Development, 55,* 1671–1686.

Spinetta, J. (1974). The dying child's awareness of death: A review. *Psychological Bulletin, 81,* 256–260.

Spinetta, J., Rigler, D., & Karon, M. (1973). Anxiety in the dying child. *Pediatrics, 52,* 841–844.

Spinetta, J., Swarner, J., & Sheposh, J. (1981). Effective parental coping following the death of a child from cancer. *Journal of Pediatric Psychology, 6,* 251–263.

Spitz, R. (1965). *The first year of life.* New York: International Universities Press.

Stack, J. (1984). The psychodynamics of spontaneous abortion. *American Journal of Orthopsychiatry, 54,* 162–167.

——— (1987). Prenatal psychotherapy and maternal transference to fetus. *Infant Mental Health Journal, 8,* 100–109.

Standish, L. (1982). The loss of a baby. *Lancet, 1,* 611–612.

Sternlicht, M. (1980). The concept of death in preoperational retarded children. *The Journal of Genetic Psychology, 137,* 157–164.

Stierman, E. (1987). Emotional aspects of perinatal death. *Clinical Obstetrics and Gynecology, 30,* 352–361.

Stringham, J., Riley, J., & Ross, A. (1982). Silent birth: Mourning a stillborn baby. *Social Work, 27,* 322–327.

Strupp, H., & Binder, J. (1984). *Psychotherapy in a new key: A guide to time-limited dynamic psychotherapy.* New York: Basic Books.

Swain, H. (1979). Childhood views of death. *Death Education, 2,* 341–358.

Swanson-Kauffman, K. (1986). Caring in the instance of unexpected early pregnancy loss. *Topics in Clinical Nursing, 8,* 37–46.

——— (1988). There should have been two: Nursing care of parents experiencing the perinatal death of a twin. *Journal of Perinatal and Neonatal Nursing, 2,* 78–86.

Taylor, C., & Pernoll, M. (1987). Normal pregnancy and prenatal care. In M. Pernoll & R. Bensen (eds.), *Current obstetric and gynecologic diagnosis and treatment* (6th ed., pp. 161–177). Norwalk, Conn.: Appleton & Lange.

Taylor, P., & Gideon, M. (1980). Crisis counseling following the death of a baby. *Journal of Reproductive Medicine, 24,* 208–211.

Tennen, H., Affleck, G., & Gershman, K. (1986). Self-blame among parents of infants with perinatal complications: The role of self-protective motives. *Journal of Personality and Social Psychology, 50,* 690–696.

Theut, S., Pedersen, F., Zaslow, M., & Rabinovich, B. (1988). Pregnancy subsequent to perinatal loss: Parental anxiety and depression. *Journal of the American Academy of Child and Adolescent Psychiatry, 27,* 289–292.

Theut, S., Pedersen, F., Zaslow, M., Cain, R., Rabinovich, B., & Morihisa, J. (1989). Perinatal loss and parental bereavement. *American Journal of Psychiatry, 146,* 635–639.

Toedter, L., Lasker, J., & Alhadeff, J. (1988). The perinatal grief scale: Development and initial validation. *American Journal of Orthopsychiatry, 58,* 435–449.

Tolpin, M. (1971). On the beginnings of a cohesive self: An application of the concept of transmuting internalization to the study of the transitional object and signal anxiety. In *The psychoanalytic study of the child* (vol. 26, pp. 316–352). New York: Quadrangle.

Tooley, K. (1975). The choice of a surviving sibling as "scapegoat" in some cases of maternal bereavement: A case report. *Journal of Child Psychology and Psychiatry, 16,* 331–339.

Turco, R. (1981). The treatment of unresolved grief following loss of an infant. *American Journal of Obstetrics and Gynecology, 141,* 503–507.

Uddenberg, N. (1974). Reproductive adaptation in mother and daughter. *Acta Psychiatrica Scandinavica* (suppl. 254), 1–115.

Van Putte, A. (1988). Perinatal bereavement crisis: Coping with negative outcomes from prenatal diagnosis. *Journal of Perinatal and Neonatal Nursing, 2,* 12–22.

Veevers, J. E. (1973). The social meanings of parenthood. *Psychiatry, 36,* 291–310.

Videka-Sherman, L. (1982). Coping with the death of a child. *American Journal of Orthopsychiatry, 52,* 688–698.

Videka-Sherman, L., & Lieberman, M. (1985). The effects of self-help and psychotherapy intervention on child loss: The limits of recovery. *American Journal of Orthopsychiatry, 55,* 70–82.

Vogel, E., & Bell, N. (1967). The emotionally disturbed child as the family scapegoat. In G. Handel (ed.), *The psychosocial interior of the family* (pp. 424–442). Chicago: Aldine.

Volkan, V. (1970). Typical findings in pathological grief. *Psychiatric Quarterly, 44,* 231–250.

——— (1971). A study of a patient's re-grief work through dreams, psychological tests, and psychoanalysis. *Psychiatric Quarterly, 45,* 255–273.

——— (1985). Psychotherapy of complicated mourning. In V. Volkan (ed.), *Depressive states and their treatment* (pp. 271–295). Northvale, N.J.: Aronson.

Waechter, E. (1971). Children's awareness of fatal illness. *American Journal of Nursing, 71,* 1168–1172.

Wallerstein, J., Kurtz, P., & Bar-Din, M. (1972). Psychosocial sequelae of therapeutic abortion in young unmarried women. *Archives of General Psychiatry, 27,* 828–832.

Walwork, E., & Ellison, P. (1985). Follow-up of families of neonates in whom life support was withdrawn. *Clinical Pediatrics, 24,* 14–20.

Weaver, R. H., & Cranley, M. (1983). An exploration of paternal-fetal attachment. *Nursing Research, 32,* 68–72.

Weiner, A., & Weiner, E. (1984). The aborted sibling factor: A case study. *Clinical Social Work Journal, 12,* 209–215.

Weininger, O. (1979). Young children's concepts of dying and death. *Psychological Reports, 44*, 395–407.

Wessel, M. (1978). The grieving child. *Clinical Pediatrics, 17*, 559–568.

Weston, D., & Irwin, R. (1963). Preschool child's response to death of infant sibling. *American Journal of Diseases of Children, 106*, 564–567.

White, E., Elsom, B., & Prawat, R. (1978). Children's conceptions of death. *Child Development, 49*, 307–310.

Whitfield, J., Siegel, R., Glicken, A., Harmon, R., Powers, L., & Goldson, E. (1982). The application of hospice concepts to neonatal care. *American Journal of Diseases of Children, 136*, 421–424.

Wikler, L., Wasow, M., & Hatfield, E. (1981). Chronic sorrow revisited: Parent vs. professional depiction of the adjustment of parents of mentally retarded children. *American Journal of Orthopsychiatry, 51*, 63–70.

Williams, M. (1981). Sibling reactions to cot death. *The Medical Journal of Australia, 2*, 227–231.

Wilson, A., Fenton, L., Stevens, D., & Soule, D. (1982). The death of a newborn twin: An analysis of parental bereavement. *Pediatrics, 70*, 587–591.

Wilson, A., & Soule, D. (1981). The role of a self-help group in working with parents of a stillborn baby. *Death Education, 5*, 175–186.

Winnicott, D. W. (1945). Primitive emotional development. *International Journal of Psycho-Analysis, 26*, 137–143.

——— (1953). Transitional objects and transitional phenomena. *International Journal of Psycho-Analysis, 34*, 89–97.

——— (1956/1958). Primary maternal preoccupation. In *Through paediatrics to psycho-analysis* (pp. 300–305). New York: Basic Books.

——— (1971). *Playing and reality*. London: Tavistock Publications.

Wolberg, L. (1980). *Handbook of short-term psychotherapy*. New York: Thieme-Stratton.

Wolfenstein, M. (1966). How is mourning possible? In *The psychoanalytic study of the child* (vol. 21, pp. 93–123). New York: International Universities Press.

Wolff, J., Nielson, P., & Schiller, P. (1970). The emotional reaction to a stillbirth. *American Journal of Obstetrics and Gynecology, 108*, 73–77.

Woods, J. (1987). Obstetrician as outpatient counselor. In J. Woods & J. Esposito (eds.), *Pregnancy loss: Medical therapeutics and practical considerations* (pp. 169–187). Baltimore: Williams and Wilkins.

Woods, J., & Esposito, J. (eds.) (1987). *Pregnancy loss: Medical therapeutics and practical considerations*. Baltimore: Williams and Wilkins.

Woods, J., & Klein, B. (1987). Perinatal support service at the University of Cincinnati. In J. Woods & J. Esposito (eds.), *Pregnancy loss: Medical therapeutics and practical considerations* (pp. 271–289). Baltimore: Williams and Wilkins.

Woodward, S., Pope, A., Robson, W., & Hagan, O. (1985). Bereavement counselling after sudden infant death. *British Medical Journal, 290*, 363–365.

Worlow, D. (1978). What do you say when the baby is stillborn? *R.N., 41,* 74.

Wyatt, F. (1975). The psychoanalytic theory of fertility. *International Journal of Psychoanalytic Psychotherapy, 4,* 568–585.

Zahourek, R., & Jensen, J. (1973). Grieving and the loss of the newborn. *American Journal of Nursing, 73,* 836–839.

Zeanah, C., Keener, M., & Anders, T. (1986a). Adolescent mothers' prenatal fantasies and working models of their infants. *Psychiatry, 49,* 193–203.

——— (1986b). Developing perceptions of temperament and their relation to mother and infant behavior. *Journal of Child Psychology and Psychiatry and Allied Disciplines, 27,* 499–512.

Zeanah, C., Keener, M., Stewart, L., & Anders, T. (1985). Prenatal perception of infant personality: A preliminary investigation. *Journal of the American Academy of Child Psychiatry, 24,* 204–210.

Zigler, E., & Glick, M. (1988). Is paranoid schizophrenia really camouflaged depression? *American Psychologist, 43,* 484–490.

Zisook, S., & DeVaul, R. (1985). Unresolved grief. *American Journal of Psychoanalysis, 45,* 370–379.

INDEX

Abortion, 119, 140, 179, 191; *vs.* perinatal loss, 63–65
Adolescence, 2, 28–29, 114, 133; in child sibling case, 159–62
Adoption: relinquishing a child for, 69–71, 181
Ambivalence: during pregnancy, 12–13, 20, 30, 49, 65; in maternal cases, 101, 105, 111–14 passim, 123, 194
Anality, 4–5, 6, 172–73
Anniversary reactions, 35, 75, 93–94, 105, 146
Anticipatory grieving, 37–38, 71–72, 75, 85, 138, 167
Anxiety: and perinatal loss, 38, 73, 75, 94, 159, 160, 185; separation, 117–18, 150–54 passim, 158–61, 178, 179. *See also* Death, anxiety
Arlow, J., 171–72
Attachment: difficulties after perinatal loss, 74–75, 163, 164, 167

Ballou, J., 2, 5–13 passim, 25, 30
Barry, M., 47, 106
Benedek, T., 3–17 passim, 25, 28, 30, 66
Benfield, D., et al., 40–57 passim, 61, 67, 74

Bibring, G., 2–13 passim, 30, 82
Birth, 19, 25, 36
Bonding, 25–26, 34, 55–56
Borderline dynamics, 124, 153
Bourne, S., 48, 75, 125
Bowlby, J., 23, 32, 134, 136, 148, 186
Brazelton, T. B., 17, 23

Cain, A., et al.: on replacement child, 11, 162, 164; on miscarriage, 40–47 passim, 131, 139, 140; on sibling loss, 137, 138, 186
Castration issues, 6, 43, 62, 96–97
Cesarian section, 68
Chasseguet-Smirgel, J., 6
Clinical sample, 54, 193; maternal, 87–88; child sibling, 141; adult sibling, 169–70, 185
Clyman, R., et al., 33, 40, 41, 52, 54, 87

Death: of a child, 37, 41, 42, 71–72, 162–68 passim; anxiety, 38, 43, 140, 146, 150–51, 158–59, 167, 181; child's concept of, 132–36, 143, 145–47. *See also* Perinatal loss; Sibling, perinatal loss